Trade unions in Britain today

John McIlroy

Manchester University Press

Manchester and New York

Distributed exclusively in the USA and Canada
by **St. Martin's Press**

Published by Manchester University Press
Oxford Road, Manchester M13 9PL, UK
and Room 400, 175 Fifth Avenue, New York, NY 10010, USA

Distributed exclusively in the USA and Canada
by St. Martin's Press, Inc., 175 Fifth Avenue,
New York, NY 10010, USA

Reprinted 1990

British Library cataloguing in publication data
McIlroy, John
 Trade unions today — (Politics today series)
 1. Great Britain. Trade unions
 I. Title   II. Series
 331.88'0941

Library of Congress cataloguing in publication data
McIlroy, John
 Trade unions today/ John McIlroy.
 p. cm. — (Politics today)
 Includes index.
 ISBN 0–7190–2654–7 : $30.00 (U.S.: est.). ISBN 0–7190–2655–5
(pbk.) : $12.00 (U.S. : est.)
 1. Trade unions–Great Britain.   I. Title.   II. Series.
HD6664.M18 1988
331.88'0941—dc19   88–11781

Printed and bound in Great Britain by
Biddles Ltd., Guildford and King's Lynn

Contents

Introduction

This book is intended to provide a brief, accessible, straightforward account of some of the key issues confronting trade unions in Britain today. Trade unionism presents a very different picture as we approach the 1990s than it did a decade ago. Relatively sudden membership decline, loss of political influence, and the challenge of continuing economic, legal, and technological change, have all produced intensive wide-ranging discussion on the purpose of trade unions and their role in British society.

The following pages try to make what has been happening more comprehensible by examining the evidence and the different interpretations of the evidence. *Trade Unions in Britain Today* looks in turn at the changing economic and industrial background to union activities, contemporary trade union involvement in politics; the new legal framework of industrial relations; the impact on unions of recent technological change; the increasingly contentious issue of democracy in trade unions; and recent developments in relation to the perennial problem of workers participation and industrial democracy. It then attempts to pull the strands together and assess some of the arguments as to what has been happening to trade unions in the age of Thatcherism and what their response should be.

This book attempts both to place important issues in the context of current political controversy and to relate them to recent research on industrial relations. It seeks to outline issues, provide evidence, and strengthen debate. It is not intended to be exhaustive either in its selection of issues or in its treatment of them. Students on a wide variety of adult education, day release, and diploma courses in industrial relations, management, trade union studies and social studies, may find it worth studying as a way-in to this area. Those taking undergraduate and higher level courses may find it of interest as a concise summary of recent trends and helpful in keeping wider issues and arguments in view as they immerse themselves in the copious detail of current industrial relations institutions.

I have found the approach taken in this book useful in teaching classes for the general public, internal students and trade unionists. It owes a particular debt to the students on the Transport and General Workers' Union Distance Learning Certificate Course mounted in recent years at the universities of Liverpool and Manchester. I would like to thank Dr Bill Jones, Director of the University of Manchester Department of Extra-Mural Studies, who suggested to me the need for a book on trade unions in the 'Today' series. And I would like to thank Barbara Littler for her help in word processing the text.

Abbreviations used in the text

ACAS	Advisory Conciliation and Arbitration Service
ACTSS	Association of Clerical, Technical and Supervisory Staffs
ADM	Annual Delegate Meeting
AES	Alternative Economic Strategy
AEU	Amalgamated Engineering Union
AFL-CIO	American Federation of Labour – Congress of Industrial Organisations
APEX	Association of Professional Executive Clerical and Computer Staff
ASLEF	Associated Society of Locomotive Engineers and Firemen
ASTMS	Association of Scientific, Technical and Managerial Staffs (now part of the Manufacturing, Scientific and Finance Union)
BIFU	Banking Insurance and Finance Union
BL	British Leyland
BSC	British Steel Corporation
CAD	Computer Aided Design
CBI	Confederation of British Industry
CLP	Constituency Labour Party
CNC	Computer Numerical Control
COHSE	Confederation of Health Service Employees
CPSA	Civil and Public Services Association
EEC	European Economic Community
EETPU	Electrical, Electronic, Telecommunications and Plumbing Union
EPOC	Equal Pay and Opportunities Campaign

EPOS	Electronic Point of Sale
FMS	Flexible Manufacturing Systems
GCHQ	Government Communications Headquarters
GDP	Gross Domestic Product
GLC	Greater London Council
GLEB	Greater London Enterprise Board
GMBATU	General, Municipal and Boilermakers Trades Union
IDS	Incomes Data Services
IMF	International Monetary Fund
IMS	Institute of Manpower Studies
IPM	Institute of Personnel Management
LRD	Labour Research Department
MORI	Market and Opinion Research International
MSC	Manpower Services Commission (*now* The Training Agency)
NALGO	National and Local Government Officers' Association
NAS/UWT	National Association of Schoolmasters / Union of Women Teachers
NCB	National Coal Board
NEB	National Enterprise Board
NEDO	National Economic Development Organisation
NEDC	National Economic Development Council
NHS	National Health Service
NGA	National Graphical Association
NUJ	National Union of Journalists
NUM	National Union of Mineworkers
NUR	National Union of Railwaymen
NUT	National Union of Teachers
NTA	New Technology Agreement
OECD	Organisation for Economic Co-operation and Development
OCR	Optical Character Recognition
POEU	Post Office Engineering Union (*now* National Communications Union)
PSI	Policy Studies Institute
SDP	Social Democratic Party
SOGAT	Society of Graphical and Allied Trades
TASS	Technical, Administrative and Supervisory Union (now part of the Manufacturing, Scientific and Finance Union)

TGWU	Transport and General Workers Union
TUC	Trades Union Congress
TUFL	Trades Unions For Labour
TULV	Trade Unions for a Labour Victory
TURU	Trade Union Research Unit
UCW	Union of Communication Workers
UCATT	Union of Construction, Allied Trades and Technicians
USDAW	Union of Shop, Distributive and Allied Workers
VDU	Visual Display Unit

Chapter 1

Trade unions: the context

Trade unions are inseparable from the society in which they operate. Historically, they came into being as a response to capitalism, a form of social and economic organisation where the ownership of the means of production is in private hands, where the object of production is the competitive pursuit of profit in a free market and where the majority, excluded from the ownership of the means of production, are compelled to sell their labour power in order to live. For workers, a reasonably paid, secure job is an essential basis for a decent life. But their wages are a cost to their employers, an important item to be set against profit, and thus to be minimised and dispensed with entirely where labour is insufficiently profitable. Trade unions, therefore, take the stage in order to redress the bargaining imbalance between employer and employee and render the conflict between capital and and labour a more equal one, replacing individual competition for jobs by collective organisation as a means to protect wage levels and the conditions and security of employment.

The society we live in today remains a capitalist society. But it is very different from the kind of society trade unionists lived in 100 or 50, even 25 years ago. Unrestrained market competition gradually gave way to the state intervention in the economy, planning and nationalisations of the post-World War II period. Today we are seeing an attempt at counter-revolution as government preaches a return to the free market, a retreat in state intervention and a restoration of 'Victorian values'. Political policies, developments in the economy, changes in management strategies and their impact on industrial relations – all of these exercise a crucial influence on the kind of trade unionism which emerges in a particular period, and the nature of the problems it must confront. The purpose of this chapter is to provide a brief sketch of recent developments in these areas which constitute the environment in which contemporary trade unionism carries on its activities.

Britain's economic decline

All the important developments in industrial relations over the past 25 years are rooted in the stark facts of Britain's economic decline. We are talking in relative terms. In the post-war period Britain remained as it is today, one of the world's richest countries. But it was losing its position near the top of the first division table of economic powers. By the 1960s, the UK was clinging precariously to a position in the top ten and today it is slipping out of the top twenty. As the sixties dawned, there was a growing acceptance across the political spectrum that the UK's progress down the ladder of international competition was accelerating and that in the absence of fundamental corrective action, it would continue.

The facts brooked little argument. Between 1945 and 1970, growth in industrial productivity in Britain averaged an annual 1.5%, compared with 3% in the USA and Germany and almost 4% in Japan. Britain is an exporting nation. Yet, in the same period, its share of manufacturing exports from the advanced economies slumped from 25% to 10%. This was related to a poor rate of capital investment in plant and equipment. The average annual growth of capital stock in the fifties and sixties was a little over 4% in the UK, compared with nearly 6% in France, 7% in West Germany and a massive 12.5% in Japan. A study of this period showed fixed assets in manufacturing industry in Japan and Germany as £30,000 and £23,000 per worker respectively, compared with £7,500 in the UK.

This problem was exacerbated by the outflow of capital from Britain to other countries. Consequently, it took longer and cost more to produce goods in the UK. Higher production costs and intensive international price competition squeezed the profit margins of British employers.

In the tight labour markets of the immediate post-war period, labour shortage led to increased labour costs. Passed on to consumers through increased prices, this 'cost plus' inflation produced a further blunting of competitive edge in world markets and further pressure on profits. These problems were softened by the long post-war boom, the expansion of world trade and the temporary post-war

Table 1   *Rates of profit for industrial and commercial companies*

Country	% before tax				
	1960	1965	1970	1973	1975
United Kingdom	14.2	11.8	8.7	7.2	3.5
United States of America	9.9	13.7	8.1	8.6	6.9
France	11.9	9.9	11.1	10.2	4.1
Japan	19.7	15.3	22.7	14.7	9.5
Italy	11.0	7.9	8.6	4.5	0.8
Germany	23.4	16.5	15.6	12.1	9.1

Source: A. Glyn and J. Harrison, *The British Economic Disaster.*

Table 2   *Economic performance in the 1970s*

	% changes 1969-79						
	UK	USA	Japan	West Germany	Italy	France	Sweden
Gross domestic product	25	32	80	38	49	49	26
Manufacturing output	7	31	69	31	40	45	21
Gross fixed investment	6	22	76	31	14	35	6
Output per hour - manufacturing.	33	34	96	54	54	69	–
Government final consumption	27	11	65	48	65	41	43

Source: Lloyds Bank Review, January 1982

dislocation of competitor economies. However, attempts by successive governments failed to transform the situation. Rather decline

was cumulative and the economy spiralled into a low investment – low productivity – low growth – low profitability – low investment cycle. In the century to 1979, gross domestic product in Britain had trebled. In the United States of America, Germany, and Japan it had grown by a factor of 7, 10 and 50 respectively.

Britain is an integral part of the world economy and its difficulties were intensified by external problems, particularly the deep recession of 1973-76. The phenomenon of 'stagflation' emerged as rising unemployment went hand in hand with an annual rate of price rises never less than 8%. Between 1975 and 1980 inflation averaged 13%, compared with 4%, 9% and 8% for Germany, the United States of America and Japan. Wage levels in Britain were not only well below these countries but amongst the lowest in Europe. Productivity rates were plunging to around half of the levels in several EEC countries.

As table 2 demonstrates, by 1979, after 2 decades of sustained deterioration, the UK economy was still in trouble. Within 2 years of Mrs Thatcher coming to power it was beset by record post-war unemployment, a trebling of the investment deficit as the outward flow of capital exceeded internal investment by £6 billion, and a dramatic collapse of manufacturing industry.

Explanations

If there is broad agreement on the reality of Britain's economic decline, explanation of its roots has engendered a wealth of controversy. Much of the analysis insists on the necessity of taking a historical view. Britain had the first capitalist revolution and became the first industrial nation. The headstart and protected markets that its industrial and military power guaranteed produced an economic dominance which bred conservatism and complacency. Competitors were able to industrialise later, utilising more advanced techniques and developing social and political structures better adapted to economic needs. Resistance to innovation in Britain was strengthened by the lack of any major upheaval such as revolution or defeat in war.

Within a framework which stresses the importance of the UK'S pioneering industrial role and the stability of its society over 3 centuries, different accounts give different weight to a diverse range of factors. Many commentators see Britain's powerful trade unions pushing up wages, applying restrictive controls to work and thwarting management's ability to plan and innovate as the prime factor in economic crisis. Others claim that incompetent management, the fragmentation of the economy into small units, or the tendency of capitalists to put consumption and dividends before investment, or investment overseas before investment at home, are to blame.

Others emphasise a debilitating split between the interests of finance capital and industrial capital, so that borrowing, lending and currency speculation took precedence over what is really important as the basis for a thriving economy, building factories and producing goods. Also cited are excessive military expenditure; excessive spending on the welfare state; a liberal, elitist system of education and research, inadequately synchronised with industrial needs; and an antiquated and abstentionist state.

The Right emphasise the role of trade unions in creating inflation and cramping productivity. On the left, many of the causes of economic problems have been laid at the door of greedy and incompetent employers. But there is sometimes surprisingly little consensus amongst those sharing similar ideologies. On the right, criticism of the unions (Joseph, 1979) has been accompanied by emphasis on the way the economy is organised and the role of government (Bacon and Eltis, 1976). On the left, union strength is cited (Kilpatrick and Lawson, 1980) but so is union weakness (Harris, 1985). Marxist accounts, which underline the role of wage increases in eroding profits, have been criticised by other Marxists on technical grounds, and because this view legitimises an assault on working-class living standards (Glyn and Sutcliffe, 1972).

There is often an overlap between the explanations of those who hold very different views. From a Marxist viewpoint, Perry Anderson argues that the conservative aspects of British society which conditioned decline had their origins in the political dominance of the landowning aristocracy and merchant capital, the victors of the Civil War, over the industrial manufacturers who developed under their wing and were moulded in their image. This constrained the development of a thrusting entrepreneurial culture, a modern political system and an interventionist state (Anderson 1965, 1987). From the centre, Martin Wiener has argued that an aristocratic disdain for commerce, and the hostility the education system and the civil service held for industry, crippled the entrepreneurial spirit and produced the cult of the gentleman amateur, seriously affecting economic performance (Wiener, 1985). Whilst from the right, we find Sir Keith Joseph, the prophet of Thatcherism, declaring that

Britain 'never had a capitalist ruling class or a stable *haute bourgeoisie* ... bourgeois values have never shaped thought and institutions as they have in some countries' (Joseph, 1975, 501).

The political economy of industrial relations

The second key factor moulding today's industrial relations has been the political reaction to economic decline. In the post-war period the 2 major political parties accepted that there should be a significant move away from the *laissez-faire* philosophy, in which economic decision-making was left to the free play of market forces. Instead, the state should take responsibility for the economic and social welfare of its citizens. *The post-war consensus* involved the maintenance of a capitalist economic system modified by a greater degree of nationalisation and the creation of a comprehensive welfare state. Government would intervene to a far greater degree in the economy, using Keynesian policies of demand management. These entailed the state increasing public spending by using deficit budgeting. It should spend more than it collected in taxes in a recession but damp down demand in an economic upturn. This would produce sustained full employment, economic growth and rising living standards.

In this model, industrial relations could be left largely to self-regulation by employers and trade unions. The *voluntary system of industrial relations* required that the resolution of conflicts in industry was undertaken through collective bargaining between employers and trade unions. Collective bargaining, according autonomy to employers and unions to adjust industrial issues to the wider economic situation, was seen as a democratic and efficient method of social decision-making, and its primacy was noted as evidence of the maturity of our industrial relations.

This system, underpinned by the long post-war boom, always involved a greater degree of state supervision than its supporters allowed. As the economic situation deteriorated, however, it came under increasing criticism. What happened in industrial relations had an important influence on the country's economic performance. Industrial relations, it was now accepted, were simply too important to be left to employers and unions. Spending on the welfare state increased and public expenditure took a greater share of gross national product. It was financed by tax increases which bore more and more heavily on those around and below average earnings. To compensate, they looked for wage increases. The power full employment gave the unions enabled them to push up wages which, in turn, pressurised employers to put up prices, stimulating inflation and disrupting the attempts of the state, using Keynesian methods to manage demand. There was less agreement on how the growing economic problems should be resolved. Different policies were applied, initially within the framework of the post-war consensus. As successive attempts at reform faltered, the search for superior solutions led to the post-1945 *welfare compromise* being undermined.

Strategies of reform

The 1964 Labour government, led by Harold Wilson, ushered in a new era of reform in industrial relations. An attempt was made to involve unions and employers together with the state in a greater degree of economic planning. A Department of Economic Affairs was established, a National Plan was published and a voluntary incomes policy was agreed with the trade unions.

However, Wilsonian planning crumbled in the face of successive sterling crises. The government first resorted to deflation and then to a statutory incomes policy. Trade unions were increasingly perceived as the major barrier to economic change. A Royal Commission on Trade Unions and Employers Associations was appointed in 1966 and reported 2 years later. The Donovan Report saw the failure of incomes policy as strongly related to the way unions operated the decentralised system of collective bargaining and the strength of workplace organisation. There was a need for employers and union leaders to re-establish control through a reformed more formal and centralised system of industrial relations. The Royal Commission urged *voluntary* reform, which it felt would be more effective than the use of law.

The government, however, was not prepared to wait on this long-term approach. The same year it formulated plans for legislation to control union activities. TUC attempts to hold their members in line on wage restraint were increasingly ineffective. From 1968, both union membership and militancy accelerated. The plans for union legislation were defeated by a coalition of the TUC and leading Labour Party politicians. By 1970, the strategy was in ruins. Britain's underlying economic situation had not been improved and wider social problems showed, as did the new assertiveness in the unions that the post-war boom was at an end.

The incoming Conservative government of Edward Heath determined on a firmer stance. Trade union power and the new militancy were now to be dealt with by legislation intended to weaken and institutionalise union power and reduce strikes. There was to be no formal incomes policy but the government would set its own gradually decreasing norm in the public sector. This approach appeared to represent an important break with the pattern of post-war politics. However, the resurgence of liberal conservatism was temporary. As unemployment increased, the Chancellor Tony Barber turned to expansionary fiscal policies and a dash for growth. In early 1972, the government was rocked off course by a successful miners' strike. The crucial Industrial Relations Act was unmasked as a paper tiger. By the autumn the 'U-turn' was complete as the Prime Minister held talks with TUC and CBI leaders at Downing Street, in an attempt to agree an incomes policy. The endeavour was unsuccessful and the government imposed a 3-month wage freeze. The new policy was undermined by the inflationary consequences of the world situation and the oil crisis of late 1973. When the miners again went on strike Heath called an election on the issue of 'who rules the country'. This produced, in February 1974, a minority Labour government.

The social contract
A decade of intensive assault on the problems of Britain's productive base had, it seemed, yielded few positive results. Attempts to reform industrial relations and weaken trade union power appeared to have been, if anything, counter-productive. They appeared to have encouraged and politicised militancy. The leadership in key unions had swung to the left. The period 1968-72 saw the biggest outbreak of militancy since 1919 and the rebirth of the political strike. Shop steward organisation spread to new industries. It was contended that the publicity surrounding incomes policies had stimulated aspirations, and that consequent erosion of differentials had fuelled the growth of white collar trade unionism. Trade union membership grew from a little over 10 million in 1968, 44% of the labour force, to almost 12 million, or 50% of the labour force, in 1974. During the Heath years, real take-home pay was increasing annually at 3.5%, 4 times the rate in the previous decade. The disintegration of the boom

and government attempts to reverse economic decline had stirred up a hornet's nest in industrial relations.

Nevertheless, the impact of the radical mood in the unions, as well as the lessons of the decade of government failure, were discernible in the policies of the Wilson government re-elected in October 1974. They represented a deeper, more serious attempt to bring off the project of 1964. At their centre was an accord between government and unions which was projected as the basis for a new social contract. In return for the TUC taking economic circumstances into account in collective bargaining, the government was to introduce a wide-ranging programme of legislation which would extend union rights and underpin many of the reforms advocated by the Donovan Commission. There would be a major redistribution of income and wealth, more industrial democracy and a National Enterprise Board which would provide funds for the regeneration of industry. The unions would again be involved in tripartite decision making through a system of 'planning agreements'. Labour's economic and industrial relations policies met a similar fate to their predecessors in the previous decade. The radical cutting edge of the industrial strategy was blunted by economic problems, and the TUC's sustained attempts to police voluntary incomes policy collapsed in the strike wave of the 1978-79 'Winter of Discontent'.

Thatcherism

The commitment to Keynesianism, full employment and the welfare state had been progressively strained under the 1974-79 Labour government. It was now to be terminated. Thatcherism originated in the revival of the liberal wing of the Conservative Party in reaction to the 'U-turn' of Heath and the influence of thinkers of the 'New Right' such as F.A. Hayek and Milton Friedman. At its base is a belief that the market can do things more efficiently than the state. State expenditure was seen as cramping initiative and negating choice. The tax burden it necessitated generated inflation and reduced profits, investment and growth as the economic actors strove to increase wages and prices to compensate. The job of a radical government is to restore the free market and limit inflation by acting on its cause – the too rapid growth of the money supply. This must be controlled through reducing state expenditure and through higher interest rates. The latter makes credit more expensive and pressurises firms to become more competitive, reorganise production, and resist union demands. Because of the monopoly power of the unions there will be a need to reduce their interference with the market mechanism. Similarly, controls and regulations constraining entrepreneurial thrust must be dismantled. State withdrawal from industry will also require cutbacks in the welfare state and privatisation.

The application of these policies in a world recession sent unemployment soaring to more than 3 million by 1981 and precipitated the destruction of important sections of manufacturing industry. A programme of union legislation was successfully implemented and an impressive list of state enterprises sold off. Exchange controls were abolished and the stock exchange deregulated. The war of attrition on trade unions culminated in the victory over the miners in 1985. The spending powers of local authorities were successfully reined in but targeted reductions in public expenditure have not been attained, largely due to the massive rise in unemployment, and consequent increases in Social Security spending, electoral considerations and fear of public unrest. Inflation has been curbed but wage increases have not. Many observers doubted the degree to which industrial relations had permanently improved and the extent to which attitudes in industry had changed. They doubted whether there had been a general and significant decrease in trade union power, and were unsure as to its durability where it had occurred. The government has been returned at the polls twice with generous majorities. Yet its record in solving the UK's economic and industrial problems still remains questionable.

By 1986, monetarism appeared to have been abandoned. In a conventional pre-election boom, interest rates were cut and public expenditure increased. Despite the free market rhetoric employers had received subsidies. The Bank of England had arranged help for almost 40 important companies facing financial problems. In 1982, public expenditure in support of industry reached its highest ever level.

Whilst government supporters pointed to an increase in company profits, critics countered that they were only back to their deflated 1978 level. When Conservatives argued that manufacturing productivity had increased annually at 3.5% since 1979, compared to a less than 1 percent a year increase under the last Labour government, their opponents claimed that this increase was almost completely the result of the destruction of 2 million jobs, and asserted that by 1986 output in manufacturing was still below the levels in 1979. If economic growth between 1983 and 1986 averaged almost 3%, it averaged a mere 1.4% a year over the whole period of Thatcherism and, by 1987, manufacturing investment remained at almost 20% below its 1979 level, despite the benefits of the oil money. Many believed that the real problems of the British economy and of British industrial relations had not been solved. The deterioration in the balance of payments was severe and the UK remained badly placed to deal with a further world recession. Their resolution had been merely postponed at the unacceptable and dangerous cost of large-scale unemployment.

The state and industrial relations

The strategies adopted by the state since the early sixties to deal with the problem of industrial relations boil down to 2 main approaches. However, within these 2 broad frameworks there may be different emphases. For example, the 1974- 79 Labour government combined a limited corporatism with a modified monetarism.

Corporatism
This strategy is informed by the belief that from the early 1960s, the 'welfare compromise' and Keynesianism broke down because of a decay of 'traditional' values, an extension of workers' horizons and a consequent pressure on unions to maximise militancy to achieve higher, real wages. In response, the state needed to construct new machinery for economic planning which could maintain the benefits of the post-war consensus Keynesianism had failed to sustain. The path taken in the 1970s by the Wilson-Callaghan governments has been seen as a limited move in the direction of corporatism. This term denotes a system where the key interest groups, the trade unions and employers' organisations are given a formal role in the creation of economic and industrial policy. In return for this privilege, they are then expected to take on the responsibility for ensuring that agreed policies are implemented, by exercising discipline over their members.

In place of unregulated competition between interest groups and consequent economic and political disorder, corporatism substitutes the concertation by the state of conflicting interests which are harnessed in the management of the economy. The predictability and planning of corporatism, it is claimed, represents a superior means of allocating economic goods than the hidden hand of the market. Corporatism provides a means by which sectional goals, such as increased wages or increased profits, can be related to wider objectives such as price stability, increased investment and full employment through the state, employers and unions bargaining across the whole economic and political canvas.

Corporatism, it is asserted, avoids the situation where government attempts to manage the economy are thwarted by the mobilisation of maximum trade union power in a plethora of sectional struggles, which ultimately undermine long-term economic objectives. Abandoning the voluntary system of industrial relations enables unions to restrain their collective bargaining power in return for concessions in other areas which, added together, maximise the interests of their members to a greater degree than 'free collective bargaining'. Corporatism is preferable to 'free collective bargaining' precisely because it gives unions a voice in wider aspects of economic policy which can undermine, or render temporary, the gains of collective bargaining.

Neo-laissez-faire

The advocates of this strategy argue that corporatism failed in the past and it will fail if tried in the future. The welfare compromise broke down because Keynesianism, the welfare state and nationalisation involved state intervention which stoked inflation and inflated expectations. To deduce from this failure the need for further state intervention is to compound the initial grievous error.

Even within its own terms, the pathos of corporatism lies in its optimistic assumption that unions will be able to restrain the most effective deployment of their members' bargaining power. Every incomes policy has broken down because the internal process of bargaining in the unions which corporatism demands was ineffective. The unions were not able to transcend sectionalism, nor should they. Wage deals should depend not upon nationally set norms but upon what the employer and the market can bear. The structures of British unions are particularly ill-adapted to ensure that what leaders agree in Downing Street will be delivered in Durham and Devon. Moreover, corporatism legitimises the role of union leaders in political decision-making and increases their appetite for greater involvement in what should be the prerogatives of elected governments.

Supporters of neo-*laissez-faire* agree with corporatists that the main problem for the state in industrial relations is the control of trade union power. This, they argue, can be optimally achieved not by increased, but by diminished state involvement. What makes the economy work efficiently is not the intervention of state bureaucracies placating the excessive demands of trade unions but entrepreneurs pursuing profit unimpeded in an open market. The role of the state is to recant on its responsibility for the economic welfare of citizens and to liberate entrepreneurs from restriction and the market from regulation.

The artificial privileges of unions and the economically debilitating rights accorded by the state to employees must be removed. Employers must be encouraged to make the performance of the firm the touchstone of employees' economic reward and develop a more flexible labour force, hired and fired in immediate relation to economic demand. This strategy, which embodies the idea of the 'residual state', is being pursued gradually by the Thatcher governments. As yet, its supporters would assert, it has not been adequately pursued. A corporate bias remains, as TUC-CBI involvement in a variety of bodies demonstrates. However, persistence in present policies and their extension will ensure a superior context for wealth creation and an eventual solution to the UK's economic and industrial relations problems.

Capital: ownership and control

It is commonly asserted that, today, the majority of enterprises are controlled not by proprietorial entrepreneurs, nor by those who own shares in the company, but by professional managers. Shareholding, it is argued, has become increasingly widespread, and this trend has accelerated since 1979. As shareholdings became dispersed, no single shareholder, or group of shareholders, was able to exercise effective control over the enterprise. Control passed into the hands of a new elite of managers whose knowlege and expertise became increasingly valuable as the size and complexity of business grew. Increased share ownership has created a 'property-owning democracy', and 'the managerial revolution' has professionalised the operation of business and ensured that it is conducted not simply in pursuit of profitability, but in accordance with the canons of social responsibility.

This view is not borne out by the evidence. There has been an extension of share ownership but, as yet, it remains limited. One recent study estimates that the proportion of the adult population owning shares declined from 7% in 1958, to 4.5% in 1979. It then increased to 19.5% in 1986. However, the proportion of the stock market directly owned by individuals fell from 54% in 1963, to 25% in 1981. In that year, the Inland Revenue estimated that 400,000 people, around 1% of the population, owned 75% of the value of all shares in private hands. In fact, '... the interesting feature of the recent growth in share ownership is that although it involves a surpisingly large number of people it is almost as thin as it possibly could be' (Grout, 1987, 5).

This point is illustrated by the recent privatisations. British Telecom's 1986 accounts showed that 1.2 million of the 1.5 million shareholders have holdings of fewer than 8,000 shares, worth less than £1,500, and own just over 7% of the company (Rentoul, 1987). Moreover, whilst British Gas after the sell-off had more than 4 million shareholders, by the end of 1986, 1.5 million of these had sold their holdings and the general public's stake in the company was under 30% (*Labour Research*, April 1987). The 1987 stock market crash is also likely to inhibit further dispersal of shareholdings.

Recent research documents, moreover, that 'there is little evidence to support the conventional view of the divorce between ownership and control' (Scott, 1985, 259). Rather, the pattern of control in large British companies represents control by a small group of powerful shareholders who together control a substantial block of shares, while the remainder are more widely dispersed. This 'control by a constellation of interests' occurs when a movement towards democratisation is replaced by a movement to concentration and is quite distinct from the pattern which could produce 'managerial control'. Strategic control over the fundamental decisions in the enterprise is still concentrated in the hands of directors and chief executives, directly responsible to capital (Scott, 1985).

Directors hold more shares than any other social group (Westergaard and Resler, 1976). This is likely to have been encouraged by the recent vogue for share option schemes. Shareholdings constitute a large proportion of the personal wealth of top managers. They come from the same background as other important shareholders and they share the same objectives, ideology and social environment

(Nichols, 1969). Growth and profitability remain the key performance indicators and the professionals are often more dedicated to profit than the owner-manager (Pahl and Winkler, 1974). All managers must ultimately answer the imperatives of competition and the market. If they do not measure up to the yardstick of profit, in the end they will go under (Westergaard and Resler, 1976). Critics from different political perspectives agree that the idea of the 'managerial revolution' does not hold water (Blackburn, 1965; Child, 1969).

The upper class

This has led a majority of sociologists to argue that the pluralist model of a dispersal of power through a variety of interest groups is not an adequate characterisation of the situation in Britain today. Rather, analysis discloses 'the existence of a socially cohesive economically dominant class which dominates most significant elite positions ...' (Bilton et al, 1986, 218). The controllers of capital, those who are actively involved in determining corporate strategy, constitute the core of the upper class who stand at the apex of the hierachies of wealth, income and power in Britain (Scott, 1982, 1985).

The upper class is seen as bound together and recruited through inheritance, shared education, ideology, lifestyle and material interest. Its business core is inextricably linked on this basis with the top civil servants, judges, army officers and politicians. For example, 155 of the 305 outgoing Conservative backbench MPs in 1987 were company directors with more than 400 directorships between them, whilst nearly 70% had attended public schools.

If strategic control over investment and resource allocation in the enterprise is in the hands of a small minority of top executives, operational control of the day-to-day use of resources has to be delegated to middle-level managers, technical experts and administrators. This group may own no capital themselves but they exercise authority, expertise and surveillance on behalf of those who do. The exact social characterisation of this 'managerial' or 'service class' has given rise to intense debate and to some extent remains an unsolved question (Wright, 1978, 1985; Goldthorpe, 1982).

These managerial and technical functionaries have to sell their labour to live. But they are different from the majority of workers in terms of the degree of trust, independence, privilege, security and prospects of advancement attached to their jobs. This ambiguity has led analysts to argue that this group 'occupy a contradictory location between the bourgeoisie and the proletariat' (Wright, 1978, 63). The degree to which those in contradictory class locations, 'the new middle class', identify themselves with capital or labour will depend on political factors and organisation.

Management and industrial relations

Writers on industrial relations have suggested that different managers operate with different perspectives.

1. The *unitary* perspective views the enterprise as essentially a harmonious, integrated team whose objectives are common and unproblematic and whose interests are shared. The possibilities for structured conflict are limited and when problems do occur they are imported from outside, the product of troublemakers, or the consequence of misunderstandings or poor communications. Whilst many managers who operate within this perspective recognise and deal with unions, they do so with a measure of mental reluctance which inhibits an effective commitment to making the relationship work.

2. More realistic managers regard the enterprise as composed of a variety of groups with different interests and goals. The *pluralist* perspective, therefore, accepts conflict as an inevitable part of life at work. Trade unions are seen as legitimate representatives of employee interests and conflict between different groups in the enterprise, if recognised and channelled through adequate procedures, is considered relatively amenable to resolution satisfactory to all parties.

   The pure type of the unitarist is the small backwoods man owner-manager. The pure type of the pluralist is the up-to-date personnel manager. But Fox (1966), who developed this framework, argued that many managers oscillate between these two perspectives, which can be related to wider political and economic factors, as well as the organisation, past traditions and present markets of firms and industries. Fox later abandoned the pluralistic perspective as a useful means of understanding industrial relations in favour of a *radical* perspective. He argued that the pluralist view of a dispersal of power between management, shareholders and different groups of employees, producing a rough equilibrium of power between all groups, represented a distortion of reality. Conflicts at work were structural and deep-seated and ran essentially along a division between capital and labour with the former immensely more powerful than the latter. The resilience of conflict at work, despite the pluralists' attempts to institutionalise it out of existence, lay in the inequalities and subordination employees face not only at work but also in all aspects of economic and social life. Satisfactory conflict resolution, therefore, depended on a far deeper industrial and social transformation than pluralists were prepared to consider (Fox, 1973).

Industrial relations theorists have also attempted a more detailed classification of management styles.

1. The *traditionalists*, often managers of small businesses, like George Ward of Grunwicks, forcefully oppose unions and, acting within a unitary frame of reference, adopt an authoritarian approach.
2. The *standard moderns* represented at least until recently the dominant approach in Britain. Unions are recognised and industrial relations specialists appointed. But no great attention is paid to industrial relations unless it intrudes and there is no sustained strategy.
3. *Sophisticated paternalists*, such as Marks and Spencer or IBM, operate within a unitary perspective. They seek to keep unions out of the enterprise and compensate employees for their absence by detailed personnel policies, participative arrangements and generous reward structures.
4. *The sophisticated moderns* are simon pure pluralists who foster and legitimise unions, encourage the closed shop, sponsor strong workplace organisation and take a keen interest in union activities. They view joint regulation of industrial relations as the best vehicle for management control. Ford and ICI are cited as examples (Purcell and Sissons, 1983).

Wealth and income

The ownership of wealth – shares, property and savings – has always been concentrated. However, the share of the top 1% wealth owners fell from more than 50% in the 1930s to 42% in the 1960s and to under 30% in the 1970s. The proportion of wealth owned by the top 5% declined over the same period from 86% to 55%. The share of wealth owned by the top 50% of the population, however, gradually increased to over 60%, whilst the other half continued to own hardly anything (Atkinson, 1972, 1975). Since 1979, there seems to have been little change. This still leaves us with the top 1% of the population owning 20% of all personal wealth in the UK and the bottom half of the population owning only 14% of the total. Because the value of total personal wealth has increased, the rich have got richer without increasing their proportional share (Rentoul, 1987).

Income distribution has been more egalitarian. The proportion received by the top 1% fell during the post-war period from 12% to 6-7%. However, the share of income of the top 10% remained constant at around 30%. This process has been reversed since 1979.

Table 3   *Distribution of income, 1977–83*

% share of income	1977	1983	Change as % of 1977
Top 10%	21.2	23.7	+11%
2nd 10%	14.8	15.0	+1%
3rd 10%	12.5	12.3	−2%
4th 10%	10.9	10.7	−2%
5th 10%	9.6	9.4	−3%
6th 10%	8.5	8.2	−4%
7th 10%	7.5	7.0	−7%
8th 10%	6.5	5.9	−9%
9th 10%	5.2	4.8	−8%
Bottom 10%	3.2	3.1	−3%

Source: N. Morris and I. Preston, *Taxes, Benefits and the Distribution of Income, 1968–83.*

As table 3 shows, the share of the top 10% has increased significantly at the expense of the middle and bottom of the table during the first period of Thatcherism. This trend has continued. By 1987 it was estimated that the top 10 percent of income earners took almost 30 percent of total pre-tax income (Central Statistical Office, 1987). And it was argued that 'the shift in the distribution of personal incomes is unprecedented in recorded British economic history' (Huhne, 1987). Outside the top 20 per cent of income earners there has been a decline in overall share since 1979 and the further down the table you go, the greater the loss: since 1979 income has been redistributed away from the bottom 20% so that '...income in Britain is now distributed as unequally as that in the United States, which has one of the more unequal distributions of income among indus-trialised countries' (Rentoul, 1987, 15).

The deterioration in the overall situation can be seen in the growth of poverty. The numbers dependent on Social Security increased from 4.6 million in 1979 to 7 million in 1983. There were another 7 million people whose incomes were up to 40% of supplementary benefit levels so that the view that around 14 million people are living in poverty would appear sustainable. By 1986, the Child Poverty Action Group claimed that more than 9 million people were living on or below supplementary benefit levels.

Inequalities at work

The most obvious inequality at work relates to pay. In 1987, the average gross weekly wage of a full-time, male manual worker was on average £185, and this compared with an average of £266 for a white collar male. The range of differences is greater; in 1986, the average for a male manual worker in catering and cleaning was £140, compared with £297 for a white-collar male in the professional and administrative category. There are also important variations in the pay of men and women. The average gross weekly wage of a full-time, female manual worker in 1987 was £115, well behind that of her male comparator, as was that of a female white collar worker, averaging £157. Of course, many white collar workers doing routine jobs earn less than manual workers. The real differences lie in the work situation of the mass of employees and those in the higher management and professional grades. Wage differentials increase as we go up the tree. In 1986 Ralph Halpern, a director of Burtons, had a salary of over £1 million, having received an 80% wage increase, and 2 of his fellow directors had salaries of over £700,000 and 70% wage increases. Whilst there is evidence that absolute living standards for those in work have increased this decade, there is also evidence that differentials have increased, as table 4 illustrates.

This picture is confirmed by the *New Earnings Survey* which shows weekly earnings of the lowest paid 10% of men falling from 68% of the median in 1977, to 59% of the median in 1987: over the same period, earnings of the best paid 10% have risen from 158% of the median to 176%. At the extreme, the 20 highest-paid directors in 1979 earned as much as 454 average male manual workers. By 1983, they earned as much as 722 such workers (Nichols, 1986,238). This is partly because the better-off have received bigger wage increases in recent years. It is also partly related to tax changes since 1979. For the 'typical household' of a married couple with two children, on half average earnings, an extra 4.2% of their gross earnings has gone in tax; a couple on 75% of average earnings have seen their tax burden increase 2.5%, whilst for those with above average earnings, it has declined, so that those earning 5 times the average pay 6% less in tax. A further factor in increasing differentials has been government labour market policy. For example, the Young Workers' Scheme was changed in 1986 to provide a subsidy to employers who took on young people at £55 a week, or less.

Table 4   *Increasing differentials*

Annual pay	1979	1987
10% earned more than	£13,170	£16,470
25% earned more than	£10,340	£12,420
50% earned more than	£8,070	£9,150
25% earned more than	£6,160	£6,700
10% earned more than	£4,920	£5,200

Note: Full-time adult men and women employees' gross earnings, 1979, adjusted to 1987 money.

Source: J. Rentoul, *The Rich Get Richer.*

The higher up the scale one goes, the greater the premium placed on job security. At one end of the spectrum is the growth in golden handshakes – Sir Michael Edwardes received £380,000 from ICL in 1983 and £200,000 from Dunlop in 1985. At the other end of the scale, a recent survey found that only around a third of those made redundant received any pay above the statutory minimum entitlement, and 35% of all those made redundant received nothing because of insufficient service (Anderson, 1981). Employees at the bottom of the pile are the subject of greater work discipline. They still often have to 'clock in' at work or suffer deductions. They work more unsocial hours. The better-paid employees are, the better their chances of receiving perks connected with their job. *Social Trends 1986* stated that more than half of all semi-skilled and unskilled manual workers did not have a holiday from home in 1984;1 in 5 in the professional managerial category had 3 holidays. The lower-paid suffer discrimination in relation to a variety of benefits such as sick pay and pensions, yet they are more likely to suffer injury at work, to retire later and to die earliest. Men and women in semi-skilled and unskilled occupations are 6 times as likely to die before the age of 64 than those in higher professional, managerial or administrative occupations. They are employed in more dangerous environments, have less autonomy over the jobs and less satisfaction in their work (Blackburn and Mann, 1979).

Concentration of capital

Until 1979, British industry was characterised by an increasing size of enterprise. By the early 1970s, the top 100 manufacturers accounted for 42% of output. Two-fifths of employees in manufacturing industry worked in establishments employing 1,000 or more workers. By that time, more than a third of the private sector work force worked in companies employing 10,000 or more. Since 1979 there has been a decline in the size of establishment. By 1983, the proportion of the work force employed in enterprises of 10,000 or more was down to 30%, compared with 35% in 1978. The proportion of the work force in establishments of more than 500 employees declined from 54% in 1978, to 48% by 1983. In manufacturing industry, 768 establishments employed more than 1,000 workers in 1984, compared with 908 in 1979. Moreover, a growth is reported in the number of small businesses. It has been estimated that nearly 5 million workers are now employed in companies with a work force of less than 50 and that the figure will increase to over 6 million by 1990.

Technical change and an attempt to find cheaper, more manageable sources of labour have led firms to establish smaller plants on 'greenfield sites', located away from traditional industrial areas. The belt across the South from Bristol to East Anglia, colonised by small hi-tech operations, is seen as an example of this. So is the establishment of Japanese companies in South Wales and the North-East. The decentralisation of clerical work to low-wage, low-rent areas, the growth of subcontracting and the division of large plants into small specialised production units, have also been noted. These factors can be important for unions. The bigger the enterprise and establishment, the more work regulation tends to be impersonal and bureaucratic and the greater the possibilities are for trade unionism.

Internationalisation

By the late 1970s, between 500 and 700 giant multinational companies dominated international investment, technology and production. A mere 160 companies controlled more than 80% of foreign investment in the UK and more than a quarter of the 4,000 largest private companies. More than half of UK based enterprises employing more than 2,000 workers had overseas operations and 60% hired more labour abroad than in Britain. By 1984, foreign multinationals owned 402 of the 1,000 largest companies in the UK, nearly 4 times as many as in 1970, accounting for 15% of total employment in manufacturing and 20% of national output. US companies had by far the greatest involvement. Economic decline and the pattern of outward investment were underlined by the fact that between 1979 and 1986 the top 40 British manufacturing companies cut their UK work force by more than 400,000, whilst increasing their overseas work force by more than 125,000.

Multinational companies can influence industrial relations by means of their economic strength and their strategic ability to resist control by government and unions. Some of these global companies have a budget greater than that of many nation-states. They can suddenly withdraw investment and transfer production. Sophisticated procedures for accounting and transfer pricing inhibit union bargaining and state planning of the economy. In the UK foreign-owned firms have been credited with an innovatory approach to industrial relations, pioneering productivity deals, the flexible firm, and single union deals.

Changes in industrial structure and the labour force

Decline in production industries

A major development since 1979 has been the serious decline in manufacturing. The numbers employed dropped from 7.1 million in 1979, to 5.2 million in 1986. Only 24% of employees work in manufacturing today, compared with 31% in 1979. This decline has hit hardest in traditional areas such as metal manufacturing, the car industry and textiles. Even in hi-tech sectors, such as electronics, there has been an overall drop in numbers employed. There has also been a fall in employment in the non-manufacturing production industries such as energy, water supply and construction.

Growth in service occupations

In contrast, there has been a significant increase in professional services, distribution banking, insurance and finance, and leisure services such as hotels and catering. In these 2 sectors, increases in

WORKING POPULATION AND EMPLOYED LABOUR FORCE: Great Britain

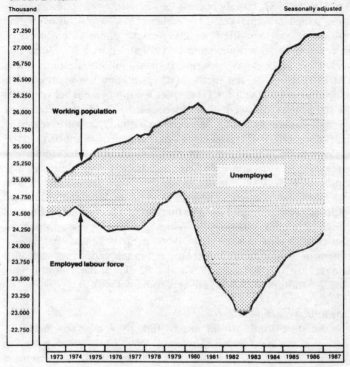

Figure 1   *Source: Department of Employment Gazette*, October, 1987

employment of 12% and 14% respectively were registered between 1979 and 1986. In banking and finance alone, the work force increased by almost 25%. The public sector employs almost a quarter of the employed labour force but is threatened with cutbacks and privatisation. Around 5 million employees work in public sector services. Overall almost 70% of employees work in the services sector. This compares with almost 60% in 1979 and 45% in the 1950s.

The implication for the unions of a change from manufacturing, where they are strong, to services, where they are weak, requires little emphasis.

Changes in employment

The working population has increased from 25.9 million in 1979, to 27 million in 1987, largely because of the numbers of young people entering the labour market. The number of employees, however, has gone down by 1.5 million, largely because of increased levels of unemployment. Unemployment in 1979 stood at 1.2 million. For most of the 1980s it has remained at over 3 million, despite no less than 18 revisions to the methods of calculating the figures which artificially depress the total. From 1986, unemployment began to fall. The fall in the employed labour force since 1979 shields a fall until 1983 and growth since then. More than a million jobs were created in the second period of 'Thatcherism', partially through a growth in the numbers of self-employed. The majority of new jobs created by employers in this period have substituted part-time women employees for full-time males. Almost 25% of the workforce now work part-time compared with 15% in 1970. Home-working and temporary employment have also increased. The various Manpower Services Schemes, such as the Youth Training Scheme, absorbed almost half a million workers in 1986. A further factor has been a growth in the number of those self-employed. This category increased by 31% between 1979 and 1984. Out of the overall labour force, 2.5 million, or 9.2 %, are now self employed.

Growth in women workers

With the shift from full-time to part-time jobs, men now make up 55% of the work force and women 45%. Male employment is projected to fall by a further 600,000 by 1990, while female employment will rise by 400,000. So women will shortly constitute half the work force. This is a remarkable development when we recall that as recently as the 1950s, women made up a quarter of the employed work force. The big growth area is part-time work in services. Here women's jobs have increased by 9% during the Thatcher years. Recent estimates claim that men make up 69% of full-time employees and women 31%, but when we look at part-time employees we find that 38% are men and 62% women. In 1987, the median weekly rate for full-time male employees was £198.40,

compared with £132.90 for full-time women, and since 1979 the
differential had increased. A full-time female manual worker, for
example, earned on average only 62% of her male counterpart's
gross weekly wage. Nor must we overlook the gap between black
workers and their white comparators. Unemployment rates for non-
white ethnic groups are double those for the white population.

North and south
Table 5 demonstrates the differential impact of unemployment in
different parts of the country. In 1987, average weekly earnings in the
South East were £224. Within the other 8 regions they varied
between £183 and £188 a week – and the gap was growing. The
number of jobs in the three 'prosperous areas' – the South East, East
Anglia and the South West – have increased, whilst jobs in the rest of
the country have decreased. More than 90% of the jobs lost in

Table 5   *Regional unemployment, 1979–86*

Region	1979–82	1982–86
South-East	−4.4	2.8
East Anglia	−3.3	12.2
South-West	−4.6	2.8
West Midlands	−11.6	2.0
East Midlands	−6.6	4.5
Yorkshire	−10.1	−1.6
North-West	−11.4	−4.6
North	−12.4	−1.5
Wales	−12.3	−5.3
Scotland	−7.2	−3.2

Source: Department of Employment Gazette Historical Supplement, 1987.

manufacturing industry since 1979 were situated outside these 3
regions. More than 60% of the new jobs created in the service sector
have been in these 3 areas. It is the South which shows most
dramatically recent change, with a large increase in part-time and
temporary workers concentrated in the fastest growth sectors such as
business and financial services, hotels and catering and distribution.
Nonetheless, in some of the new towns in the South, unemployment
is well above the national average, whilst in northern areas there are
belts of relatively full employment and high earnings. Industrial

change is more complex than the simple North/South view allows. Wealth and power is flowing to the South. By the end of the 1970s, 75% of the top 500 companies had their headquarters and top personnel located in the South East. But the decline of the older industries in the cities has also hit London, which is a classic example of urban deindustrialisation, having lost three-fifths of its manufacturing jobs since 1960. The pattern of movement from the big conurbations to small-town, greenfield sites, affects the South as well as the North. Nonetheless, many would claim that if present trends continue – and the increasing location of hi-tech industry in the South is crucial – then the divide will become an important reality.

Decline of the manual worker

Another important development, much commented on by industrial relations experts and political pundits, is the decline of the 'traditional working class'. Manual workers – 70% of the work force in the 1950s – today make up less than half of Britain's employees, but half of all male workers are still in manual occupations and so are 35% of women workers. Whilst there has been a big decline in manufacturing where manual workers are strong, we should remember that many service occupations involve manual work. In contrast, the number of white collar workers in the labour force has almost doubled since 1950, moving from just over 6 million to around 12 million today.

Industrial restructuring

To summarise, recent change represents the response of state, capital and labour to the pressures exercised by increasing international economic competition. We are witnessing important shifts in the pattern of industry from production industries to service industries, from low-tech to hi-tech, from the public sector to the private sector, from large enterprise to small businesses, from location in the North to location in the South. These developments have brought in their train changes in employment. There is a decline in the participation of men in the labour force, an increase in the involvement of women, a shift from manual to white collar work, a decline in full-time employment, a growth in part-time and temporary employment and a far larger pool of unemployment. All of these trends have implications for politics, industrial relations and the future of work.

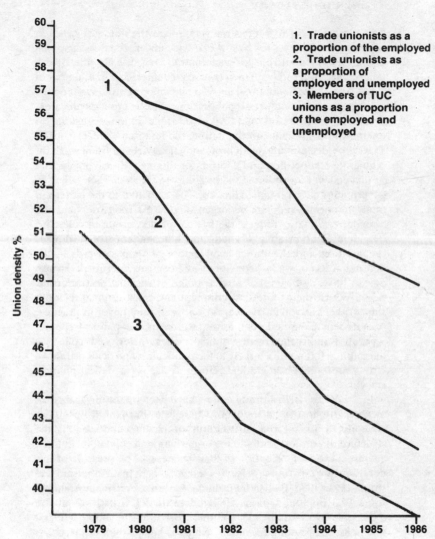

Source: G. Bain and R. Price 1983; *Department of Employment Gazette*

Figure 2   *Union Density in Recession*

Trade unions today

The context of British industrial relations, with wide disparities in wealth, income, control over work and power, would suggest an important potential role for trade unions. Historically, the British unions have differed from their overseas counterparts in a number of ways. They have maintained unity in one union centre, avoiding the fragmentation on industrial, political or religious grounds prevalent in other countries. Around 90% of trade unionists belong to organisations affiliated to the national federation – the TUC. The TUC provides affiliates with professional services, a framework for regulating competition and a forum for forging political policy. But its powers over its affiliates and its ability to speak on their behalf to government have remained limited. This is related to the pattern of multi-unionism, with unions organising across industries and job boundaries. It also reflects the system of decentralised collective bargaining, the relative strength and independence of workplace organisation and the direct involvement of shop stewards in the determination of wages, conditions and controls over work. British unions have also adopted a wide range of socialist and reformist goals. Whilst their united commitment and constitutional relationship to the Labour Party is again unusual, they have, in practice, operated in a limited, defensive fashion in the political sphere; separated industrial from political issues; prioritised collective bargaining; left politics largely to the politicians; and demonstrated a strong preference for gradual reform as against a radical political stance.

In the 1980s, British trade unions have been operating against an increasingly hostile background. Changes in the political position, economic policies, the distribution of income and wealth, the structure of employment and the organisation of capital, all militate against successful execution of their purposes. The pressure of this deteriorating environment is reflected in changes in membership and structure. In 1986, British trade unions had an overall membership of some 10.8 million. Unions affiliated to the TUC had 9.2 million members. More than 40% of the work force – employed and unemployed – belong to unions, which is higher than in the USA, Germany, Japan, France or Italy, but lower than in the Scandinavian countries, Belgium, Australia and New Zealand. This represents a significant decline on 1979, when more than 50% of the work force were members and 11.5 million employees were members of TUC-affiliated unions.

Table 6 Membership of TUC unions

Union	1979/80	1986	% change
TGWU	2,086,281	1,377,944	−33.00
AEU	1,217,760	857,559	−29.58
GMBATU	1,096,865	839,920	−23.00
NALGO	753,226	750,430	−0.37
NUPE	691,770	657,633	−4.93
ASTMS	491,000	390,000	−20.57
USDAW	470,017	381,984	−18.73
EETPU	443,621	336,155	−24.22
UCATT	348,875	249,485	−28.49
TASS	210,000	241,000	+16.60
COHSE	212,930	212,312	−0.29
SOGAT	197,000	199,594	+1.30
UCW	203,452	191,259	−5.65
NUT	290,740	184,455	−36.56
BIFU	131,774	158,746	+16.99
NCU	131,000	155,643	+15.83
CPSA	223,884	150,514	−32.77
NGA	116,000	125,587	+7.63
NUR	170,294	125,000	−26.60
NAS/UWT	152,222	123,945	−18.58

Source: TUC Annual Reports.

Whilst 87 unions are affiliated to the TUC, membership is highly concentrated with more than half belonging to the top 5 unions and over two thirds being in membership of the top 15 unions. This pattern has been strengthened by a growth in amalgamations since 1979. There are 25 fewer unions in the TUC than in 1979. Often based upon political compatibility rather than the logic of the industrial structure, the amalgamations of the 1980s have not qualitatively diminished the complexity of British trade unionism.

Loss of membership since 1979 has caused many problems. The 3 biggest unions have all suffered. The TGWU has seen its membership fall from 2 million to 1.3 million; the AEU has declined from 1.5 to 1.1 million members and the GMBATU's membership has gone down from over a million to 800,000 (see table 6). Other unions, such as the NUM, have been even harder hit, losing more than 60% of members.

Unions in the public sector, such as NALGO or NUPE, have not suffered to this degree and others, such as BIFU and the CPSA, have increased their membership.

The proportion of employees who are in trade unions varies by sector and industry. Of the TUC's affiliated membership 44% now work in the public sector and 70% of employees there belong to TUC unions, as compared with 35% in the private sector. Within that sector, only 10% of employees in distribution, hotels and catering and 18% in banking, finance and insurance are union members, compared with more than 50% in transport and communications and 67% in metal goods, engineering and vehicles.'

These are the bare bones of trade unionism in Britain today as it faces its greatest challenge since the Second World War. It is clear that all in all, these changes, particularly the decline of manual work and manufacturing industry, the reduction in the size of establishment, the development of part-time work and a large pool of unemployed, can exercise a detrimental impact upon trade union organisation and power. In succeeding chapters we look in more detail at that challenge and how unions are reacting to it.

Further reading

A. Glyn and J. Harrison, 1980, and P. Armstrong et al, 1984, are essential reading on the background to Britain's economic decline. An excellent collection, representing almost all viewpoints, is D. Coates and J. Hillard (eds), 1986. Historical background is contained in M. Wiener, 1985, and P. Anderson, 1987.

A very useful analysis of recent state policies in a range of different countries is J. Goldthorpe (ed), 1984. The following provide helpful analysis of different aspects of recent industrial change: J. Stoford and L. Turner, 1985; J. Gershuny and I. Miles, 1983; D. Masse and R. Meagan, 1982; D. Massey, 1984.

J. Scott, 1985 is an excellent examination of the arguments about ownership and control in industry. See also P. Stanworth and A. Giddens, 1974; T. Nichols, 1969; E. Wright, 1978, 1985.

A. Atkinson, 1972, is a detailed study of trends in the distribution of income and wealth. J. Rentoul, 1987 is an up-to-date and readable analysis.

Chapter 2

Trade unions and politics

 Are trade unions too involved in politics? Do they exercise too much political power? These are perennial questions wherever trade unions are discussed. Yet unions have been deeply immersed in politics since their early days, and despite the strenuous efforts of recent governments they remain so. This chapter looks at some of the issues. We start by examining the links between trade unions and the Labour Party and some of the arguments about whether, to what degree and how, unions should intervene in the political arena. We then discuss the 1984 Trade Union Act's requirements for political ballots and evaluate the campaign mounted by the unions to maintain their political funds. The fortunes of the unions in relation to recent Labour and Conservative governments are then scrutinised, and we conclude by looking briefly at some of the recent theories about Thatcherism and the decline of the Labour Party.

Unions and the Labour Party

From its birth in the Labour Representation Committee of 1900 to its formal incarnation with the election of 30 MPs in 1906, the Labour Party was financed by the trade unions. Whilst some unions made provision for its upkeep by means of a special 'Parliamentary Fund', others contributed money from their general funds. The threat to the established Conservative and Liberal parties soon attracted unfriendly attention. In 1908 W. V. Osborne, a branch secretary of the Railway Workers, went to court to halt trade union political expenditure. Osborne was a member of the Trade Union Political Freedom League, a forerunner of today's Freedom Association. The case progressed to the House of Lords, which held that unions were only entitled to spend money on legal objectives, those objectives laid down in the Trade Union Act, 1876. This act accepted that unions had only *industrial* purposes: to spend money on *political* aims was beyond their powers. An order was granted against the Railway Workers restraining them from spending money on political purposes.

The unions mounted an intensive campaign to convince the Liberal government that the Osborne judgement should be reversed. Companies met no legal obstacles whatsoever when they wanted to finance the 'big two' political parties. The unions, it was urged, should be in the same position – they should be entitled to spend money on whatever they wanted. The Liberals were not prepared to accept this argument. Instead, they arranged a compromise: the 1913 Trade Union Act allowed unions to spend money on politics, but on certain clear conditions.

Political objectives had to be specifically laid down in union rules. Cash spent on party political purposes had to come from a special political fund, quite separate from the union's general funds. This fund had to be financed by a political levy on members distinct from ordinary dues. Unions could only introduce this system after agreement from their members in a secret ballot. Individuals would also still have a right to contract out of paying the political levy. Finally, if the legal requirements were not followed, members could complain to a special ombudsman – today the Certification Officer – and eventually to the courts.

Until the 1940s the policy of both the TUC and the Labour Party was the restoration of the status quo prevailing prior to the Osborne judgement. Nevertheless, the 1913 settlement endured until the 1980s. There were 2 important changes. In 1927, in retaliation for the General Strike, the Conservatives introduced a Trade Disputes Act. Instead of trade unionists having to *contract out* of paying the political levy, they now had to *contract in*. It seems that the 'inertia effect' is quite considerable. Partly because of this change, the percentage of members of unions paying the levy dropped by more than 30% between 1927 and 1946. In the latter year, Clement Attlee's Labour administration restored the 1913 position – members once more had to opt out.

The party of the unions
The establishment of a political fund and affiliation to the Labour

Party were legally two separate things: unions could, in theory, use their political funds to make donations to the Conservative or Liberal parties. In practice, political funds and support for Labour went hand in hand. In 1983, 58 unions, covering 8 million members, had political funds and 47 were affiliated to the Labour Party. Unions asked members for a political levy varying from 20p a quarter in UCATT, to £2.70 annually in the GMB. They then paid an annual sum – 75p in 1987 – for each member they affiliated to the Party. Labour Party election funds were particularly dependent upon donations from the unions. In 1978, an umbrella organisation *Trade Unions For a Labour Victory* (TULV) was established to raise funds. In the 1983 election, the unions contributed more than £2 million to Labour's fighting fund. The unions also helped the Party by sponsoring between 150 and 200 Parliamentary candidates. The TGWU, for example, has more than 20 sponsored MPs. The union pays up to 80% of the candidate's election expenses and they often contribute to the salary of the full-time agent. They also make direct payments to sponsored MPs.

In the recent past, the unions have contributed more than three-quarters of Labour Party funds. One problem has been the changing nature of trade union membership and, of course, its overall decline. By 1983, the number of trade unionists affiliated to the Labour Party had fallen by 500,000 on its 1979 level and was down to 6 million. The NALGOs and the CPSAs, the white collar, unaffiliated, unions were doing far better in maintaining members than Labour's traditional backers, the manual unions. In 1982 and 1983, when they conducted ballots, both NALGO and the CPSA registered 2:1 majorities against the establishment of a political fund. At the time of the Osborne judgement, 90% of union members affiliated to the TUC were affiliated to the Labour Party. Now the figure was down to 50% and declining further.

Trade union control

In return for paying the piper, the unions called the tune. Votes at the Party's annual conference are awarded to the unions on the basis of the number of members on which they affiliate. Unions, moreover, do not have to affiliate on the basis of the number of members paying the political levy. Some unions, such as the TGWU, have always affiliated *less* than the number of levy payers, whilst others, such as ASTMS, have affiliated *more* than those contributing to their political fund. This block-vote system means that a union like the TGWU has more than a million votes at conference, more than all the consistuency delegates put together. It means that the unions with around 6 million votes, compared with around 600,000 allocated to CLP delegates and around 60,000 to the small affiliated socialist societies, dominate Labour's policy-making.

The unions are also allocated 12 of the 29 seats on the Labour Party National Executive. Moreover, their votes dominate the choice for the five women seats and the Party treasurer. When it comes to electing the leader and deputy leader they have 40% of the votes in the electoral college, compared with 30% for the Parliamentary Party and 30% for the constituencies. Branches of affiliated unions can affiliate to constituency parties and send delegates to their General Management Committees. Because unions can send delegates to District and Regional Labour Parties they can control the party at every level.

Since the 1970s, the unions have developed more direct methods of influencing party policy. The TUC-Labour Party Liaison Committee was established in 1972, consisting of members of the TUC General Council, Labour's NEC and the shadow cabinet. It has played a central role in policy formation. The formation of TULV was an admission that the formal party union structures were not working as far as finance was concerned. TULV was soon being criticised, on the grounds that it was a self-appointed and unaccountable club of union bosses which was interesting itself in policy-making. It has now been replaced by another body, *Trade Unions for Labour* (TUFL), which has concentrated on fund-raising but which, prior to the 1987 general election, appointed trade union officials as co-ordinators to help CLPs in all the key marginal seats. TUFL's performance seems to have been a mixed one. There was a £1.3 million gap between what the unions promised and what was deposited in Labour's campaign chest. Moreover, there were divisions within TUFL. Some unions refused to contribute to its campaign. Many argued that an increase of 4% in the numbers of trade unionists voting Labour compared with 1983 represented a very inadequate harvest.

Unions and politics

The Labour Party and the TUC gradually came to accept the 1913 compromise. The right wing of the Conservative Party did not. It

was, however, only with the election of Mrs Thatcher as party leader
and victory in the 1979 election that they were in a position to do
anything about it. From the late 1970s, trade union involvement in
politics once again became an issue.

The case for the prosecution

1. Trade unions are essentially industrial organisations. Their
   intense involvement in politics is questionable in constitutional
   terms. Unions exercise direct influence over government but they
   represent less than half the work force – fewer still are in Labour
   Party-affiliated unions. There is, moreover, little evidence –
   1974-79 is a good example – of their link with the Labour Party
   improving wages and conditions. The Labour Party may do
   something for union leaders; it has done little to improve the
   situation of the average member. The millions spent on politics
   might be better spent on employing more full-time officials,
   improving union organisation and providing superior services to
   their members.

2. It is unhealthy that one of the major parties should be in hock to
   one sectional interest group. Strong political parties are vital to a
   democratic system, yet a year after Mrs Thatcher came to office a
   Commission of Enquiry reported that the Labour Party had no
   reserves, a thoroughly inadequate income and is moving into
   serious deficit and debt. The history of the Labour Party is a
   history of financial crisis. With unions in decline, this problem is
   likely to intensify. The Labour Party must look for more secure
   sources of income.

3. The link with Labour is a classic example of union leaders
   misrepresenting their members. In 1979, a bare majority of trade
   unionists voted Labour. By 1983, this had declined to 39%. Why
   should the preferences of the majority of trade unionists who are
   anti-Labour not be reflected in financial and political support for
   the other parties? That, surely, would be the democratic way to go
   about things. A system by which, in 1983, 3.4 million trade
   unionists voted Labour but the affiliation fees of 6.1 million
   clinked into that party's coffers is all wrong.

4. The political levy system is indefensible. A study in 1974 of the
   Communications' Workers Union showed that only half of the
   members paying the levy realised that they were doing so (Moran,
   1974). In 1983, 98% of the members of the TGWU and NUPE

paid the levy. In the AEU, it declined to 65%, going down to around 35% in ASTMS and 7% in the Cine Technician's Union. Such differences can only be explained by manipulation. Many unions deliberately make it difficult for members to contract out of the political levy; industrial and political payments are often compounded into one subscription fee. Membership application forms obscure the fact that there is a right not to pay the levy. Three unions, the TGWU, NUPE and the GMBATU, control almost half the union block votes. A study of union constitutions demonstrates that there is little membership control over their disposition. The political levy is, in between 50% and 70% of cases deducted from a trade unionist's wages at source together with the rest of the union subscription, and dissidents are required to seek a rebate from the union. This, like the initial opting-out, requires application, time and courage.

5. The system of block votes is particularly indefensible. Union bosses can buy in as many votes as they require to further their political ambitions, regardless of how many members pay the political levy. The constituency party activists, who do the real day-to-day hard political slog, are disenfranchised by the union cuckoos and end up a minority in their own party. The system is seen in its true colours when parliamentary candidates are chosen. Union representatives from poorly attended union branches, with a tiny membership in the constituency, suddenly appear. All too often *they* determine who will represent the constituency in Parliament. Moreover, because those who decide union policy are often not members of the Labour Party, policy is in fact being decided by outsiders, some of whom will be members of other groupings, such as the Communist Party.

6. The system also has implications for participatory democracy. Whilst statistics on membership are unreliable, the Houghton Committee on Financial Aid to Political Parties, reporting in 1976, estimated that the Conservatives had 1.5 million members, 5 times the number of individual Labour Party Members. The obvious deduction is that citizens are not prepared to be active in an organisation which fails to empower them. Union domination inhibits political involvement.

7. There is a need for legislation to deal with all these problems.

The case for the defence

1. The industrial and political purposes of trade unions are indivisible. Unions need MPs just as much as they need full-time officers. Government policies, not only on the level of public expenditure, taxation, interest rates, price and incomes, but on education, health, housing and defence, affect the state of the economy, the position of employers, the bargaining power of unions and the livelihood of their members. Unions which operated only through collective bargaining would be walking on crutches when they had two good feet. The industrial/political split reinforced and developed by the 1913 Act is an artificial and unhealthy one. If union involvement in politics *is* essential, then having their own Labour Party represents the most logical and intelligent form of political involvement. A report by the NEC to Labour's 1987 conference recorded that the selection of the Party's candidates for that year's general election had involved only 8.4% of the individual membership. In one third of constituencies, less than 30 people voted at each selection meeting.

2. Conservatives' criticism of Labour for its dependence on sectional interest represents a chronic case of the pot calling the kettle black. Unlike the unions, who publish and publicise their political expenditure, employers hide their lights under a bushel. It is difficult to establish exactly what they spend. Nonetheless, *Labour Research* estimated that, in 1983, 338 companies donated £2.7 million to the Conservative Party, £432,000 to *British United Industrialists*, a conduit pipe to that party and £223,836 to *Aims of Industry* and similar right-wing pressure groups. In 1984, *The Economist* studied 1,500 companies which made donations of £2.5 million to the Conservatives and allied bodies. In 1986, *Labour Research* found 255 companies donating £1.85 million to the Conservative party. These figures underestimate the true position. They provide business with a means of influencing Conservative Policy and securing preference for its interests. Big companies are richer than big unions. Tory dependence on the far less democratic employers is far more unhealthy than Labour's dependence on the unions.

3. There is nothing to stop supporters of the Conservative party in the unions securing a revision of rule if they get sufficient support. But the policies of alternative parties are less satisfactory to the unions than those of Labour. And neither of these parties would

allow the unions such a privileged role in their internal constitutions. Union influence, therefore, would be diminished. Finally, the unions are not a cohesive, homogenous block who always agree on policies for the Labour Party. There are big differences between unions like the Miners and the Electricians, just as there are between different sections of the Parliamentary Party. Moreover, for most of Labour's history, the Parliamentary Party has maintained a sturdy autonomy from direct union influence.

4. The political levy system is indeed indefensible. Why should unions have to meet a legal obligation to ballot, whilst companies have to meet no such criteria? If critics of the union/Labour Party link were coherent, then they would support legislation to ensure that companies held ballots to get their shareholders' support for a political fund, which could only be 'supported by part of the dividends of those shareholders who decided not to contract out of the scheme. To give the Alliance their due, they have supported this approach, but the Conservatives have not. The only obligation companies have, now contained in the 1985 Companies Act, is to disclose in their annual report donations in excess of £200.

5. Perhaps unions *should* do more to raise the whole question of political expenditure, including the system of exemption, with their members. But the system of exemption is, itself, highly illogical and undemocratic. Democracy is about the wishes of the majority. If the majority of a union's members support political expenditure as essential to the union's purpose, why should those who disagree be enabled to opt out and be assured of a free ride at the expense – literally – of their fellow members?

6. There is a devastating dearth of evidence to backup allegations about abuse of the political levy. In 1982, when Frank White, MP for Bury, asked the Director-General of the Engineering Employers' Federation whether he possessed evidence of these allegations, he was told: 'not anything that I think you would recognise as evidence, no'. That seems to sum up the position of the critics and of discontented union members who, of course, possess full rights to complain of abuse to the Certification Officer. On average there are about a dozen to a score of complaints each year. In 1982, at the height of the intense public discussion, there were 24 complaints of abuse of the political levy and 21 the following year – from 6 million levy payers.

7. Perhaps there *should* be more frequent ballots – as long as they are binding on *all* participants – and perhaps there *is* a need to review the internal procedures of the Labour Party. It is certainly arguable that the block vote inadequately rewards the efforts of constituency activists and restrains involvement. But the Labour Party has changed its internal arrangements periodically, often in reaction to pressure from the constituencies. In the 1980s, for example, it has introduced the collegiate system for electing its leadership, mandatory reselection and 'one person, one vote' in the selection of parliamentary candidates. The real point is this: it has changed under its own efforts. Voluntary change – through self-government, not state intervention – is what true participatory democracy is about. The need for legislation is, therefore, a moot point. But if there is legislation it should, in terms of basic equity, embrace companies as well as trade unions.

The 1984 Trade Union Act

Mrs Thatcher, in the wake of her 1983 election victory, moved into action. Initial ideas of simply changing contracting-out to contracting-in were dropped in return for an agreement that the TUC would ask affiliates to circulate information on the right to contract out. In keeping with their general philosophy of 'giving the unions back to the members', the government focused instead on the question of ballots. To minimise accusations that it was acting in partisan fashion to bankrupt its main competitor, it addressed the unions' political expenditure, not political affiliation. Too crude and draconian an assault might, it was felt, draw attention to the legally untrammelled position of companies.

The 1984 Act, therefore, required unions to ballot all their members every 10 years, not on whether the union should affiliate to the Labour Party, but on whether it should maintain a political fund. All unions with political funds had to hold such a ballot within 12 months of March 1985. In future, these ballots should have to be held once every 10 years. If no ballot was held, or if no majority was attained, then political expenditure had to stop.

The Act also extended the definition of the purposes for which a political fund was required. NALGO's campaign against the cuts was seen as a classic case of a union without a political fund spending £1 million to predispose voters against the re-election of Mrs Thatcher.

The objects on which only political fund money could be spent were now extended to include not only expenditure on political parties, but on the production of any material whose main impact is to persuade people to vote, or not to vote, for a particular party or candidate.

There were teasing glimpses of another agenda. 'What would please me immensely,' Mrs Thatcher was quoted as saying, 'would be if the TUC were not and the unions were not a part of the Labour Party, or the Labour Party a part of the trade union movement. That connection, I must say, I think is wrong'. Later she went even further and stated that she favoured a US-style system where both major parties operated 'within the same framework of free enterprise'. Some Conservatives were more explicit. Back-bench MP John Townend pointed to the need 'to have an alternative government to the present one, who will not take the country down the irreversible road to Marxism ... (this amendment) could result in speeding up the Labour Party's decline and its replacement by the Alliance as an alternative to the Conservative Government'.

The political fund ballots
The Labour Party and the unions were acutely aware that one or two major reverses could set in train a dynamic of disintegration. Three important initiatives strongly influenced the outome of the ballots. Firstly, a Trade Union Co-ordinating Committee was established to oversee the progress of the ballots. Secondly, the Committee's decision that the ballots should be phased, with the unions most likely to win going first, to establish a momentum, proved to be excellent strategy. It exploited to the hilt what turned out to be the government's miscalculation in allowing the ballots to take place over 12 months, rather than going for one 'big bang'. A fickle press, with a limited time span of attention, soon lost interest. Thirdly, there was a decision to play down the link with the Labour Party and keep Labour Party personnel out of the limelight.

This low-key approach was suggested by polls, which showed far more support for unions financing political activities than for financing affiliation to the Labour Party. There were differences in emphasis between the unions. Whereas NUPE and TGWU, at least in several regions, did argue for the Labour Party link, the line in unions like ASTMS was 'Labour Party? What Labour Party?'.

On the whole, there was little discussion of specific political policies. The central theme was the unions' ability to successfully protect their members and the need for a political dimension to this function. The campaign was professional. A key to success was the emphasis on reaching members where they worked. The defensive, limited nature of the campaign, its peaceful co-existence framework – if you don't want a political voice, OK, but vote 'yes' to let other members have a political fund – and its streamlined efficiency, contributed to its resounding success.

In what was one of the few unquestionable union success stories this decade, Mrs Thatcher was handed a 38-0 drubbing. Moreover, 2 unions which did not have political funds took advantage of the way the wind was blowing to ballot successfully for their inception. Overall, 83% voted for political funds, as against a derisory 17% who opposed them, on a very reasonable 51% turnout. In unions like the Miners and the Transport Workers, singled out for criticism by the government, the 'yes' voters were more than 90% and more than 80% respectively. Even in unions like ASTMS, where a minority of members paid the levy, there was a majority vote to keep the political funds.

Employment Secretary, Tom King, branded the unions' campaign as a 'blatant example of deliberate disinformation and misleading propaganda'. His complaint was that the vote should have been about the union links with Labour. Perhaps it should. But it was pointless crying foul when his administration had clearly established the rules of the game. Within the Labour movement, some felt that the unions had, nonetheless, been excessively coy over the link with Labour and had lost an opportunity to re-argue the need for a trade union party. Others felt that the campaign's orientation, given the fact that if you could not have a political fund then you could not affiliate to Labour, was the right one. But the unions should now take a more political approach. By 1987, 6 unions without political funds in 1984 had voted to establish them. Half a dozen others were said to be preparing for ballots. The CPSA, having voted to establish a political fund, voted for a further ballot on Labour Party affiliation. NALGO, having had its 'Make People Matter' campaign prohibited by the courts, during the 1987 election campaign on the grounds that its real message was 'vote Labour', balloted its members successfully on establishing a political fund.

Mrs Thatcher had observed the growing strength of the white collar unions. Their members, according to the opinion polls, were antagonistic to political involvement and their leaders seemed moderates. The political fund ballots were intended to extend the influence of these unions in the TUC. Instead, they had misfired, and many white collar unions were now turning political. However, as the 1987 election affirmed, the political fund ballots demonstrated members' support for a political voice. They did not demonstrate support for a particular mouthpiece in the shape of the Labour Party. This was underlined by the failure of Labour to attract more individual trade unionists into membership and activism. The Party's individual membership declined from 323,292 in 1984 to 297,364 in 1986.

Influencing the state

The TUC, in the 1950s, pithily summed up their political rationale: 'It is our long-standing practice to work with whatever government is in power .. to find practical solutions to the social and economic problems facing the country.' Union leaders have enthusiastically participated in the corporate bias of the British state. Their involvement increased until it reached a high point under the 1974-79 Labour government. This period was widely characterised as 'corporatist' and the unions were seen as 'running the country'. Yet the degree to which the state institutionalised direct representation of capital and labour, and the degree of success this period yielded trade union politics have been exaggerated. An overestimation of what happened on both these counts leads to an exaggeration of the political change that has ocurred since 1980, and an overestimation of the decline in trade union power under the Conservative governments.

Labour, the unions and corporatism
Against the conventional view, it can be argued:
1. Corporatism requires the involvement of capital in the planning process. This occurred minimally during this period. Bodies such as the NEDC, 'the little neddies', the sector working parties, were discussion bodies, not instruments for directive planning. The system of Planning Agreements between government and companies were castrated once it was agreed they would not be compulsory, and they never really got off the drawing board. The National Enterprise Board fell far short of its initial objective of controlling a leading company in each key sector of industry, and

failed to act as a stimulus to private investment. Rather than acting as examples of the benefits of planning, work intensification and large-scale redundancies were the pattern in publically-owned industries. The saga of the Bullock proposals on industrial democracy summed up the limits of Labour's attempt to plan capital.

2. The social contract was basically an agreement between the government and the unions, not a mechanism of concertation between the state and the two 'social partners'. Moreover, it increasingly became simply an instrument for the control of wages. There was no open and formalised bargaining between the state, capital and labour, where broad social objectives and counter objectives were articulated, analysed and bargained over. There was no national economic forum, no national economic assessment and no national economic plan. Instead, the economic crisis of June 1975 was utilised to 'bounce' the TUC General Council into agreeing the 'voluntary' £6 pay policy. The temporary, imposed and fragile nature of the process was underscored when one year later, in September 1976, the TUC voted for a phased return to free collective bargaining.

3. The distance this style of policy-making takes from corporatism, is highlighted by the lack of agreement within the unions to the wage restraint that was the core of the social contract. From the start, there was opposition from prominent leaders. Others who accepted it saw it as a temporary, piecemeal expedient, not as the germ of a more comprehensive system of long-term planning.

4. The history of the 1974-79 government was not a history of a growth of corporatism, but of the gradual *breakdown* of what was initially little more than a corporatist *tendency* or *inflection* in a policy-making whose central thrust was increasingly conventional and focused on wage control. After 2 successful years, wage restraint became increasingly imposed and disrupted. The 1977-78 bargaining season produced challenges from the Leyland toolroom workers and the fire-fighters – and the TGWU ceased to support the policy. When James Callaghan attempted to enforce a 5% limit for 1978-79, the dam burst as a wide range of groups sought to compensate for 3 years of belt-tightening. The role of employers is also noteworthy. Companies like Fords were not prepared to abide by government norms any more than their employees.

5. The lessons for any future corporatist experiment would appear to include the need for formalised tripartite bargaining across the economic spectrum and the necessity for the government to deliver on *its* promises. Whether this is possible in a situation of economic decline and whether such formalised bargaining stimulates a heightening of aspirations are arguable issues. A key question is whether bodies like the CBI and the TUC, given their traditions and structure, and Britain's devolved and fragmented system of collective bargaining, are in a position to undertake the orchestration of intra-organisational bargaining required for meaningful and enduring concertation. A further problem is the unions' control of the Labour Party.

6. Another fundamental criticism contends that corporatism, even of the very limited type practised in the 1970s, compromises the independence of trade unions, weakens the links between leadership and rank and file and undermines activism. Union leaders spending a greater proportion of their time on quangos would be better occupied building up the strengths of their unions. Their influence on these bodies is limited and they become increasingly estranged from their members and any conception of activist trade unionism. It is not simply that the results trade unions achieve in corporatist-style arrangements don't justify the price. Such policies have demobilised trade unionism and partially explain the election of the Thatcher government and the unions' fumbling response.

Union power in the 1970s

It is often claimed that the election of the 1979 Conservative government marked a sudden and decisive decline in the fortunes of the unions who, in the period 1974-79, dominated government policy making. This view is open to question on the following grounds:

1. It is difficult not to agree with the assertion that 'the year 1975 marked a high point of union influence as rare as it was brief' (Coates, 1980, 71). The employment legislation, particularly the provisions on recognition and the closed shop, provided means for consolidating and extending the growth in union density since 1968 (see chapter 3). There were soon more than 2,000 nominees installed on tripartite bodies at national and local level. There were high hopes of the Industry Act. And the TUC leaders were, it seemed, never out of Downing Street.

2. After this it was downhill most of the way. By early 1975, Chancellor Callaghan was already stating: 'Britain must now accept lower average wages or face mounting unemployment'. By the summer, the unions had accepted the trade-off, for it was clear that acceptance of the £6 maximum would involve a fall in living standards for many trade unionists. Henceforth, the real power the unions were able to demonstrate lay in delivering 24 months of tight wage control which reduced real earnings by around 10%. Moreover, the trade-off did not work. By 1977, the unemployment figure had more than doubled, there was disillusion with the employment laws and the government had traded off the maintenance of public expenditure they had promised the TUC to the International Monetary Fund, in return for a large loan.

3. Corporatist bargaining involves unions in restraining the economic power of their members in return for the maintenance of full employment and welfare expenditure. Yet under Labour, school-building programmes were cut by 60%, hospital-building was reduced by 30% and fewer council houses were built than under the previous Tory Government. Moreover, it was Labour, in defiance of union policies, which ruptured the post-war commitment to full employment and Keynesianism. As James Callaghan told the 1976 Labour Party Conference: 'We used to think that you could spend your way out of a recession by cutting taxes and boosting government spending. I tell you in all candour that this option no longer exists.'

4. If Labour was not converted to monetarism, they increasingly utilised, from 1976, a monetarist approach, cutting public expenditure as a proportion of gross national product, reducing the budget deficit and introducing monetary targets. They differed from monetarists in their reliance on incomes policy, in the large subventions to firms in trouble, such as British Steel and Chrysler, in their limited programme of nationalisations, and in their close links with the trade unions. Nontheless, scrutiny of Labour policies illustrates the need to see the degree of continuity as well as change in Thatcherism. Also the reluctant acquiescence of the unions in a modified monetarism, designed to placate the IMF, shows the distance between the rhetoric of trade union power and the very limited reality.

5. Far from the unions dictating policy, trade union power was used to secure members' acquiescence in a policy very different from

that union conferences advocated. However, the limits of the unions' power of restraint was also evident. As we have seen, any corporatist-style strategy requires a reconciliation *within* the key interest groups of competing demands and interests. Until 1978, Labour's incomes policy favoured semi-skilled workers in the private sector and manual workers in the public sector. This eroded differentials which created opposition to the policy, opposition to Labour and a growing level of support for Mrs Thatcher's promise of a return to free collective bargaining.

6. What trade union leaders gained under the Labour government was not so much 'the power to determine the substantive drift of policy, as the ability to participate in a new set of *procedural* rights which created the very impression of influence that the resulting drift of policy so often belied' (Coates, 1980, 203). The negative power of trade unionism was demonstrated in the strikes of 1978-79. Its positive power was essentially demonstrated in subordination to Labour's leaders rather than domination of the party.

Thatcherism and the unions

Within the broad contours of a strategy developed prior to coming to office, Mrs. Thatcher's industrial relations policy has been cumulative and adaptive. Its details were not graven on tablets of stone. The policy developed and evolved. Far from rushing her fences like Edward Heath, she has worked for success in one area before building on it in another. She has been prepared to retreat, or trim her sails when expedient, while successful policies have yielded further alternatives.

For example, in 1979, the Tory leader felt constrained by the balance of forces in the party to appoint Jim Prior Secretary for Employment. Prior still supported the ideas of Heath's post-1972 experiment and looked to revise the social contract with a stronger TUC and CBI, policing a voluntary incomes policy and exercising greater control over plant and company bargaining on the German model. Prior was determined that union legislation should be cautious and limited and that confrontation should be avoided. However, Prior increasingly found himself out of sympathy with other ministers as the leader's domination increased. Having waited patiently until the time was ripe, Mrs Thatcher despatched Prior to

Belfast, replacing him with the far more radical Norman Tebbit. He was then able to quickly start where Prior had hoped to finish, supplementing the 1980 Employment Act with the 1982 legislation.

In general terms, policy has required the transformation of trade unions, not their extirpation. The models of US business unions and Japanese enterprise unions have been periodically cited. In the interests of restoring a market economy, industrial relations policy has involved a range of measures.

1. At its heart, Conservative policy demanded the decisive weakening of the bargaining power of the unions. There were, therefore, to be limitations on industrial action and the closed shop. Mrs Thatcher aimed at a decisive reduction of union membership and the development of new hi-tech non-union and strike-free small businesses. Partly to serve these ends, public corporations should be sold off, public services privatised and changes in the industrial structure accelerated.

2. The government wished to develop a non-political business unionism. This required not only a weakening of links with the Labour Party, but a diminution of conceptions of trade unionism as a *movement*, a loosening of solidaristic bonds across industry and a greater identification of the union and its membership with the needs of the enterprise. 'In the nineties,' Norman Tebbit stated, 'I believe that managements and work forces will have to come closer together, seeing that their common interest is in the firm – not the national union.'

3. These objectives required a severe attenuation of any conception of unions as a 'fourth estate' in society. Union leaders were to be excluded from the corridors of power and returned to their proper place in the industrial field. Here, they should show themselves more responsive to the aspirations of their ordinary members at the expense of the concerns of irresponsible activists, a change to be facilitated the introduction of systems of plebiscatory democracy into the unions.

4. Artificial constraints on wage determination, Mrs Thatcher argued, should be removed and wages should find their market level related to productivity and profitability, not comparability and the 'going rate'.

5. Many trade unionists had a stake in the *old* system of a swollen public sector, subsidies to industry and privileges for unions. Whilst waiting for the new market to deliver increased prosperity,

schemes for employee shareholding, profit sharing, employee involvement, as well as wider measures such as council house sales, should be implemented to give workers a stake in the *new* system.

6. Employers must to these ends, restructure industrial relations and reorganise the work process through the introduction of new technology, increased flexibility and no-strike deals.

7. The precursor of a residual state must be an activist state, intervening in the labour market to prepare the conditions for an eventual and final withdrawal. The government must set an example to the private sector through its actions in the public sector. Strict cash limits on public sector pay would give unions and management a straight choice between more pay and less jobs. Unemployment would be allowed to rise and the government would refuse to bail out struggling employers. This would undermine unions' ability to resist change and dampen down expectations. However, a number of set-piece confrontations between the government and public sector unions were budgeted for.

This policy has been adroitly applied. The government gritted its teeth in the face of rising unpopularity between 1979 and 1981 and waited until unemployment had blitzed the private sector unions before taking a tougher line in the public sector. It intensified wage control and job loss policies only in 1982. Within this approach, the government was willing to take on the already weakened steel union in 1980 but retreat before the still strong miners in 1981. Haunted by the experiences of the Heath administration, they were determined to avoid both a public sector union alliance and an even broader alliance between unions in the public and private sectors.

If required, Mrs Thatcher was quite prepared to make concessions to strong groups as she did to the water workers in 1980 and 1983 and to the railway workers during the miners' strike, when fears of a united front were particularly strong. Each public sector case was examined in power terms. Those who could cause disruption got a better deal than groups with weaker bargaining power – until the government was ready to take *them* on.

Out in the cold

Union leaders in the 1970s had direct access to ministers. They were also meshed into social decision making via a network of industrial and economic bodies such as the NEDC; the Industrial Training Boards; the Advisory Conciliation and Arbitration Services; the Health and Safety Executive; the Manpower Services Commission; and the National Enterprise Board. They were well represented on the boards of nationalised industries. TUC nominees also sat on bodies such as the Schools' Council, the Health Authorities, the two Equality Commissions and the panels of Social Security and industrial tribunals.

Direct contact with government immediately decreased. With the passing of Prior, it almost ceased. In one sense, there was no point in ministers holding talks with union leaders; they were simply not prepared to trim their policies for, in Mrs Thatcher's words, 'there was no alternative'. Conservative economic policy was premissed on the fact that there was no margin available for concessions and the concessions the unions wanted would impede imperative change. Also involved was a removal of the unions' *legitimacy* as participants in social decision-making.

The restoration of individualism and the free market required government and management to address citizens directly, not through the good offices of bureaucrats. Not only was there no such thing as a free lunch, this process legitimated the collectivism which so urgently required surgery.

The unfruitful nature of the few contacts there *were* and the TUC boycott of talks over the employment legislation further cooled the atmosphere. As Conservative industrial relations policies gradually achieved success, there was less need to seek the co-operation of the unions. In retrospect, the government only agreed to talk with the TUC leaders when they smelt trouble, as over the 1981 inner-city riots and over GCHQ. And even then, the union leaders claimed, it was simply to enable Mrs Thatcher to read them a lecture.

The union role on state sponsored committees has also been scaled down. ACAS' legal role in securing union recognition and the extension of collective bargaining was scrapped. Mrs Thatcher made it clear that union representation on public bodies would be limited to those which required industrial relations expertise. Even on industrial tribunals, the TUC monopoly of nominations was broken. The NEB and most of the training boards were abolished. The Health and Safety Executive was starved of resources. Nonetheless, NEDC, the MSC and ACAS remained in place. But the power of union representatives on these bodies to influence government policy was at an all time low. Immediately after the 1987 election, the government announced, with no consultation, that the NEDC would in future meet only quarterly. The Chancellor would only chair one meeting, there would be a severe reduction in staffing and 20 of the 35 development committees, 'the little Neddies', would be axed. The foundation-stones of corporatism was being significantly eroded. Mr Fowler, the new Employment Secretary, decided that the 3 employers' representatives on the MSC, who balanced the 3 union representatives, would be trebled. Employer representation on the 7 remaining training boards would also be increased.

Wages

Since 1979, the government has sustained an attack upon key institutions of collective bargaining such as the annual pay round, comparability, national negotiations and job evaluation. As Employment Minister, Kenneth Clarke, said in 1986, 'if we can move to a system where pay increases are based primarily on performance, merit, company profitability and demand and supply in the local labour market, we will dethrone once and for all the annual pay round and the belief that pay increases do not have to be earned'.

In the public sector, the Standing Commission on Pay Comparability was terminated. The Civil Service Pay Research Units, which linked pay with the private sector, were also abolished, as was the National Water Council, which co-ordinated pay rates. The argument that public sector pay should be determined by supply and demand was taken to extremes in 1986, when the government removed the schoolteachers' rights to negotiate. A further concern has been the removal of institutional constraints such as minimum wage-setting machinery, which has been seen as 'pricing people out of jobs'. As the Conservatives started their third term, the insistant emphasis was on the need to end national pay bargaining. The government was frustrated by the inability of large-scale unemployment to exert downward pressure on wages and the limited extent to which regional disparities in employment were reflected in pay levels. It was terrified of what would happen to already buoyant wages if unemployment started falling significantly or if inflation gathered momentum.

Whilst many employers had moved from national multi-employer to company bargaining, few appeared to be pressing pay determination down further to local plant level – there were exceptions such as

Lucas and GEC. In response to appeals from the Chancellor, Nigel Lawson, at the NEDC, many employers' organisations declared their support for national bargaining. They claimed that it helped to hold down pay increases and avoid leap-frogging through unions targeting profitable plants and companies. Many non-pay issues were more efficiently administered at national level. Smaller companies lacked the resources for single employer bargaining and national disputes procedures were particularly useful in limiting disputes. In its 1986 *Annual Report*, ACAS emphasised the advantages national bargaining possessed. The TUC also contended that national wage deals made for stability. They claimed that pay levels did reflect regional differences and a greater link would do little to reduce unemployment.

Privatisation
The Conservatives regarded the public sector as, in itself, an important constraint on the development of a free market economy and as a sanctuary from which militant trade unionism could extend its corrupting influence to the private sector. Mrs Thatcher felt she needed to cut the size of the public sector to reduce public expenditure, to provide the greater efficiency private ownership would bring and to increase the choice open to consumers. But the privatisation strategy also had the inestimable advantage of opening monopoly trade unionism to the cutting edge of the free market. Unions would be flushed out of their strongholds – 90% of public sector employees in 1979 were unionised, a far higher density than in the private sector. Judging by the opinion polls, the policy was popular and greater employee share ownership would give workers a greater stake in the free enterprise system.

The first Thatcher government took action over enterprises such as Britoil, Cable and Wireless and British Aerospace and piecemeal action to privatise NHS and local authority services. By 1982, it encountered opposition from NALGO over the sale of gas show-rooms and from the British Telecom unions. Moreover, unions attempted to organise boycotts on share sales and, in 1983, the POEU took industrial action. Nonetheless, the government pressed on, circumnavigating scandals over give-away sale prices along the way. In 1984/85, Scott Lithgow, Inmos, Jaguar and 51% of British Telecom were sold off. Increased competition was injected into the public sector in the same gradual fashion. In Mrs Thatcher's first term, private coaches were licensed to compete with the public company. In her second term, local bus transport was deregulated. After her third victory, the Prime Minister was ready to take a bite at some of the larger morsels. Water, electricity and steel were targeted for a return to private ownership. Rail and postal services were ruled out for the moment, but coal was under consideration.

The privatisation programme constituted a limited success. Union opposition had been faced down. Labour's initial policy on rena-tionalisation had to be modified. Both the unions and Labour had to give up on attempts to lecture employees on the evils of share ownership and go some way towards adapting Conservative ideas in their own programmes. Against this, however, there is already a rising stream of complaints regarding the service offered by newly privatised concerns and the 1987 stock market crash.

The unions' political response

During the 1980s, the unions' response to Thatcherism has boiled down to a continued assertion of their right to a key role in the corridors of power. They have urged opposition to the government's policies in an attempt to pressurise it into change. These efforts have been carried on within a policy framework whose major imperative was increasingly the return of a Labour government. The TUC saw the need to temper its opposition with responsibility and to ensure that it did not develop into a political challenge to a constitutionally elected government.

In the immediate aftermath of the 1979 election defeat, impetus for change in the Labour Party came from the left-wing constituency activists who felt betrayed by the policies of the Wilson/Callaghan governments. Their mood was given form by the pressure group, the Campaign For Labour Party Democracy. Coining the phrase 'never again', they pushed for constitutional reforms, such as mandatory reselection of MPs, the election of the leadership by the whole party, not just the MPs, and greater powers for conference. The left turn also involved enthusiasm for what became known as the Alternative Economic Strategy. This had four main ingredients: a far greater degree of state control over industry; a far greater planning of foreign trade and control over finance capital; a policy of aggressive redistribution of income and wealth; and the mobilisation of workers to support and implement the policies of a future Labour government.

The leadership of unions such as the TGWU, NUPE, ASTMS and the NUM shared the new mood to some degree. Others, such as the EETPU and AEU, staunchly supported resistance from Labour's right wing. Many unions were far from opposed to proposals which would, in the end, because of their block votes, strengthen their control over the Party, even if they had little in common with the proposers.

The decision to give the unions the lion's share of the votes in the new electoral college was more the result of accident and manoeuvre than strategic foresight, but a union like the TGWU supported Tony Benn on the second ballot in his bid for the deputy leadership against Dennis Healey. This election, in the autumn of 1981, represented the limits of the swing left. Concerned at the formation of the SDP in March 1981, and the divisions in the party and, more importantly from their point of view, their spilling-over into the unions, union chiefs presided over a truce, arranged at Bishops Stortford in early 1982. By that time, the Right had re-established control over the NEC but continuing divisions within the party contributed to Labour's ineffectual campaign in the 1983 election.

The TUC initially failed to understand the decisive political change Mrs Thatcher's victory represented. Encouraged by Prior's appointment and the continued presence of the Tory 'one nation' wets in government, they foresaw a 'U-turn'. Once unemployment reached a certain figure, Mrs Thatcher, like Heath before her, would be forced to reverse her policies and revert to the norms of post-war consensus. The pendulum would soon swing. A short dose of Thatcherism would quickly turn the electorate leftwards once more. The TUC's job, meanwhile, was to propagandise against Tory policies, organise their affiliates into the posture of antagonism which had proved so successful in the 1970s, and involve themselves in detailed policy-making against the day when Labour was returned to power.

The TUC was not prepared to lead direct action any more than in the previous decade. But if such action occurred, the key calulation was the degree to which it embarrassed Mrs Thatcher, as against its consequences for a Labour victory at the polls. So the General Council was prepared to support days of action, rather than strikes, against legislation and in support of the NHS workers in 1980 and 1982. But, in the latter year, it moved fast to instruct ASLEF to call

off action which could have embroiled the unions in a confrontation
with the government.

The TUC-Labour Party Liaison Comittee was soon meeting
regularly and produced two major policy statements, *Trade and
Industry: A Policy for Expansion* (1980), and *Economic Planning
and Industrial Democracy* (1982). Whilst they made some concessions to the rhetoric of the AES, these documents basically
rehearsed, with slight refurbishment, most of the policies some
partially implemented, some never tried, of the previous decade.
Their ideas found their way into Labour's 1983 manifesto. But the
proposals for a revived National Enterprise Board, renovated
planning agreements, a radical extension of industrial democracy,
the reduction of unemployment by increases in public spending and
the use, if necessary, of selective import controls, failed to convince
the electorate. After 4 years' intensive propaganda and condemna-
tion of Thatcherism, the TUC had failed to convince even a majority
of trade unionists to vote for the Labour Party.

The new realism
After Labour's worst post-war defeat, the unions got behind the new
leadership of Neil Kinnock and Roy Hattersley. At the TUC, Len
Murray vocally supported by right-wing leaders such as Frank
Chappell of the EETPU and Alistair Graham of the CPSA, outlined
plans for a 'new realism'; the post -1979 strategy of antagonism had
failed. The unions must accept the reality of Thatcherism, be
prepared for a more conciliatory approach, accept that they were
not, in Murray's words, 'some sort of alternative government,
Brother Bonnie Prince Charlie waiting to be summoned back from
exile'. Unions had to represent their members' interests *now* and
hold out the hand of co-operation to Mrs Thatcher. This would
involve the unions distancing themselves to a greater degree from
Labour.

The problem for the unions was to what extent identification with
Labour should inhibit involvement with the Conservatives. In the
1950s, for example, the TUC did not divulge to the Labour Party the
content of its discussions with the Churchill government. The turmoil
of the 1960s and 1970s had increased the bond between party and
unions, and so had Mrs Thatcher's early stance. But, of course, a
growing proportion of the TUC's membership was in white collar
unions not affiliated to Labour whose leaders wanted to talk to the

Tories and to the Alliance. They argued strongly that their members expected them to protect their interests by doing business with whoever had power. But the insuperable problem was that the political basis for a new accord between the Conservative Party and the unions, in which the TUC would play a stripped-down subaltern role, was non-existent. Mrs Thatcher had never wanted the unions. By 1983 she did not need them. Murray's refusal in December 1983 to support the NGA in its dispute with Eddie Shah was a clear signal that 'Barkis was willing'. It alienated many union leaders.

In January 1984, Murray co-authored a charter for the new approach, *TUC Strategy*. Whilst it reasserted TUC opposition to Conservative legislation, it also stressed the utility of trade unions to employers in increasing efficiency. Strikes were harmful. Trade unions accepted 'the need to sustain the enterprise as a thriving concern'. Employers and government, in their turn, 'have to take note of unions because they are the vehicle for winning the consent of individuals, as workers, for policies employers and governments wish to pursue and that they need the co-operation of workers if they are to succeed'.

The document went on to recall the historic links between the unions and the Tories: 'TUC involvement in government owes much to Churchill's war-time coalition government and to the Conservative Governments that established the NEDC and the MSC'. If the TUC, since 1979, had criticised Conservative policies, it had 'drawn a clear distinction between the use of industrial action for industrial purposes, and its use for political purposes insisting that governments, no matter how distasteful their policies, are to be changed through the ballot box, not industrial action'. Governments, whatever their complexion, had to involve the TUC because of the important section of society it represented.

Cogent, corporatist and conciliatory as this offer of partnership was, Mrs Thatcher wasn't having any of it. The storm in January 1984 over her attempts to ban trade unions at the GCHQ signals centre in Cheltenham produced the TUC's clearest gesture yet. If the government withdrew the ban, they promised a *voluntary* 'no strike' agreement. Mrs Thatcher met the TUC leaders and turned down flat their handsome offer. In the face of such intransigence, Murray was unable to hold the line for 'new realism'. The TUC withdrew its representatives from the NEDC and whilst this proved temporary,

the miners strike then dislocated the normal rhythm of trade
unionism for a good 12 months.

Murray's subsequent resignation and the defeat of the miners
produced a new situation. The Left was now on the run, as the defeat
of municipal socialism and the expulsion of 'Militant' supporters
made clear. As most of Labour's 'left wing' regrouped behind Neil
Kinnock, the TUC, under Norman Willis, eschewed any dramatic
new initiative. They were too busy trying to maintain a united front,
for asserting their authority on the industrial – let alone the political –
front was becoming increasingly difficult.

The TUC's growing impotence was illustrated in the miners'
strike, and it was soon caught up in the in-fighting over whether the
unions should accept government money for ballots, and the rumpus
between the EETPU and the print unions over the dispute at Rupert
Murdoch's Wapping plant. There was a real and continuing danger of
a split-off by the engineers and electricians. The TUC's reduced
political role was highlighted when, during the 1987 election
campaign, Labour Party leaders reiterated that union influence in a
Neil Kinnock government would be clearly limited. That there would
be no return to the days of Jack Jones and Harold Wilson was
confirmed by the attempts of Labour luminaries to distance themselves from the unions during the campaign. The gloominess of the
unions' political failure was underlined by Labour's third defeat in a
row.

The trade union electorate

The future of the Labour Party as a party of government is central to
the question of the unions' future in politics. Table 7 illustrates the
broad problem; a majority of trade union members no longer vote for
the trade unions' party. Decline is gradual until 1979, but Labour is
still the choice of more than half the trade union electorate. Then a
sharp decline sets in. Labour's union vote collapses in 1983 and only
marginally recovers in 1987. The situation is worse amongst white
collar trade unionists. Moreover, a new factor in the last two
elections is the emergence of the Alliance, which took 29% of the
union vote in 1983 and 26% 4 years later. Despite the success of the
political fund ballots, it is clear that the politics of trade union
members are very different from those represented in union policies.

Table 7

A   *How the electorate voted (%)*

Party	1964	1966	1970	1974(Feb)	1974(Oct)	1979	1983	1987
Labour	44	48	43	37	39	37	28	31
Conservative	43	42	46	38	36	44	42	42
SDP/Liberals	11	9	8	19	18	14	25	23

B   *How trade unionists voted (%)*

Party	1964	1966	1970	1974(Feb)	1974(Oct)	1979	1983	1987
Labour	73	71	66	55	55	51	39	42
Conservative	22	25	28	30	23	33	31	30
Others	5	4	6	15	16	13	30	26

C   *How social groups voted (%)*

Party	*Professional/Managerial*			*Office/clerical*		
	1974	1983	1987	1974	1983	1987
Conservative	63	62	59	51	55	52
Labour	12	12	14	24	21	22
Liberal/SDP	22	26	27	21	24	26

	Skilled manual			*Semi-skilled manual*		
	1974	1983	1987	1974	1983	1987
Conservative	26	39	43	22	29	31
Labour	49	35	34	57	44	50
Liberal/SDP	20	27	24	16	27	19

In the past, the basic determinant of voting behaviour appears to have been social location. The majority of manual workers voted

Labour and the majority of white collar workers voted Conservative. This identification with the parties was not complete. Up to a quarter of manual workers voted Conservative and up to a fifth of white collar workers voted Labour. This pattern, with nearly 90% of the vote being split between the two big parties, began to disintegrate in the 1970s. Both parties have lost votes. Labour recorded almost 49% of the vote in 1951 and the Tories 48%. Even in 1970, the figures were 43% and 46%. Yet, in 1987, the Tories won a massive victory with 43% against Labour's 31%. Labour has clearly lost out more than the Conservatives. To some degree, this is related to the emergence of the SDP, but this does not completely explain why so many voters have deserted Labour. Labour has suffered, as table 7C discloses, a stiff drop in its support from manual workers, particularly skilled manual workers.

Many people have looked for explanations to the changing class structure. The manual working class, although still the biggest single occupational group, is declining, while white collar workers in particular the managerial–professional category, are growing fast. It has been argued that the drop in the number of manual workers, in itself, explains Labour's reduced vote. There is still a correlation between voting Labour and being in a union, even if it is a weaker one than in the past. Yet today, there are 3 million fewer trade unionists than at the start of the 1980s.

Others have stressed a weakening of old allegiances and argued that a process of *partisan dealignment* has taken place. Rather than identifying with one party, voters are more willing to shop around. Still other writers have stressed the importance of new divisions in society between those who are dependent on the state, whether because they work in the public sector, are unemployed or live in council housing, and those who are not. This, it is claimed, could explain why skilled manual workers in the private sector, with private houses and minimal dependence on welfare benefits, vote Conservative. It was pointed out in the 1979 and 1983 elections that the Conservatives attracted more private sector votes than they did in the public sector, particularly among non-union members. In 1983, 46% of the public sector workers voted Labour compared with 29% voting Conservative, whilst in the private sector the figures were 37% and 36%.

The 1987 election illustrates many of the problems. Labour's campaign was one of the most professional ever mounted. Yet it had minimal impact; the positions of the parties hardly changed from start to finish. The Conservatives had scored in 1979 an orthodox victory, well within the normal range of success registered by victorious parties in the previous 2 decades. Nineteen eighty three represented not so much a real breakthrough for Thatcherism – although it did consolidate its newly found support amongst skilled manual workers – as a collapse of Labour's vote. The changes in 1987 were small. Mrs Thatcher lost 17 seats, the Alliance lost 5 and Labour gained 21, pushing up its vote by 4 points. Compared with 1983, the Conservatives lost votes in the middle -class and white collar categories – down 3% in the managerial/professional group – but received 53% of the vote in the skilled manual category, compared with Labour's 34%. In the last election Labour won in 1974 the comparable figures were Labour 49%, Conservatives 31%.

Labour increased its vote amongst the semi-skilled and the unskilled and gained an overall majority amongst the unemployed. The 1983 split between North and South was even more glaring. In the north of England, Scotland and Wales, Labour was an overwhelming victor. In the South, its vote declined in London and it had no presence outside the metropolis. Many analyses of the election saw the working -class vote split along the lines of whether voters lived in the North or South, were owner-occupiers, and worked in the public or private sector.

Thatcherism triumphant?

Some commentators have emphasised the radical nature of Thatcherism as a novel set of ideas. Stuart Hall has claimed that at the centre of Thatcherism is what he terms 'authoritarian populism'. The Thatcher wing of the Conservative Party, he argues, took up important, popular concerns such as the rate of inflation, the rise of crime, the fact that the education system was not providing children with the skills they needed, the fact that unions were too powerful, as well as a desire for greater economic freedom, less taxation, and so forth. Thatcher orchestrated these concerns, which Labour had failed to answer, in a politics which fused together a more powerful and coercive 'strong' state with a more open market system in the economy and the social services. By responding to people's anxieties and systematising answers to them, Thatcherism won over key sections of the electorate. Thatcherism is, therefore, essentially a powerful, compelling, new set of ideas which grips the imagination of many working-class voters.

Critics have counter-claimed that Thatcherism represents little that is new; many of its preoccupations were inherent in the philosophy and politics of the Heath government before its 1972 'U-turn'. Further, there is a certain continuity with the policies of the Callaghan government. Hall, it is felt, exaggerates the power, coherency and reach of Thatcherism. Firstly, its success is limited. In the 3 elections of the 1950s, the Conservatives' percentage vote was 48%, 50% and 49%. In the 3 elections under Mrs Thatcher, it has been 44%, 43% and 42%. This represents serious decline rather than breaking new ground. If Thatcherism is so popular, why has it not significantly increased its vote compared with 1979?

Secondly, it is asserted that the Conservative victories in the 1980s are largely due to the emergence of the SDP. In that sense they owe more to luck than to the development and success of a revolutionary new creed. The fact that Mrs Thatcher remains in office represents the failings of Labour rather than a positive endorsement of her ideas. Thirdly, Hall's view that Thatcherism represents 'an exceptional form of the state' also confuses appearance with reality. Mrs Thatcher may have taken a strong line on law and order, increased the numbers of police and used them against trade unions, most dramatically during the miners' strike, and shown little respect for civil liberties and open government, but Britain is still a parliamentary democracy and if there is more of a 'strong state' under Mrs Thatcher than there was under Stanley Baldwin (and that is arguable) the change is one of *quantity* rather than quality.

Finally, what success Mrs Thatcher has had, it is claimed, has more to do with canny political strategy and material changes than her success in the battle of ideas. Skilled workers voted Tory in 1979 simply to get more money. Under Mrs Thatcher they have got it, as well as, in some cases, council houses at give-away prices; and it looks more than it is when their neighbours are unemployed. This is illustrated by the opinion polls which show majorities opposing tax cuts if they are paid for by reductions in social expenditure. However, rising living standards for the majority leads them to opt for the status quo particularly when there is little confidence in the alternatives on offer. In reality, what success Thatcherism has had is based upon *material* not *ideological* factors. It is difficult to see where the mass support for Thatcherism is in Liverpool, Glasgow, Newcastle or Manchester. And the difference in voting patterns between North and South is to be explained, in the end, by material differences rather than differences of ideas.

This view receives some support from analysis of the 1987 election results. Evidence indicates that had the electorate voted on the issues they selected as most important, unemployment, the NHS, education and defence, Labour would have won. But the election in the end was fought and won on economic issues. From the autumn of 1986, surveys showed a big increase in the number of those believing that the economy in general, and living standards in particular, were improving and a close, positive correlation between holding this belief and voting Conservative and a close negative correlation between holding this belief and voting Labour. In a situation where wages were outpacing prices, complemented by pre-election tax cuts, increases in lending and extra money for the social services, people voted on the basis of their perception of the material situation.

The forward march of Labour halted?

Eric Hobsbawm has argued, in the book *The Forward March of Labour Halted?* and in a series of articles, that the Labour Party's recent problems are part of an historic crisis facing the Labour movement. The advance of party and unions was halted between 1948 and 1951. According to Hobsbawm, important changes since that time have centred on the decline of the manual working class, the disintegration of traditional communities and common lifestyles and levels of affluence undreamt of in the past. These developments have produced a growth of sectionalism in the Labour movement and a militancy focused largely on sectional wage demands, symptoms of a decine in class-consciousness which has produced a diminished attachment to trade unions and the Labour Party. From his analysis Hobsbawm concludes that there is a need for Labour to adopt policies acceptable to its right-wing and middle-class voters, and attempt to win back the SDP which should never have been forced out of the Party. There should be an electoral arrangement with the Alliance and, indeed, with all those opposed to Mrs Thatcher, on the model of the Popular Fronts of the 1930s.

A basic criticism of Hobsbawm takes up his 'march' metaphor which, it can be argued, unhelpfully simplifies what has been more of an historical ebb and flow in the fortunes of a Labour movement, going forward at one time on one front, being driven back on another. The unions were severely defeated in 1926, yet Labour was elected 3 years later. The collapse of the 1929 government and the retreat of the Labour movement in the 1920s and 1930s, moreover, shows just how questionable Hobsbawm's idea of a forward march until the 1950s is. It was only in Hobsbawm's period of decline that many of the strengths of British trade unions, such as the edifice of workplace trade unionism, surely a vital expression of working-class self -activity and combativity, for all its flaws and limitations, was constructed.

It was, after all, in 1966, a time when prosperity for many areas of Britain was at its height, that Labour won 48.8% of the vote, almost equalling its all-time greatest performance of 1951. How, 16 years into the reversal of the forward march, did Labour do better than it did in 1924, 1929 or 1935? How, in the age of the affluent worker, flower power and the Beatles, did Labour do better than it did in the depressions of the 1930s and the 1980s? Moreover, had Hobsbawm pointed out to Edward Heath in the early 1970s that the forward march of Labour had halted more than 2 decades before, the Conservative Premier, faced with the battles over the Industrial Relations Act and the miners' strikes, would have, surely, been less than impressed.

The strikes over legislation in the 1960s and 1970s raise questions about the sectional and economistic nature of the militancy of that period. But if Hobsbawm is basically correct in his overall estimation of that period, it is difficult to see any significant increase in sectionalism compared with past strike movements such as that of 1918-22. Trade unionism embraces a far greater section of the working class in the 1980s than it did in the 1920s, including many of Hobsbawm's white collar groups, whilst the entry of women into the labour force provides the potential for greater unity and power than when they were cut off from the work process and corralled in the home.

The situation is, thus, more complex than Hobsbawm allows. He tends to see the past through rose-coloured spectacles, and focuses on changes in prosperity and the social structure at the expense of politics. He places very little weight on the policies of the Labour governments of the 1960s and 1970s and Labour's failure to provide any coherent, convincing policies essentially different since 1979.

Any account of Labour's problems surely needs to place more emphasis upon the way the 1974-79 government attempted to control and discipline its working class base without delivering any meaningful reforms. It is working-class votes that are essential to Labour. It is these votes it has lost since 1979. And, given their last experience of Labour in power, this should not be too surprising.

Hobsbawm's advocacy of an electoral arrangement with the Alliance has also provoked dissent. The idea of an anti-Thatcher majority is certainly simplistic. A MORI poll after the 1987 election asked Alliance voters for their preference if the election produced a deadlock: 25% wanted another quick election; 43% wanted a Conservative/Alliance government; only 29% wanted a Labour/ Alliance administration. Moreover, the 1987 result and subsequent events show the Alliance in disintegration. Labour, it would appear, if it gets its act together, can recover *some* lost ground by going it alone. And the price which would be asked of Labour in terms of giving up vital policies is a constraint on any electoral arrangement. Against this, Labour has to face one chilling fact: if it is to replace Mrs Thatcher in the next election, it will have to engineer a swing against her greater than any registered in the post war-period.

Conclusion

The political influence unions wielded in the early 1970s was real, if susceptible to exaggeration. From 1975, a decline set in. Since 1979, the unions have suffered a severe loss of political power. They have been forced to abdicate their role as the direct voice of working people in the political process. The significance of this development should not be underestimated. Many of the structures of corporatism remain in place but their power is qualitatively reduced and the influence on them of the unions insubstantial. Having failed to achieve their objectives under Labour, the unions under the Conservatives have been pushed out of the centres of power on to the margins. If British unions never became such a firm fixture in the political firmament as their Swedish or German counterparts, their fall is no less dramatic. Their political arm has been excluded from power for a decade. Their overtures to Mrs Thatcher have produced no response. Economic and industrial relations policies have been developed and implemented with no union participation. Contacts with ministers have been limited and the only bargain the TUC has

struck with this government has been the agreement to police
political funds more closely.

The victory in the political fund ballots meant that the unions
staved off a decisive reverse. It enabled their battered battalions to
stabilise the front but at a crucial distance from the boundaries they
occupied in the 1970s. Unless we wish to revise accepted views of
trade unionism which, across a broad spectrum, insist on the need for
unions' industrial power to be complemented by successful political
pressure, we must agree that an important change has occurred. How
important, how enduring and for what reasons all remain contentious
questions. However, before we can come to a further estimation of
the impact of Thatcherism on the unions and look at the future
direction union strategies might take, we need to examine what has
been happening in the legal and industrial spheres since 1979.

Further reading

K. Ewing, 1982, is a good detailed analysis of the 1913 Trade Union
Act and the background to political funds. More recent developments in the relationship between unions and the Labour Party are
covered in K. Coates and T. Topham, 1986; D. Fatchett, 1987; and
A. Taylor, 1987. P. Hain, 1986, is a good analysis of the whole area.

J. Prior, 1986, provides some interesting insights into the policy of
recent Conservative governments. A good survey is P. Riddell, 1985.
For some of the arguments about Thatcherism, see S. Hall and M.
Jacques, 1983; and E. Hobsbawm, 1981 and 1984.

The best detailed account of the last Labour government is D.
Coates, 1980. An extensive discussion of corporatist developments in
a range of countries is contained in J. Goldthorpe ed, 1984. A good
criticism of both corporatism and neo-*laissez-faire* is P. Armstrong et
al, 1984, whilst L. Panitch, 1985, discusses some of the arguments
about corporatism in the 1970s. Different views as to what is
happening to voting patterns and why are covered in P. Dunleavy
and C. Husbands, 1985, and A. Heath et al, 1985. B. Jones and D.
Kavanagh, 1987, gives a good brief account of the 1987 position.

Chapter 3

Trade unions and the law

The 1980s have seen a revolution in labour law. The dramatic tide of change of the previous decade, which saw the law give new protection to trade unions and individual workers, has been halted and put into reverse. The enduring legal framework for trade union activities erected between 1870 and 1906 has been remodelled. The Conservative government has carried through a rolling programme of labour law reform, unparalleled in breadth this century.

Intellectual influences on the new Conservatism, such as F.A. Hayek, argue that trade unions 'are the prime source of unemployment. They are the main reason for the decline of the British economy in general' (Hayek, 1980, 358). Law is at the root of the trade union problem: 'trade unions' legal privileges (are) the chief cause of unemployment ... There can be no salvation for Britain until the special privileges granted to the trade unions three-quarters of ago are revoked' (Hayek, 1980, 363). The manifesto on which the Conservatives were elected in 1979 took up this theme. It asserted that 'by heaping privilege without responsibility on the trade unions, Labour have given the minority of extremists the power to abuse individual liberties and to thwart Britain's chances of success'.

Mrs Thatcher's governments have acted upon these words. Before examining the changes in legislation introduced since 1979 it is important to scrutinise the view that, at the core of British labour law, there has lain a set of artificial, unjustified privileges, boosting union power to the detriment of both individual and economy and requiring drastic surgery if both constitutional and economic strength are to be restored to Britain.

Labour law and history

When trade unions emerged in Britain they faced illegality under both the criminal and the civil law. The Combination Acts of 1799 and 1800 were only part of a battery of more than 40 statutes which criminalised workers' organisation. Combination was viewed not only as a threat to the free workings of the market which guaranteed the well-being of society but, with the French Revolution sweeping Europe, as a threat to the social and political **status quo**. The penal legislation outlawed agreements or organisation to influence terms and conditions of employment, and prosecutions before the magistrates were common. The Masters and Servants Act re-enacted in 1766 and 1823 made a breach of contract by an employee a criminal offence, whereas an employer had to be suid in the civil courts. As late as between 1858 and 1875, more than 10,000 prosecutions for breach of contract occurred each year in England and Wales. Legislation also made most forms of industrial action and picketing criminal 'intimidation' or 'molestation'. Even when, in 1824-25, the Combination Acts were repealed, the new legislation re-enacted a list of criminal offences. Under both criminal and civil law, the unions were judged by the courts to be *conspiracies* and under the civil law they were associations *in restraint of trade*.

The judges did not recognise *collective* relations: the regulation of industrial life began and ended with the market and the individual contract of employment between employer and employee, which was the legal manifestation of *laissez-faire*. Ignoring the imbalance of power, the fact that the employer was already a combination who dictated terms rather than negotiating them with another party of equal bargaining power, the judges deemed illegal any attempt at combination, as collective bargaining was anathema to the common law and its custodians. When they were forced by Parliament to recognise trade unions they cavilled at their essential methods.

The 1859 Molestation of Workmen Act ushered in a period of gradual, if slow and grudging reform. The unions and their middle-class supporters pressurised the Liberal and Conservative Parties, fought every step of the way by the judges. The 1871 Trade Union Act and the Criminal Law Amendment Act of the same year protected unions from criminal liabilities, particularly from criminal conspiracy. Unions were immunised from certain actions 'in restraint of trade' and given civil status and tax and administrative advantages. The resilience of the judiciary was soon reflected in the case of *R v*.

Bunn where the organisers of a gas strike were found guilty of criminal conspiracy. Union pressure led to the 1875 Conspiracy and Protection of Property Act. This crucial legislation repealed the Master and Servant Acts. It protected unions from conspiracy where they were acting 'in contemplation of furtherance of a trade dispute', defined in terms of disputes centred on terms and conditions of employment.

The judges quickly turned their attention to civil law. Union activities were now branded as civil wrongs or torts. In a series of cases, the courts held that organising a strike to secure 100% trade union membership and the dismissal of non-members was a civil conspiracy to injure; and instructing or urging workers to withdraw their labour could constitute the tort of inducing breach of contract. In 1901, the decision of the House of Lords in the famous *Taff Vale Case* open trade union funds to attack. A further campaign by the unions led to the enactment of the 1906 Trade Disputes Act. Unions were to be protected against the torts of civil conspiracy and inducing breaches of employment, so long as they acted in contemption or furtherance of a trade dispute. Their funds were also to be protected against civil actions by employers.

Trade union privileges?

The argument against the Edwardian legal settlement is simply put. Companies, or individual citizens, cannot go around committing civil wrongs such as inducement to breach of contract. If trade unions are allowed to do so then they are the subject of special privilege, privilege which enables them to bring business to a halt, inflate wage levels, feather-bed jobs and debilitate the economy. Yet it is difficult to see how the argument that the protections place unions above 'the ordinary law of the land' can be sustained.

The 'ordinary law of the land' is not a fixed category but is constantly developing to take account of economic and social change. It is at any one time a product of political pressure by different interests. For example, in the early years of the last century, the factory owners mounted a successful campaign against the earlier system by which wages were fixed by the magistrates. Did the resultant system of free market regulation give employers special privileges or raise them above the general law of the land? Did the creation of limited liability for companies give *them* special privileges and put *them* above the ordinary law of the land on debt which applies to all individual citizens? Few adherents of the 'New Right' would accept that this was so. Yet the trade unions, by asserting the need for legal change to protect their organisation and activities, were simply asserting working-class political economy against *laissez-faire*, just as the supporters of that creed had sought to break down older structures of economy, property and law. If wage fixing by the courts is not regarded as immutable, why should wage regulation by individual bargaining be viewed in this light? If capital could not develop effectively under the absolutism of the monarchy, trade unions were unable, under the legal ordinance of *laissez-faire*, to function in any efficient fashion. If 'the ordinary law of the land' had continued to govern union activities, union organisation would have had only a twilight existence.

The argument is not really a legal argument but a political one. If one is for trade unions then one must be for their exemption from 'the ordinary law of the land'. The argument can only be about the degree of exemption. When, 10 years before the 1906 Act, Lord Justice Lindley commented that 'you cannot make a strike effective without doing more than is lawful', he was summing up the fate of trade unionism if the common law was *not* overridden by the legislature. As the Solicitor General pointed out, during the second reading of the 1906 Bill, the proposed legislation was not intended 'to confer any exceptional immunities, far from it; it was in order to remove exceptional disabilities imposed on those trade unions, disabilities which are contrary to the general spirit of our law' (von Prondzynski, 1986, 192).

Lumley v. *Gye* (1853), which introduced the civil wrong of 'inducement', involved an impresario seducing an opera singer to break a contract. The courts did not hesitate to press union support for industrial action into the same mould. But trade unions were not impresarios. Had the tort been applied in full measure, industrial action would have been generally outlawed. There was no compelling reason why the decision in *Lumley* v. *Gye* should have been applied to the very different situation of a union procuring industrial action. The 1906 Act, which protected unions from inducement to breach of contract, did not confer on the unions special privileges. It simply accepted that what was good for impresarios was not good for unions and that without protection from the fallacious analogies of the judiciary, unions could not fulfil their legitimate social and economic roles.

The interim injunction, moreover, continued to cause problems for trade unions. If an employer could make out a *prima facie* case that a tort had been committed, the judges were prepared to issue an injunction restraining industrial action until a full trial if they felt that 'the balance of convenience' favoured the employer. Invariably the courts decided that this was the position. It was more convenient to halt the action and freeze the status quo than allow economic loss to continue, leaving the employer to recoup it in damages if he succeeded at the full hearing. It was relatively easy to make out a *prima facie* case. The courts also failed to accept that the granting of an injunction could be inconvenient for the union. Yet if the strike was over a dismissal, the injunction did not restore the status quo. It did not reinstate the dismissed employee. If the strike was over wages, then the issue of an injunction normally ensured that the trade unionists had to bargain, deprived of the strike weapon, accept a settlement below what they thought possible or return to the fray months later, in circumstances perhaps less favourable to the mobilisation of industrial action.

The system of immunities

Despite its lack of substance the 'privilege' argument gains some colour from the *form* that the protections took. Parliament did not give the unions *rights*. Britain's law has never known a developed code of 'positive rights' – to organise, to bargain, to strike – such as exists in other countries. In Britain, trade unions sought 'exclusion' or 'immunity' from the common law doctrines created by the judges. The doctrine of conspiracy, the tort of inducement to breach of contract, continued in being. Under specific circumstances, the unions were exempted from their jurisdiction.

The British working class, the first in the world, lacking previous examplars and an alternative philosophy, made their way in the same piecemeal, pragmatic fashion as capital had. Their leadership was cautious and accomodative, more interested in *ad hoc* compromise than the creation of a new economic or legal order. The empiricism of British society was reflected in the lack of a written constitution. The unions, in this key formative period, with universal suffrage some way off, had no political party to articulate an alternative legal framework. They were dependent on the advice of middle-class reformers and the good will of the Conservatives and Liberals who believed in a limited role for the state. Given their experience with the law, trade unionists wished to protect themselves by retreating beyond its reach, rather than positively penetrating the legal universe. The result was a compromise with the common law rather than its transformation (Fox, 1985; Wedderburn, 1986).

The system of immunities was, therefore, simply a method of insulating the unions from judicial law-making, a means by which unions were guaranteed essential protection. The content of those protections was extremely limited. Strikers had no protection against dismissal. Pickets had no right to stop a driver or pedestrian to put their case. Industrial action to oppose government policies was not protected by the golden formula of a 'trade dispute'. Moreover, the fact that 'conspiracy' and 'inducement to breach of contract' continued to apply outside the field of industrial relations gave continued sustenance to the view that unions were being treated as a special case. Also, the fact that the common law doctrines still existed meant that they could still be developed by the judges.

The judges

In the conventional view, the judges are seen as neutral referees, deciding disputes by reference to an established body of law, in an impartial fashion. Whilst the judges are, in reality, ultimately answerable to Parliament, their relative autonomy from the political process enables them to mediate between individuals and the state and, at times, restrain the excessive deployment of political power. Marxists, in contrast, have long argued that the judiciary is an integral part of the ruling class, that 'the judicial elites, like other elites of the state system, are mainly drawn from the upper and middle layers of society and those judges who are not have clearly come to belong to those layers by the time they reach the bench' (Miliband, 1969, 138). The apparent independence of the law, whose content is determined by the state of the class struggle, but which is ultimately an instrument of capital, strengthens illusions in the neutrality of the state.

A recent distinctive critique of the conventional view notes that over the last century the dominance of the upper and middle class in recruitment to the judiciary 'is overwhelming ... four out of five full-time professional judges are products of public school and of Oxford or Cambridge' (Griffith, 1985, 26). Legal training, practice, renumeration and selection constitute conservatising factors. Judges cannot be politically neutral because they are often placed in situations where they have to make political choices. In reality,

their interpretation of what is in the public interest and therefore politically desirable is determined by the kind of people they are and the position they hold in our society ... this position is a part of established authority and so is necessarily conservative and illiberal. From all this flows the view of the public interest, which is shown in judicial attitudes such as tenderness towards private property and dislike of trade unions, strong adherence to the maintenance of order, distaste for minority opinions, demonstrations and protests ... (Griffith, 1985, 226).

The judges themselves have periodically been willing to gnaw at the edge of these problems. In the 1920s, Lord Justice Scrutton mused that:

the habits you are trained in, the people with whom you mix, lead to your having a certain class of ideas of such a nature that when you have to deal with other ideas you do not give as sound an accurate judgements as you would wish ... Labour says 'where are your impartial judges? They all move in the same circle as the employers and they are all educated and nursed in the same ideas as the employers. How can a labour man or a trade unionist get impartial justice?' It is very difficult sometimes to be sure that you have put yourself in a thoroughly impartial position between two disputants who are of your own class and one not of your own class (Abel-Smith and Stevens, 1967, 117).

Half a century later, the Lord Chancellor, Viscount Hailsham, observed that 'there is no such thing as a value-free or neutral interpretation of the law'. Whilst a prominent judge, Lord Devlin, observed that 'Judges are inevitably part of the establishment and the establishment's ideas are those which are operating in our minds ... I think the law has to be part of the establishment' (McIlroy, 1983, 15, 16).

The history of judicial law-making in relation to the trade unions certainly provides grist for the critical mill, whilst also supporting the view that 'the avoidance of outrageous bias is much more likely in periods of relative social calm than in periods of acute social conflict and stress '(Miliband, 1969, 141). As the bitter class conflict of the early years of the century gave way to the enforced quiescence of the inter-war period, the judges, in cases such as *Reynolds* v. *Shipping Federation* (1924), and the *Crofter Case* (1942) accepted as legitimate unions' objectives which they had earlier deemed unlawful. The post-war boom, too, produced few confrontations between the unions and the courts. As its disintegration led to a renewal of class struggle, judicial activism re-emerged.

The judges today

When the 1974 Labour Government clarified the 1906 position, judicial concern reached an intensity unparallelled since 1914. The judges began to pick apart Labour's legislation. Lord Salmon was early to speak out against the introduction of legislation he might later have to impartially interpret. In the House of Lords debate on the Trade Union and Labour Relations (Amendment) Bill he gave an insight into judicial thinking: ...

there are groups very small numerically, but extremely cohesive and tenacious, who have infiltrated the unions with the intention of seizing power if they can. Their objectives and ideas are entirely different from those of the trade unions which we all know and respect. Their avowed purpose is to wreck the social contract and the democratic system under which we live (Griffith, 1985, 47).

The 'moral panic' which was to culminate in the 'Winter of Discontent' was already on as far as the judiciary was concerned. Lord Justice Lawton likened the National Council of the NGA to 'a political commissar in a communist state'. Parliament, Lord Denning said, in *BBC v*. Hearn, 'has conferred more freedom from constraint on trade unions than has ever been known to the law before. All legal restraints have been lifted so that they can now do as they will.'

Although, as Lord Scarman pointed out, in the case of *NWL* v. *Woods*, the law was simply 'back to what Parliament had intended when it enacted the Act of 1906', the Court of Appeal, in a series of judgements such as *Express Newspapers* v. *McShane* (1979) and *Duport Steels* v. *Sirs* (1980), rendered the immunities meaningless. In 1979-80, these cases were reversed on appeal by the House of Lords. It was clear that they felt that the creativity demonstrated by the Court of Appeal under Lord Denning could bring the whole legal apparatus into disrepute.

Nonetheless, Lord Diplock noted that 70 years after the Trade Disputes Act, the immunities still 'tended to stick in judicial gorges'. The conclusion in *Duport Steels* that they applied to secondary action was, he felt:

intrinsically repugnant to anyone who has spent his life in the practice of the law or the administration of justice. Sharing these instincts, it was a conclusion that I, myself, reached with considerable reluctance, for, given the existence of a trade dispute, it involves granting to trade unions a power which has no other limits than their own self-restraint to inflict, by means which are contrary to the general law, untold harm.

Lord Salmon stated ominously that the time had come for the law to be altered. Mrs Thatcher and the 1980 Employment Act were happily at hand.

Voluntarism

Most of those who studied the British system of industrial relations until the 1970s termed the system a 'voluntary' one. They noted that unions supported legislation to ensure their right to exist, bargain and strike. For the rest, they feared that more extended legal enactment would, because of the plasticity of statute in the nimble fingers of the judges, lead to a greater – and from a union view – more harmful regulation of industrial relations by the courts. A reliance on law could sap union independence and pave the way for later restrictive legislation. If the state played too great a role in providing rights for workers they might question the rationale for union membership.

Employers too, the voluntarists argued, accepted collective bargaining as the preferred means of industrial regulation. Voluntarism emphasised employer autonomy in a capitalist culture which was resistant to all but the most limited state intervention. Employers, in this view, preferred to solve their own problems, even at the cost of industrial action. The law could not succeed in forcing large numbers of strikers back to work and its intervention could sour future industrial relations. From the state's point of view, voluntarism nurtured belief in its essential neutrality. There was no need for the state to overload itself with functions which could be left to unions and employers. The nature of the immunities and the judiciary, and the latter's brief as secondary legislators, provided a system for fine-tuning existing law to the problems of the moment and drawing attention to the need for broader legislation.

An examination of British industrial relations certainly seemed to justify its description as a 'voluntary system'. Until the 1970s the enduring legal landmarks in British industrial relations were few. There was no law giving trade unions rights to recognition and no law requiring employers to bargain with them. Collective agreements were not directly, legally enforceable. The state provided some auxiliary legislation but the Conciliation Act of 1896 and the Industrial Courts Act of 1919 constituted the most limited props. Health and safety legislation such as the Factories Acts provided a minimum floor of civilised working conditions and regulated the hours of women and young people. The Fair Wages Resolutions dating from the 1890s and legislation such as the Terms and Conditions of Employment Act (1959), provided limited machinery for extending the terms and conditions arrived at in industries regulated by collective bargaining. Wages Council legislation, dating from 1909, laid down minimum wages in weakly organised industries. Taken together with the immunity statutes, they made the British system of industrial relations one of the most minimally legally regulated in the world.

By the post-war period, voluntarism or 'collective *laissez-faire*' was seen as *prescriptive*. The system embodied a cherished set of values, a 'great idea' which represented the best way of ordering industrial relations in an advanced economy. The extended legal regulation represented by the 1971 Industrial Relations Act was a passing cloud and even the deluge of labour law under the Wilson and Callaghan governments was not viewed by certain supporters as striking at the roots of voluntarism. As late as 1979, the traditional analysis, albeit somewhat supplemented, was seen as adequate to characterise British industrial relations (Kahn-Freund, 1979).

The limitations of voluntarism

In recent years analysis has focused on the *limits* of state abstention and self-regulation in the British system. It has been pointed out that the state introduced in both world wars powerful measures to control trade unions such as the Munitions of War Act, 1915 and Order 1305, 1940. The latter legislation lingered on until 1951, when its use against members of the TGWU provoked its repeal. The Emergency Powers Acts 1920 and 1964 and the Trade Disputes Act, 1927, were not inconsiderable pieces of legislation. The latter legislation limited union membership for certain categories of public employee, imposed criminal penalties on political strikes, restricted the range of lawful picketing and replaced 'opting-out' of the unions' political levy with 'opting-in'. The 1920 Act and its 1964 successor gave the state extensive powers to intervene in strikes and use the military to do the work of the strikers.

Between 1963 and 1968, and 1972 and 1974, under both Labour and Conservative governments, incomes policy legislation controlled the price of labour. This legislation provided for criminal penalties but, dealing with wages, it went to the root of collective bargaining and industrial relations, and can only be ignored at the expense of a most restrictive definition of labour law. Moreover, the 1963 Contracts of Employment Act, and the 1965 Redundancy Payments Act, marked the mid-1960s as the end of an era. Since 1964, every government has aspired to interject a greater degree of legal regulation into the British system of industrial relations and the majority have succeeded. If by 1976 this trend appeared irreversible, it appears even more so in the 1980s.

If voluntarism is used in the narrow sense of an abstention of the law, its proponents appear to be correct in analysing the situation in these terms, at least until the 1960s. If we are talking more broadly of voluntarism as a shared set of values, the view that voluntarism only adequately describes particular periods of British industrial relations and that its maintenance was always conditional upon a certain power balance appears convincing. Some writers have argued that as 'an ideological belief common to both sides of industry' voluntarism was largely a post-war phenomenon, in which case we are talking of a very limited time span indeed – around 20 years (Lewis and Simpson, 1981, 9, 16). Certainly, the inter-war period saw an abstention of the law, but the weakness of the unions left management with a relatively open field. There was little rationale, from their point of view, for greater state intervention, whilst the unions lacked the power to impose it. The fact that the disintegration of economic stability went hand in hand with the disintegration of voluntarism raises the question of whether this approach represented, from a trade union point of view, the best means of regulating industrial relations.

By its emphasis on the procedures of collective bargaining and the value of legal abstention, voluntarism obscures questions of power and substance. What kind of law are we talking about, with what kind of content and what kind of administration? The absence of one kind of law may help trade unions. The absence of another kind of law may handicap them. An extended system of favourable legal rights administered by a reformed judiciary may further union purposes more efficiently by comparison with a voluntarist system. Can we favour self-regulation through collective bargaining, as against a greater measure of legalism, without some sort of assessment of the *outcomes* of collective bargaining? Looked at in this light, the abstention of the state in the 1920s and 1930s may be seen as acquiescence in a distribution of power which strengthened the employers and reinforced the subordination of workers. And the growing state intervention since the mid-1960s, when unions were stronger, may be seen as the state attempting to re-order, in the interests of capital, a situation capital could no longer control.

Collective bargaining redresses the inequality of power between employer and individual worker but it does not significantly affect the structures of power, ownership and control (Fox, 1985b). Voluntarism can, therefore, be seen as shaped by both the needs of capital and pressures from the labour movement. Its acceptance represented a defensive compromise, organic to the unions' separation between economics and politics, which left existing structures of ownership and law intact. It gave workers the means of civilising their subordination, but played a role in distracting workers from an attention to the structures of power and domination which might have produced more wide-ranging social change. The legislation on immunities solved little. The terms on which the judiciary were excluded from intervention premissed their periodic re-entry into the field to the detriment of trade unions. Had this unsatisfactory compromise been rejected in favour of more thoroughgoing reform, which replaced defensive measures by a positive code of rights and democratised the judiciary, the unions might have had a greater impact on the disequilibrium of power in industrial relations. It is by no means certain that voluntarism was the best way for the unions – or that a return to voluntarism today would represent the optimum solution.

The Donovan Report and 'In Place of Strife'

The Report of the Royal Commission on Trade Unions – the Donovan Report, 1968 – represented a strong defence of the voluntary system. It argued that collective bargaining was still the most efficient method of giving workers a voice in decisions which affected their working lives, and that the problems its operation was throwing up, such as wage drift and unofficial stoppages, could be solved by a voluntary reform of industrial relations procedures and institutions. Donovan wished to keep the legal wolf from the door in the sense of opposing new restrictive obligations on trade unions.

Nonetheless, the report argued that if voluntary change failed, then penalties on strikes should be considered.

Its main thrust argued for more comprehensive and more formal collective agreements at company and plant level; more formal procedures to deal with grievances, discipline, redundancy and union organisation within the workplace; a reform of wage payment systems; and greater integration of shop stewards within the union. These reforms, which should be stimulated by a new tripartite Commission on Industrial Relations, would strengthen managerial control over industrial relations, make renumeration and the labour process more susceptible to efficient planning and, thus, facilitate the operation of incomes policy and government economic policy.

The extension and renovation of collective bargaining could also be stimulated by the enactment of legislation on union recognition and unfair dismissal, as well as provisions for the registration of collective agreements plugging in to the Contracts of Employment and Redundancy Payments legislation and the Prices and Incomes Acts.

This recipe for patient, long-term action was not to the liking of the Wilson government. Its 1969 White Paper *In Place of Strife* proposed to introduce legislation covering many of Donovan's proposals. There was to be new law on dismissal, recognition and disclosure of information. However, the unions questioned certain of the 25 proposals, such as the establishment of a body which would review trade union rules. They also bitterly opposed proposals to allow the government to suspend unconstitutional stoppages for 28 days, while conciliation took place, and trigger compulsory ballots before official strikes.

In the spring of 1969, the government sought to rush through a short bill covering 'the penal clauses'. This was totally opposed by the TUC, by members of the cabinet and by many back-bench MPs. After the TUC held a special conference which gave the General Council new powers to intervene in unofficial strikes, the government withdrew the Bill in return for a 'solemn and binding undertaking' by the TUC that they would take a more forceful line in future.

The Industrial Relations Act

The Conservative Party, by the mid-1960s, had undergone a

conversion to 'legalism'. The philosophy of their 1968 policy document *Fair Deal at Work* was clear: extensive legislation was required to restrict trade union power and to remould collective bargaining. The parties themselves were incapable or unwilling to reform industrial relations without a greater degree of legal intervention than the country had ever previously witnessed. The 1971 Industrial Relations Act marked a clear and final rupture with voluntarism.

A key to the legislation was its provisions on registration. Unions which registered would be subject to a certain degree of state supervision. In return, they could avail themselves of a range of rights to recognition, bargaining and disclosure of information. Reinforcing this 'reform' emphasis were clauses presuming collective agreements to be binding, in the absence of evidence to the contrary, a series of unfair industrial practices, limiting unions' rights to take secondary action and to picket, and powers granted to the Secretary of State to apply for orders prohibiting industrial action harmful to the economy. Compulsory ballots on industrial action and 'cooling-off periods' could also be ordered. A new National Industrial Relations Court was established to deal with the collective provisions of the legislation. Individual rights, such as unfair dismissal, were enacted.

The legislation was attempting to achieve an awful lot. Not only was it comprehensive to a fault, it was also contradictory. Titbits such as unfair dismissal and recognition procedures were offered to the unions. But this approach was undermined by provisions allowing workers to opt out of union membership. There were problems in the drafting of the act – crucially, uncertainty as to the unions' legal responsibility for the activities of shop stewards. The legislation provided backwoodsmen employers with an opportunity for provoking a widespread confrontation with the unions. Some, indeed, saw the act as informed by two not completely compatible philosophies embodied in two phantom draftsmen: one 'a civil servant concerned mainly to bring order and a tidy structure into collective British industrial relations; the second is quite different, a Conservative lawyer imbued above all else with doctrines of individual rights' (Wedderburn, 1972, 270). Not for the first time, the Conservatives found their commitment to the individual contaminating their approach to the reform of collective relations.

These factors were important, given the relatively powerful position of the unions and the belief, confirmed by the *In Place of Strife* furore, that legal initiatives could be seen off. A series of one-day strikes and a co-ordinated campaign by the TUC built opposition. However, several important unions refused to accept the TUC's instruction to de-register under the Act. Some had to be expelled. Whilst the policy of withdrawing union representatives from industrial tribunals was largely observed, the fact that unions still took cases before the new employer-dominated bodies limited its rationale. Moreover, as soon as the boycott of the new court posed problems, the TGWU appeared before it.

Nonetheless, rank and file opposition was reinforced by the TUC's posture and by the success of the miners in punching holes in the Heath government's wage restraint policies. The government's use of the pre-strike ballot against railway workers in early 1972 produced an overwhelming vote in favour of strike action. The imprisonment of 5 dockers in Pentonville gaol in the summer of 1972 provoked a major political confrontation. The TUC called the first one-day general strike since 1926 and a rolling strike movement began. The House of Lords published, with unprecedented haste, a judgement reversing the Court of Appeal decision which had led to the dockers' contempt, of court and incarceration. Despite the fact that they had taken no steps to purge their contempt they were immediately released.

The Act was halted in its tracks. Its impact on day-to-day industrial relations had been minimal, '...the central analysis about the nature and causes of industrial conflict upon which the Act was based was often not shared by management, unions or workers'. Management connived in the insertion of exclusion clauses which kept collective agreements non-enforceable and joined with the unions in maintaining the closed shop. 'Employers generally refused to see their industrial relations as a problem and the "disorder" described by others was often defended by managers because it gave them flexibility ... Management seemed anxious to avoid the loss of control to outsiders which they felt the use of the new legal institutions implied ... the Act had little influence on the general practice of industrial relations' (Weekes et al, 1975, 223, 232).

The lessons drawn by some were the old lessons; the law should be kept out of industrial relations. It was inherently anti-union but it could not defeat mass opposition. This disastrous episode had

brought the legal system into disrepute and stoked up militancy.
Others saw the mistakes as strategic and tactical. Heath had gone
about things the wrong way from the start and backed down
ignominiously when the going got tough.

Social contract and employment protection

As recently as 1966, in its evidence to the Donovan Commission, the
TUC had reaffirmed its support for voluntarism. But the unions'
conversion to a more detailed legal framework had been proceeding
through the 1960s. For its part, the incoming 1974 Labour government saw legal concessions as a relatively unproblematic and
inexpensive means of purchasing acquiescence in wage restraint.
There was to be no return to the pre-1971 position.

The Trade Union and Labour Relations Act, 1974, and the Trade
Union and Labour Relations (Amendment) Act, 1976, refurbished
the immunities and extended the protection against the tort of
inducing breach of contract to cover commerical contracts.
Employers were protected aginst unfair dismissal actions where they
dismissed non-union members in a closed shop. The TUC established an Independent Review Committee to hear appeals from
those expelled from unions, or refused admission, who worked in
closed-shop employment.

The Employment Protection Act, 1975, placed the Advisory
Conciliation and Arbitration Services on a statutory footing. A
Certification Officer was established to take over many of the
functions of the Registrar of Friendly Societies and to adjudicate on
whether trade unions met the criterion of independence, a prere-
quisite for receipt of many of the new legal rights.

ACAS was given a broad brief to extend the scope of collective
bargaining. Unions could refer recognition issues and disputes over
disclosure of information to ACAS which would then follow a
statutory procedure, culminating in compulsory arbitration.
Employers had new duties to provide information to unions and to
consult with them in redundancy situations. There were new
provisions for the extension of 'recognised terms and conditions of
employment' on the model of the old 1959 Act. Union representatives were given time off for union activities and training and facilities
to help them in their union work. The unfair dismissal provisions
were strengthened and extended to embrace dismissal for union

activities. There were new rights to guarantee payments for employees when laid off, protections for workers suspended for medical reasons and rights to itemised pay statements. The wages council system was strengthened and new Codes of Practice produced by ACAS on discipline, time off for shop stewards and disclosure of information.

The Health and Safety at Work Act of 1974 was an enabling act intended to stimulate a renovation and codification of the whole field of welfare legislation. It provided, moreover, for a new system of workplace safety representatives and safety committees. Pensions were dealt with by the Social Security Pensions Act, 1975, and equal rights by new provisions on maternity leave and maternity pay, the Sex Discrimination Act, 1975, and the Race Relations Act, 1976.

The impact of employment protection
This legislation was seen by many as providing an important increment to trade union power. The Conservatives complained in their 1979 manifesto that 'between 1974 and 1976 Labour enacted "a militants' charter" of trade union legislation. It tilted the balance of power in bargaining throughout industry away from responsible management and towards unions and sometimes towards unnofficial groups...'.

What strikes us more today is its limitations. It lagged behind the standards set in most EEC countries. The legislation on the closed shop, for example, involved no substantial change in the position that had pertained prior to 1970. The legislation on unfair dismissal lacked any strong spine, as it failed to give tribunals powers to enforce orders of reinstatement against employers. By 1980, reinstatement was the remedy in less than 1% of cases. The median award of compensation, the remedy in the other 99% of unfair dismissal cases, was £375 in 1978. £410 in 1979 and £963 in 1981. In that year, more than half of the awards were for amounts under £1,000 and workers had less than a one in four chance of winning an unfair dismissal case. The situation is even more limited in relation to the discrimination statutes. By 1983, 46% of successful applicants under the Sex Discrimination Act and 62% of successful applicants under the Race Relations Act received less than £500. There were only 575 applications under both jurisdictions, whilst equal pay claims fell from 2.742 in 1976 to 35 in 1983.

Tribunals, generally, became increasingly legalistic (Dickens et al, 1985; Hepple, 1983). If many of the new rights were limited to begin with, many students felt that their handling by tribunals and courts had deprived them of much of the efficacy they initially possessed: 'The law of unfair dismissal has been sterilised to such an extent that, it is reasonable to conclude that far from controlling managerial discretion and, therefore, protecting the interests of workers in job security, the law generally endorses and legitimates a strong conception of managerial authority' (Collins, 1982, 170).

Much the same could be said in relation to the 'collective rights'. The procedure which unions could utilise to secure recognition was lengthy and lacked teeth. If pursued to the bitter end, it guaranteed not recognition but only compulsory arbitration of certain terms and conditions of employment. ACAS made recommendations for recognition in 158 out of the 247 cases it reported on under the procedure. But in only 58 cases did ACAS know of compliance before the change of government. Moreover, 'although the sanction was weak in intention and weaker still in operation it was perceived differently by the judges. They compared it with the powers of compulsory acquisition of property and described it as "as interference with individual liberty" which "could hardly be tolerated in a free society unless there were safeguards against abuse" ' (Dickens and Bain, 1986, 92).

Just as they whittled down the revived immunities, so the judges after 1975 turned their attention to the new rights. By 1979 a series of judgements in the Court of Appeal, *Grunwick* v. *ACAS, UKAPE* v. *ACAS* and *EMA* v. *ACAS,* led the chair of ACAS to inform the government that the recognition procedure was no longer operable to any satisfactory degree.

Labour's legislation, then, was far from 'a militants' charter', particularly if it was set in context as part of the social contract. It should be seen, rather, as a continuation of the reform approach which started with the Contracts of Employment and Redundancy Payments legislation and continued through the Donovan proposals. The Redundancy Payments legislation, for example, was described by Labour Minister Ray Gunter as having 'an important and necessary part to play in allaying fears of redundancy and resistance to new methods and economic change ... our object is to increase mobility of labour by reducing resistance to change' (McIlroy, 1983, 25).

The law on unfair dismissal was intended to stimulate formal disciplinary procedures and increase the efficiency of management and the legitimacy of their decisions, thus avoiding industrial disputes, as well as to provide compensation for dismissed employees. The procedures for recognition and disclosure of information were intended to extend, formalise and professionalise collective bargaining, as were the provisions on the closed shop and time off for shop stewards. If an element of employment protection was, in relation to pressures from the EEC, an end in itself, it was also a weapon in modernising management and restoring management control over collective bargaining.

In this objective, the social contract legislation appears to have met with some success. It has encouraged the growth of procedures and influenced management's handling of problems. The professionalisation of shop steward organisation and the growth of full-time convenors has also been linked to the social contract legislation. The degree of change in certain areas is highlighted by one survey's report that only 8% of private sector establishments had a formal written disciplinary procedure in 1969, compared with over 80% in 1980 (Daniel and Millward, 1983, 162-3; Daniel and Stilgoe, 1978; Dickens et al, 1985).

By 1980, there was a clear trend 'towards the juridification of individual disputes ... Matters which were once entirely within the sphere of managerial prerogatives or left to collective bargaining are now directly regulated by positive legal rights and duties' (Hepple 1983, 393). If the degree to which the conduct of industrial relations was regulated by the law was still limited compared with other countries, it was substantial compared with the position in 1960. Some observers drew a distinction between individual protective law and the law relating to collective labour relations. The growth of the former category, it was argued, was consistent with traditional policies of voluntarism. The 1974-79 Labour government had been careful not to intrude into the latter. The rupture with the past occurred in 1980, not in 1974 or 1964 (Clark and Wedderburn, 1983).

Others have argued that the social contract witnessed the enactment of a substantial corpus of collective labour legislation. Had traditional philosophy applied in 1974, the trade unions would have demanded a small act restoring the immunities they would not have supported legislation on recognition, disclosure of information, the closed shop or rights for shop stewards (von Prondzynski, 1985). It was certainly clear by 1980 that the distinction between individual and collective labour law had become increasingly blurred and its utility as a tool of analysis was increasingly questioned. The law on the closed shop or shop stewards' rights, for example, was essential to collective purposes but was defined in terms of the individual. Redundancy consultation was a collective issue which gave the union the right to take a case, yet required the tribunal to formulate a remedy for the individual. The impact of individual rights such as unfair dismissal, were to be measured in terms of collective agreements, and it was these that tribunals had to scrutinise to adjudicate on individual issues.

Neo-*laissez-faire* and the law

The Conservatives' policy was based upon a reading of where Heath had gone wrong. There was to be no one central piece of new legislation, no new labour court to focus opposition, no devices such as registration which the unions could exploit. Where the Heath legislation had promised a remoulded, registered union movement, a role as responsible social partners with employers and government, the legislation of the 1980s was based in a far more straightforward fashion on reducing the power of the unions. The measures contained in the 1979 orders in council, the 1980 and 1982 Employment Acts, the 1984 Trade Union Act, the 1986 Wages Act and other ancillary measures, covered a wide and dispersed front.

Undermining employment protection
The qualification for bringing a case of unfair dismissal was increased, in 1979, from 6 months' to one year's continuous employment. Special provisions were made for workers in small businesses. In 1985, the qualification for all employees was raised to 2 years. These changes removed several million workers from legal protection. The minimum length of a fixed-term contract under which the employer may exclude employees' rights to protection was sliced from 2 years to 1 year. The onus of proof in tribunal cases which favoured the employee was neutralised. In determining the fairness or otherwise of dismissal, tribunals now had to consider the size of the enterprise and the employer's administrative resources. The 'basic' award of compensation was reduced. A 'pre-hearing assessment', which could be used to scrutinise the validity of an applicant's case, was introduced and the basis on which costs could be awarded was extended. Guarantee payments were cut, the arrangements for

maternity leave and maternity pay were weakened and made more complex. The provisions for redundancy consultation were limited and the Redundancy Payments Fund abolished.

In 'getting the state off the backs of business' the government ignored studies which demonstrated that the burdens placed on industry by employment protection were minimal (Clifton and Tatton-Brown, 1979; Daniel and Stilgoe, 1978; Evans et al, 1985). Moreover, membership of the EEC exercised a contrary pressure and forced the government to introduce measures such as the Transfer of Undertakings (Protection of Employment) Regulations, 1981, the Equal Pay (Amendment) Regulations, 1983, and the Sex Discrimination Act, 1986, which gave employees enhanced, if still flawed, protection.

Weakening collective bargaining

In order to facilitate labour market 'deregulation', the 1980 legislation abolished the procedure dealing with trade union recognition and axed schedule 11 of the Employment Protection Act, which provided for the extension of recognised terms and conditions to comparable workers by compulsory arbitration. In 1983, the Fair Wages Resolution was rescinded and, in 1986, young workers were removed from the protection of wages councils. The Truck Acts were abolished and the restrictions in the Factories Act of women's hours of work repealed. The legislation supporting the collective bargaining system has been dismantled and statute law replaced by the common law.

Limiting the immunities

The definition of a trade dispute – the golden formula which is the gateway to trade union protection – has been restricted in important aspects. To attract protection disputes must now not merely be *related* to the list of employment issues contained in the formula, but they must be *wholly or mainly* about these issues. Disputes must now be between employers and *their workers*. Disputes between *workers and workers* are no longer protected and support for disputes outside the UK minimally so.

The picketing protection was narrowed to workers picketing their own place of work and a restrictive Code of Practice promulgated to guide the courts. Protection for trade unionists taking secondary or sympathetic action has been severely restricted and this area turned into a legal minefield by complex definitions which give free play to judicial creativity. The aim has been to limit industrial action to the workers' own employer and minimise solidarity. Industrial action to pressurise employers to recognise unions and to implement the closed shop and 'union only' practices has been severely circumscribed.

The employer's protection when dismissing workers taking industrial action has been extended, whilst unions now lose their immunities if they support or, indeed, fail to repudiate, industrial action initiated without a secret ballot. In 1987, the government reinforced its theme of disorganising industrial action when it proposed to legislate to protect workers who refused to take industrial action called after a successful ballot under the 1984 Trade Union Act. Social security measures have also been utilised: a sum deemed to have been paid by the union as strike pay is deducted from the social security benefit of strikers whether or not such payment actually exists. The Conservatives are urged on to further restriction by legal supporters who argue, with scant regard for the realities of industrial relations or legal history, that 'life without immunities offers unions an honourable and responsible role, as voluntary associations active within the limits of the ordinary law of the land to secure the interests of their members' (Tur, 1982, 162-3).

Disorganising the unions

The 1980 and 1982 Employment Acts created a structure by which closed shops were only protected if approved in a ballot by 85% of those voting, or 80% of those to be covered by the arrangement. It was, moreover, unfair to dismiss employees eligible to participate in the ballot if they refused union membership. Employees who objected on grounds of conscience were also protected. Trade unionists exerting pressures for the dismissal of non-members were opened up to legal action and the scale of compensation was dramatically increased. These measures were again accompanied by an *even more* restrictive Code of Practice. In 1987, the government announced further measures which would mean the outlawing of the closed shop.

The protection given to unions after the *Taff Vale* case has been revoked so that union funds now are open to legal action. Limits on damages in each individal case were introduced, related to the size of the union. Legislation also attempted to remould unions' internal practices by applying new restrictions to the election of executive members and to influence the unions' links with the Labour Party by modifying the 1913 Trade Union Act. Amongst the measures announced in 1987 were proposals to extend balloting in union elections, the establishment of a new commission to help union members take action against their organisations; provision to give members greater scrutiny of a trade union's financial affairs; and a proposal that the unions should no longer be able to indemnify officials against unlawful action by paying court fines or damages incurred.

Conservative legislation – the union response

The unions were confronted in 1980, not with the bumper Industrial Relations Act with its 170 clauses and 9 schedules, but with a slim measure introducing piecemeal changes. Nonetheless, the TUC mounted an educational campaign. That it underestimated the nature of the attack the government was mustering was already evident in the title of its educational publication, *Bargain to Beat the Act*. More active opposition got under way with a Day of Action on 14 May, 1980. Around a million trade unionists took industrial action in what was a patchy response. In an echo of the previous decade, the Fleet Street unions stopped the national press and successfully ignored an injuction granted to Express Newspapers. The TUC held its fire; perhaps there would be no follow up.

When this hope proved illusory and the 1982 legislation saw the light of day, a Special Conference at Wembley in April 1982 supported a programme intended to draw the teeth of the Conservative measures. Unions would not hold or participate in ballots on the closed shop, nor should they accept public funds for internal ballots. Union representatives would withdraw from tribunal hearings of closed shop cases. The TUC would establish a Campaign and Defence Fund with a levy to meet financial commitments. Crucially, the TUC General Council, when requested by a union faced with legal action, would have the power, if they were satisfied that assistance from other unions was justified, to 'co-ordinate action by other affiliated unions in support of the unions in difficulty, including, if necessary, calling for industrial action against the employer concerned, or more widely' (TUC *Industrial Relations Legislation*, 1982, 20).

It was clear that the TUC was wishfully thinking of 1972-style scenarios. But the conditions which had underpinned the 1970s response were now being undermined. As unemployment reached new heights, union confidence and the belief that aggression paid were on the wane. Workers were worried about their jobs and the threat of the new laws still appeared a rather abstract one. The initial response of all concerned was cautious. When, in August 1982, the branch secretary of the Fleet Street electricians who had struck on a Day of Action to support the NHS workers was brought before the courts for breaching an injunction, the judge contented himself with a small fine for contempt. Only a trickle of employers – Chloride and the Mersey Docks and Harbour Board were amongst the most notable – took legal action, in small disputes, and only after careful calculation. But it soon became clear that the union officials against whom injunctions were directed under the 1980 Act were anxious to comply with the court orders, as the recession took its toll on union membership (Evans, 1985a).

A change in the TUC's stance after the 1983 general election was soon discernible. As part of its campaign against privatisation the Post Office Engineering Union instructed its members not to connect the private Mercury network with British Telecom. Mercury, a new company with a lot to lose, not British Telecom, took the union to court. The High Court judge refused an injunction on the grounds that, under the new legislation, the action was related *wholly or mainly* to workers' concern over their jobs and, therefore, fell within the new definition of a trade dispute.

This decision was reversed in the Court of Appeal. The Master of the Rolls, Sir John Donaldson, accepted the argument that the predominant element in the dispute was not related to concern over termination of employment but, rather, political opposition to the government's policy of privatisation. The union's inducement to its members to break their contracts was, therefore, not protected by the definition of a trade dispute and an injunction was granted. The POEU was informed by TUC General Secretary Len Murray.that the TUC's policy was not intended to encourage breaches of the law, and they withdrew their instruction.

The next union in the firing line, the NGA, was made of sterner stuff. Eddie Shah, who ran Messenger Group Newspapers, became embroiled in a dispute with the union when he attempted to establish an open shop at his Warrington Plant. The NGA instructed all its members to boycott the Messenger Group and began to picket the Warrington Plant. Mr Shah was granted an injunction because the unions were in breach of the 1980 Act – the members were picketing a workplace other than their own – and the 1982 Act – they were pressurising advertisers and suppliers of Mr Shah in order to obtain a closed shop.

When the union ignored the injunction it was first fined £50,000 and, when it still refused to obey the course, £100,000 and eventually, a further £250,000. At the end of November 1983, the High Court ordered its total assets sequestrated – taken over by court-appointed accountants. In December 1983, the Employment Committee of the TUC General Council voted to support the NGA's stance. They were publicly repudiated by Len Murray and a subsequent meeting of the full General Council voted, amongst much bitterness, to leave the NGA to its fate. The union lost the dispute and in the full hearing of the case, in 1984, Mr Shah was awarded £250,000 damages against the union.

From defiance to acquiescence

It was now clear that the TUC was not prepared to attract legal penalties by carrying out the mandate of co-ordinating solidarity action that it had requested at Wembley. Its position now was that it could not support law-breaking. Co-ordination of supporting action would, in itself, breach the new laws. It could, therefore, never be justified. And the example of the NGA showed how unlikely it was that any individual union would be able to stand up to the full might of the law.

There were cases, such as the dispute at Shell in 1983, where the courts issued injunctions and the workers ignored them. In the dispute between Dimbleby and Sons Ltd and the NUJ, the union which instructed its members to boycott copy to the new printers of Dimbleby's newspaper, an anti-union company, T. Bailey Foreman, initially defied the injunction. But, in the end, the NUJ was forced to accept its terms. This case also showed the wide ambit of the legislation. The NUJ, the courts held, had a dispute with T. Bailey Foreman which refused to employ their members. It had no dispute with TBF Ltd, who did the printing, a separate company under law, even though both were corporate entities controlled by the same company and had the same directors and shareholders.

The *Messenger* dispute had witnessed the use of a mass police presence against the pickets, and the year-long miners' strike which erupted in March 1984 was characterised by a cautious use of the civil law and a reliance on paramilitary policing to deal with the problems of picketing. In the first days of the strike, injunctions were granted to the NCB restraining the Yorkshire Area NUM from organising members to picket beyond their own workplace. When the injunction was ignored, the NCB refused to raise the issue of contempt and adjourned the proceedings. They were concerned at the impact the use of the legislation might have in uniting a divided union. Other big state corporations such as BSC and the CEGB failed to use the law, leading to wide-ranging criticism that government influence was inhibiting the use of the new measures against the kind of situation that they had been expressly designed to deal with.

In April 1984, however, Reads, a small transport company, were awarded an injunction against the South Wales NUM who were unlawfully picketing their lorries. In July, the area was fined £50,000 and, in August, its assets were sequestrated. Nonetheless, the primary legal influences on the miners strike were not the employment legislation but the criminal law and the age-old breach of contract actions based on the union's rule book brought by working miners and their advisers, actions which eventually led to the sequestration of the national union's assets (Beynon, 1985; Fine and Millar, 1985). After the defeat of the miners it was clear, if it had not been before, that the new legal edifice – and further extensions to it – would not be defeated by direct union action.

The TUC decided to accept the provisions of the 1984 Trade Union Act. Despite a clear TUC interdict against it, officials of all affiliates closed their eyes as their shop stewards participated in ballots on the maintenance of closed shop arrangements. The disintegration of TUC defiance was symbolised in the struggle over the boycott of state funds for union ballots. Both the AEU and EETPU, because of their support for secret postal ballots and their financial difficulties, were determined by 1983 to take advantage of this financial aid. When, in 1984, the government announced that unless claims for money spent on ballots since 1980 were received by February 1985, they would not be met, both unions resolved to act.

An AEU ballot saw members vote 12 to 1 for acceptance of the state subsidy. Although the AEU's National Committee ordered a re-run of the ballot, the union, in June 1985, took delivery of more than £1 million to cover costs of balloting since 1980 and the EETPU also lodged an application. The TUC General Council voted to discipline the AEU, but the 1985 Congress produced a compromise by which the re-run ballot would explicitly refer to the TUC policy that government money was not acceptable. Despite this provision, the re-run ballot showed an 8 to 1 majority in favour of taking the money and the EETPU voted 9 to 1 in favour. In February, 1986, the TUC convened a Special Conference which voted to drop the boycott. This Conference set the final seal on the demise of any TUC defiance of the new legislation.

At the same time, the Wapping dispute was sounding the knell of active opposition from individual unions and illustrating how useful the new legislation could be to employers. The law protected Rupert Murdoch as he sacked his work force and transferred production to a new plant. The picketing and secondary action that the unions had historically used to deal with this kind of situation were now unlawful. In the space of a few weeks, News International initiated a dozen legal actions against the unions. This time the NGA was more prudent but SOGAT went to the brink. Its assets were sequestrated and it was fined for contempt. It now did something a union had ever done before: it quickly took steps to purge its contempt and gave the court assurances that, in future, it would operate within the law. The unions were, henceforth, severely impeded by the existence of the legislation in efficiently running the dispute. It certainly seemed that where Heath had failed in the 1970s, Thatcher had succeeded in the 1980s.

The impact of the legislation

A crude measure of the success of the employment legislation were the efforts and resources devoted by the unions to the political fund ballots, and the way in which union after union, chivied along by the Certification Officer, have changed their rules to meet the requirements of the 1984 Act. Surveys show that employers are using the law to a greater extent than in the past, although there is as yet no lemming-like rush to the courts. A study of 38 disputes involving picketing between 1980 and 1982 found employers seeking injunctions in 9 and seriously considering legal action in a further 7. A survey of disputes between September 1980 and April 1984 found employers seeking injunctions against picketing and unlawful secondary action in 34 cases.

The law was most likely to be used where the strikers lacked unity and were relatively isolated and uninfluential with union officers. The aim was often to demoralise strikers and restore official union control over a dispute. The law was increasingly considered as an option where industrial action put financial pressure on employers. They were interested in stopping the action through an injunction, rather than gaining financial redress. In the majority of cases, the injunctions were complied with and the industrial action halted. In the majority of cases, those taking legal action were the direct employers of those taking industrial action (Evans, 1985a; 1985b).

The employers' resort to the courts appears to have speeded up somewhat in 1984 and 1985 and a further survey found a total of 70 cases had been brought before the courts by August 1985, the vast majority arising under the 1980 and 1982 Acts. However, these statistics overestimate the extent of litigation. By 1985 a third of cases brought emanated from printing and publishing. Shipping was also well represented. In other areas there was little legal activity. There were a further 18 requests for injunctions against unions in 1986 and 8 in the first 6 months of 1987. The courts were issuing orders swiftly, often within 24 hours and, in some cases, without union representatives being present. Between 1979 and 1987, 29 unions, comprising more than 80% of the TUC's affiliated membership, had appeared before the courts (*Labour Research*, 1985, October 1987). Statistics on legal cases, however, only give us a very broad idea of the operation of the legislation. We know little about the impact of threats of litigation. And what is missing from the statistics is the degree to which, because the legislation is there and has been successfully used elsewhere, unions modify their methods, refuse to pursue certain courses of action, accept offers they would otherwise reject and follow paths that, in the absence of legislation, they would ignore. The purpose of the legislation is, after all, not to provide work for lawyers but to transform the behaviour of unions. The interim judgement based, on hints in the studies cited above, must be that it has had an impact in conjunction with the general economic and political climate.

In the year after the implementation of the requirements on strike ballots in September 1984, ACAS noted 79 ballots, of which 53 were for strike action, 23 were against and one was a draw. By the end of 1986, they reported that 246 ballots had taken place of which 189 (77%) showed a majority for action with 54 (22%) voting against, and 2 draws. In the first 4 months of 1987, 42 out of 44 strike ballots went in the unions' favour. Turnouts were high, averaging between 75 and 85% (ACAS *Annual Report*, 1986).

Over the same period, there were 12 reported legal cases involving strike ballots as unions at first ignored the law (Hutton, 1985). However, it seems that after the Austin Rover Dispute, in late 1984, where the TGWU ignored an injunction against strike action called without a ballot and was fined £200,000, there was a significant move to accept the law. Nonetheless, as ACAS points out, more than 1,000 officially recorded stoppages took place in 1986. Whilst its figures on strike ballots are far from complete, we may conjecture that they still only occur in a small minority of cases. The figures show that a strike ballot does not constitute an insuperable hurdle to industrial action. Unions seem to have few problems in winning ballots and securing a mandate. However, evidence from ACAS suggests that in an overwhelming majority of cases industrial action does not follow. Unions are using ballots as a demonstration of support to increase their bargaining power with employers.

Ballots on the closed shop appear to have tapered off after an initial spurt. From November 1984 to September 1985, ACAS noted 97 ballots, and in 75 of these the unions achieved the required 85% majority. In 1986, ACAS estimated that only 30,000 out of more than 3 million workers covered by the closed shop had taken part in statutory ballots. The evidence on the closed shop law and other areas of recent legislation shows the possibility of unions coming to terms with many of the statutory restrictions and in some cases turning them to their own benefit.

There are problems in isolating the law from other factors influencing union activity. But, of course, in Mrs Thatcher's project the law was not intended to be isolated: it is essentially related to her overall industrial relations and economic policy. In that context, it has played a limited but useful role, both practical and symbolic, in circumscribing union power and producing a more cautious and centralised union movement. The degree to which the changes that have taken place represent the impact of coercion rather than conversion and whether they would be swiftly reversed in an economic upturn remains a matter of debate. But the evidence seems to show, as yet, no halfway, lasting transformation in the attitudes of trade unionists. Behaviour has changed through fear of the consequences of confrontation with the law, not through any conviction that secondary picketing or striking without a ballot is not the way to go about things.

Alternatives

The specifics of legal settlement of the 1980s will endure as long as its political progenitors remain in power. But the framework may last a lot longer, albeit with a different content. The Conservative legislation is lopsided. It contains many of the limitations on union organisation and activities enacted in other legal jurisdictions. It lacks the correlative individual and collective rights which in other systems are balanced against these restrictions. It is in the field of such minimum rights that the Conservative system will come under increasing pressure from the EEC.

When we turn to alternatives the picture is unclear. Discussions between the Labour Party and the TUC do not appear to have established any firm detailed content for future labour law and the unions are still debating possible options. The TUC's 1986 discussion document, *Industrial Relations Legislation*, noted the demise of voluntarism and stated that 'the law is in industrial relations and cannot now be excluded'. The TUC argued for a revival and extension of the employment protection rights. It also asked for union views on abandoning the immunities in favour of a series of positive rights to organise, bargain, strike and picket. The response from affiliates was confused and divided. The consequent policy statements accepted by the 1986 Congress pledged the unions to maintain strike ballots, introduce a national minimum wage and extend employment protection rights in future legislation introduced by a Labour government, but presented a fuzzy picture of what an alternative framework of law would look like. The unions remain unclear as to whether they wish to retain closed shop and political fund ballots, whether they should forsake the immunity form for positive rights, and what the ambit of collective rights, however formulated, should be (Hyman, 1987; McCarthy, 1985; Wilson, 1986).

Lawyers have argued that the immunities should be replaced by positive rights on the grounds that these would be more readily understandable and less susceptible to judicial misinterpretation, whilst the inefficiencies of the immunities in protecting union activities are well known (Elias and Ewing, 1982). Other commentators have argued that in the context of a right to organise, take part in and induce others to participate in industrial action, the injunction or at least the interim injunction should be excluded from industrial relations (Doyle, 1979).

Given that 'it is scarcely possible to discover in the long history of the "golden formula" an important reported judgement which advanced the collective interests, as such, of workers effectively and unequivocally on a critical point of law' (Wedderburn, 1983, 15), such a radical approach would appear justified. However, attention has been drawn to the fact that positive rights are unlikely, in practice, to be unqualified and unconditional and they would still be open to judicial scrutiny (Hyman, 1987). Defining the ambit of positive rights and the exclusion of the injunction would also pose problems (Wedderburn, 1983). Having emphasised the problems involved in a radical approach, Lord Wedderburn poses even more fundamental questions when he remarks 'the root problem is not the form of the law, it is its administration', only to conclude that 'we must do our best with the judges we have and utilise whatever shape of statute seems most suitable at the time' (Wedderburn, 1983, 21, 28). He has, however, raised the possibility of a self-contained labour court system (Wedderburn, 1986, 845).

The content of any new legislation and who interprets it are crucial. The role of the judiciary still represents a problem. Any system in which a leading judge such as Sir John Donaldson can, as he did in 1983, advise the government on legal issues he will later have to adjudicate upon is open to question in terms of its own tenets of independence and the division of powers. When the same judge can play a part in reversing the important High Court decision in the *Mercury Telecommunications* case in favour of Mercury, on debatable criteria, and is then reported as holding shares in Mercury's parent company, the gravity of the problem is graphically highlighted.

Any sustainable programme of reform will have to involve reform of the judiciary or a more democratic labour court. In this context, a switch to positive rights could represent a new start and the new form could embody a new legitimacy for trade unionism. It is true, as Conservative explorations of the issue illustrate, that positive rights could be restrictive in content. It is also true that the exclusion of the injunction from industrial relations on the model of the 1932 Norris-La Guardia Act in the USA has been specifically rejected by the Labour Party leadership and has usually been legislated in tightly regulated systems of industrial relations. Yet a greater degree of legal regulation looks to represent the future face of UK industrial relations. Perhaps the best stance for the unions is to bargain within such a framework, in order to turn it to their purposes and to forge a new relationship between law and collective bargaining. There is no reason why a greater measure of legal regulation should necessarily be antipathetic to collective bargaining. Key questions are the precise nature of the regulation, who does the regulating and what the unions get in return.

A retreat to voluntarism seems both unfruitful and impracticable. The challenge for the unions is to reject the withdrawal into their own private sphere that the immunities symbolised and, instead, pin to their banner the demand for a new positive code, in the context of a programme of social renovation which would involve the extensive refurbishment of an anachronistic judiciary. The proposal for a separate labour court again smacks of the old policy of exemption. Why not tackle the problem of judicial law-making head on? If the judges cannot handle industrial conflicts adequately, what does this say for their handling of other social conflicts? If a satisfactory system of positive rights, the exclusion of injunctions and a reform or exclusion of the judiciary appear distant in relation to today's Labour Party policies, they are objectives that the unions cannot lose sight of if they are to ever forge an enduring and equitable framework for their activities.

Further reading

Lord Wedderburn, 1986, is a classic introduction to the framework and issues. R. Lewis, 1986, is an up to date and detailed survey of key aspects of current legislation. A. Fox, 1985, is essential for the historical context of legal developments. J. Griffith, 1985, examines the judiciary, whilst P. Fosh and C. Littler, 1985 is a useful collection on current problems and controversies in employment law. W. McCarthy, 1985, also contains several useful essays on the contemporary situation.

Chapter 4

New technology and trade unions

A capitalist society is a dynamic society. Technological advance is continuous and in certain periods can dramatically transform industrial organisation. In the eighteenth century, the employers in the new factories and mills of the first industrial nation developed *the division of labour* which paved the way for *mechanisation*. Machines were invented capable of performing more efficiently, more continuously and more speedily productive operations, previously performed by human labour.

The post-war period saw the emergence of a new wave of technological innovation. *Automation* involved the creation of automatic control of work tasks and the use of computers in data-processing. Mechanisation compensated for the physical limitations of the human labourer with the precision and energy of the machine. But it still required a high degree of human control. Automation carried the promise of substituting for human mental as well as physical power, mechanising human thought processes and developing the self-regulating production of goods and services.

In the immediate post-war period, automation was limited by the state of the art in electronics. Equipment used large, fragile, inefficient and very expensive valves. A computer could cost £250,000, fill a room and require as much power as a steam locomotive. Compact, cheaper transistors gradually replaced valves. Miniature transistors, working even more cheaply, led to the manufacture of integrated circuits. Eventually, the process of miniaturisation allowed thousands of transistors and other components to be packed together on a basic chip, immeasurably increasing the power and speed of the circuit and dramatically reducing costs.

By 1980, the mammoth of the 1950s had become a microcomputer, costing around £2,000 yet 10,000 times as powerful.

As developments in microelectronics were parallelled by advances in telecommunications and as the rate of innovation accelerated, people began to talk of a 'new industrial revolution'. The new technology was extremely cheap; it improved performance, was flexible and could be applied to almost every area of industry. It affected both product and process innovation. Its creation of a mechanical intelligence meant that robots could be introduced into factories to displace labour on assembly lines. Computers, assimilating, storing and transmitting information by cable or teletext and word processors, replacing typewriters, seemed to presage the 'paperless office'. Journalists could now key in their copy directly to a computer, saving the labour of compositors and proof readers. The possibilities of the 'most remarkable new technology ever to confront mankind' (Maddock, 1980, xiii) appeared to be without limit.

Yet as the newspapers began to report on computerised plants, where a handful of supervisors stationed in front of computer terminals replaced scores of process workers, clerical employees and warehouse staff, discussion of a range of potential problems began to develop. What was to happen to the workers who were displaced by the new technology? Would they find new jobs, share in the benefits of the new technology by being paid a new social wage to participate in the new leisure society, or be consigned to a long and unproductive life on the dole? Would those workers who kept their jobs find that their work had become less skilled, more intensive and more monotonous? Would the new information technology lead to more draconian, if sophisticated control of labour? Were new hazards to employees' health, safety and welfare involved in using new equipment and systems? What impact would new technologies have on the organisation of the enterprise? And what would be the reaction of trade unions to the introduction of new equipment which would affect their members' working lives in so many different ways?

The new technology

New technology is being introduced into industry in a variety of forms:
1. *The office*. The most obvious development here is the explosion in the use of the word processor. Word processors store text in an

electromagnetic bank, enable reproduction on a visual display unit (VDU) for correction, addition or consultation and improve the speed of document production by up to 50%. Optical character recognition (OCR) equipment reads and records documents directly. Computer output microfilm transforms storage of files and cable and satellite systems provide the possibility of moving towards the integrated electronic office – the aim of one third of employers purchasing new office equipment (Steffens, 1983).

2. *The factory*. Robot technology is a growth area. By the mid-1980s, more than 2,000 programmed robots were working in British industry and their numbers were increasing at around 50% per annum. Concentrated in automobile manufacture, they performed a variety of tasks – welding, spraying, joining, turning nuts and bolts, injection moulding, handling assembly and inspection. There have been other important innovations such as the introduction of computer-aided design and draughting (CAD) and computer numerically-controlled (CNC) machine tools. Further computerisation of the manufacturing process is represented by a more recent technology – flexible manufacturing systems (FMS). In the near future, integration of these systems could produce a further extension in automation. The new technology is, perhaps, likely to have less impact on already capital-intensive industries such as chemicals and oil refining. But computerised systems are speedily transforming the coal, steel, food and printing industries.

   The automation of small-batch production in the engineering industry is now on the agenda. Companies such as GEC believe that the completely automated factory, with all the individual computerised systems linked up, can be achieved by the end of the century. Products would be designed by computers, with production details programmed into computer-controlled machine tools, turning out the components. Robots would assemble the components whilst voice recognition equipment would enable people to talk to the machines.

3. *The shop*. Electronic point-of-sale systems (EPOS) which code items, record and store information on prices and sales, and print till receipts, have been introduced in many chain stores. More than a half of all grocery items made in Britain now have bar codings. These systems provide faster customer throughput at

checkouts, avoid the need to price all individual items, and provide automatic updating on stock levels. Electronic fund transfer from bank accounts minimises handling of cash and can establish a cashless shopping network. Automated warehousing and new security systems are other recent developments. Retailing will, in future, require fewer sales assistants and more employees with computer skills. The use of Prestel and Viewdata by mail order firms could presage a future boom in tele-shopping and telephone ordering.

4. *The bank*. Banks, building societies and insurance companies deal largely in information and are naturals for computerisation. Computers were first installed to record information on accounts. Direct data transmission between branches was gradually introduced. In the big banks, word processing terminals provide standard letters and customer inquiry terminals provide details of accounts. Cashier terminals provide staff with information about customers, an electronic cash book and credit clearance. Automatic teller machines supply cash on demand and allow 24-hour banking. These changes have produced a decline in the number of full branches and an increase in the number of 'satellite' branches. In the future, point-of-sale terminals in retailing or home banking could produce a further decline in establishments and manpower.

The context

This 'new industrial revolution' is taking place against the background of a world recession, intensified international competition and determined attempts to restructure British capital. Against this background the Labour Party has stressed the importance of new technologies in modernising the economy and the role of the state in planning their introduction. They have argued, in Harold Wilson's words, for 'a conscious, planned, purposive use of scientific progress to provide undreamed of living standards and the possibility of leisure ultimately on an unbelievable scale' (Benson and Lloyd, 1983, 11). This emphasis was affirmed by James Callaghan who argued that the UK must 'wake up to microelectronics'. Unless the rate of application was speeded up, Britain would fall further behind her competitors and face economic stagnation. The theme of speeding up the application of new technology in order to catch up with Britain's competitors retains a strong resonance in Labour's present policies.

The 1974-79 Labour government's stress on state regulation was reflected in the resources devoted to training through the Manpower Services Commission and the Industrial Training Boards, and the investment strategy of the National Enterprise Board. The Department of Industry established a £70 million government scheme of support for companies applying new technology and a 'micro-electronics awareness programme' for employers and trade unionists. The NEB invested in a number of electronics companies such as ICL and Ferranti. They established a mass silicon chip producer, Inmos, with an initial investment of £25 million. Labour thus started the process of building a distinctive British industry and research and development capacity in this area as a counterweight to US domination. Public funds and state purchasing policies were intended to compensate for the deficiencies of private capital.

These policies were put into reverse by the Conservatives. The NEB was merged with the National Research Development Corporation in a new British Technology Group which quickly sold off the state share in 25 companies. The new philosophy was that the application of new technology was a matter for private, not public, initiative and investment. Nonetheless, the Conservatives continued Labour's microelectronic-awareness programme, declared 1982 'New Technology Year' and, in 1983, offered loans of up to £50,000 to attract new companies into the hi-tech area.

But Inmos was sold off to Thorn-EMI in September 1984 and soon ran into serious financial difficulties. There were job losses and drops in profit levels at Standard Telephone and Cable, GEC and Plessey. British micro makers, such as Apricot Computers and Future Technology Systems, and chip makers such as National Semi-Conductors, were reported to be in trouble. The liberalisation of telecommunications and the privatisation of British Telecom stimulated further uncertainty. A 1984 NEDO Report, *The Crisis Facing UK Information Technology*, painted a gloomy picture on the future prospects of the industry in Britain. UK computer companies were facing a hard and probably losing battle against IBM and the production capacity for microchips was outstripping demand.

The Conservatives' view is that innovation is basically the business of entrepreneurs and 'the government's role is to provide the sort of economic environment which will stimulate market forces in such a way that the innovation process will be encouraged' (Coombs et al, 1987, 232). The ability of deregulation, increased competition and liberated market forces to stimulate technological development in some areas should not be underestimated. But it appears that in other sectors the lack of state orchestration will inhibit change as firms refuse to take investment risks on innovation. The Conservatives' attachment to a *laissez-faire* approach to innovation in the context of its general strategy of increasing productivity is an important influence on technological development. It is apparent that:

a technology policy guided by the principles of the market shapes the sort of technologies that are produced and applied ... the principle underpinning the design and application of *this* technology, rather than *that* one is how can we best the French, Japanese, Germans or Americans (and all these nations are operating on the self-same lines) and axiomatic considerations here are cheapening the costs of labour, controlling the labour process more effectively and increasing the output of saleable goods and services. Another is that the technologies which get manufactured are those that are marketable rather than those that are socially needed' (Webster, 1986, 391).

Technology is not neutral but embodies the economic considerations and social values of those introducing it. So today, the position of the office as the cockpit of innovation is influenced not only by the cheapness of the technology, but by pressure on profits, the low productivity of white collar workers and the escalating cost of office overheads. And Thorn-EMI decided to withdraw from the essential field of medical electronics because, in the words of its chairperson, 'there appeared little likelihood of achieving profits in the foreseeable future'.

Management and new technology

The *availability* of new technology does not mean that managers will *necessarily* purchase it. Where it is installed, managerial intentions can differ, according to a range of factors from market position and industry to the nature and organisation of the particular management and work force. International studies have shown the UK falling behind its competitors in introducing new technology because of a lack of financial wherewithal or confidence to invest, a limited awareness of equipment and its potential and shortages of suitable staff (Werneke, 1983; Daniel, 1987). Conservative management can be an important constraint (Barron and Curnow, 1979).

Other studies show management introducing new technology to improve the quality of product, create new product lines, increase productivity and establish a greater degree of control over the work process. But the key factor in most cases is the reduction in costs (Buchanan and Boddy, 1983; Steffens, 1983; Wilkinson 1983). Where, for example, the stimulus for introducing CAD comes from a wish for greater design flexibility and a desire to experiment, there is still a powerful justification in terms of saving on labour costs (Arnold and Senker, 1982).

In some cases, innovation may be strategic and well articulated in terms of changes in the employers' market position and increased competition, whilst in others it may appear confused, *ad hoc*, or the product of personal enthusiasm (Willman and Winch, 1985; Wilkinson, 1983). Some analysts argue that the idea of a conscious strategy to enhance management control is not useful. Decisions to 'go technological' are influenced by a range of factors (Bessant, 1983) and often depend upon an innovator within the management team (Buchanan, 1983). Whilst management may simply produce acceptable rationalisations to explain innovation (Jones, 1982), and whilst different levels and functions of management may have different motives and expectations (Buchanan and Boddy, 1983), so that senior management concentrate on costs and return on investment and middle line management on control of work flow, technological change ultimately seeks to answer the imperatives of the market. As one commentator observes, '... even where the primary purpose is not to cut costs, many companies have taken the opportunity to reform working practices, increase labour flexibility or reduce manning levels. This probably reflects an increased concern with competitiveness' (Willman, 1986, 48).

This is not to assert that the introduction of new technology necessarily produces certain outcomes. There are choices to be made in the implementation of change, the design of technological systems and the consequent organisation of work. The impact of technological change is mediated through the actions of management, trade unions and workers. But it would be wrong to wrench this process of choice from its essential context or to overestimate the scope of choice available. The range of technological and market opportunities provides a degree of discretion. But new technologies are constituted not by perceptions of the needs of labour, but by perceptions of the requirements of profitability. New technology may contain the potential for a great development of human potential, undreamed of living standards, unbelievable leisure and a guaranteed income for all; but these particular technologies are being introduced for particular purposes in a particular economic and political context. Undreamed of living standards and enhanced, paid leisure are not the objectives behind their present application. *This* technology is being introduced by profit seeking employers against the background of a reversal, not a reinforcement of the post-war trends towards planning and egalitarianism, and in a situation where the distribution of power over decision making is increasingly skewed against those it will most affect. The probability is that new technology will benefit the few at the expense of the many.

Technology and unemployment

Many of the initial estimates of job loss arising from the application of the new technologies were dramatic. Barron and Curnow (1979) calculated that there would be a continuing high level of unemployment of 10-15% throughout the 1980s if there was no change in the growth rate of the British economy. In *The Collapse of Work* (1979), Jenkins and Sherman assumed that the existing trend to job loss in the manufacturing sector would continue and, on the basis that employers would utilise existing innovations, forecast an unemployment figure of 4.5 million by 1990.

Other writers attempted to integrate the new developments in the long-wave theories of economic growth proposed in the 1920s by the Russian economist, Kondratiev, and popularised in the West by Joseph Schumpeter. This approach argues that the creation of important new technologies stimulates entrepreneurs to invest. Emulation by other profit-seekers fuels a boom, the creation of new firms and the development of new products. Gradually, competition intensifies, profit margins are cut, investment falls and a new techological plateau is established, waiting on the next wave of innovation. Past waves of development were associated with the introduction of the steam engine, the railways, electric power and the car.

Exponents of long wave theory have different views on what is happening today. Some predict a period of overall job loss for 3 or 4 decades which is likely to be followed by a new upswing as new technology spreads to new sectors and creates new firms and products (Burns, 1981). Others argue that problems are likely because not enough new technology is being introduced at an

adequate pace. There is a need for new investment at an unprecedented rate if the UK is to keep up with its international competitors
and maintain productivity and full employment. Sustained unemployment is being underpinned by a shortage of capital. Faster and
more extensive introduction of the new technology which is both
labour-saving and capital-saving could allow increased output and
eventually more job creation. This would require a revolution in
industrial policy and social attitudes (Freeman et al, 1982).

Other studies questioned whether the high levels of unemployment which emerged in the late 1970s were the result of technological
innovation, rather than economic trends, changes in international
competition and national markets and state policies (Stoneman et al,
1981). They concluded that, by the mid-1980s, the job loss arising
directly from technical change was relatively small, representing
around 5% of the overall drop in manufacturing employment
(Northcott et al, 1985). It was argued that, in certain cases, new
technology produced no overall job loss, with natural wastage
ocurring in some companies introducing word processors but extra
labour being hired in others (EPOC, 1980). Other work pointed out
that technological change could produce an increased demand for
certain categories of labour such as electronic engineers, craft
workers and sales staff.

There are serious problems in isolating the impact of technical
change on employment. The Jenkins-Sherman forecast, for example, was based upon projections of demographic trends and economic growth, not specifically on the effect new technology would
have – as well as on the unfounded assumption that management will
automatically use what new technology is available. There is,
moreover, difficulty in balancing job loss with the job creation which
may occur elsewhere as a consequence of innovation. We cannot
assume a *fixed* demand for goods and services because productivity
growth stemming from the application of new technology may
expand consumption and *increase* demand. Firms which innovate
may, in fact, not shed labour if demand for their products or services
rises to offset the increases in productivity that the new equipment
brings in its wake. Employers who *do* reduce their labour force
because of the greater productivity and savings in labour new
technology provides may help to create jobs in companies providing
the new equipment. Increased profits or increased wages for the
remaining labour force or lower prices for the company's product

may be fed back into the economy through higher investment and increased spending power and, thus, create new jobs in other sectors of the economy.

On the other hand, employment levels will be affected by the rate of innovation in particular areas of the UK and in other countries. If Britain lags behind, its economic performance will suffer in comparison with that of its competitors. Within the UK, differential rates of innovation may mean that the North, for example, imports unemployment from the South. Overall, there can be little doubt that certain groups of workers *will* be thrown out of work by the new technology and certain skills and occupations *will* vanish from the scene. New technology *will* restructure the job market. Moreover, if workers displaced by technical change eventually find other jobs in different occupations or new industries, this may take time, owing to lags in investment and demand, a mismatch of skills, regional disparities and a lack of opportunities for retraining. Innovation may push up unemployment in the short, medium or even long term.

In other words, complex economic arguments lie behind many of the broad predictions about job loss. Factors such as job creation, retraining programmes, regional policy, import penetration, export strategies and exchange rates all come into the overall calculation. Whether new technology 'will exert an immensely destructive impact on both existing jobs and the future supply of work' (Jenkins and Sherman, 1979, 1), whether sufficient new jobs will be created to compensate for those lost, and whether the dismissed workers will be qualified to do the new jobs that are created, ultimately depends both on the state of the British and international economy, and the way the process of change is handled.

The position in the UK

The wide range of variables involved defies precise forecasting. But it seems that at least some of the conclusions in the earlier work were exaggerated, too dependent on an imaginative extrapolation of social and economic trends. If, thus far, many predictions have been wide of the mark, we should not completely write them off. It will not do to swing too far in the other direction and underestimate the impact of new technologies. Recent *Financial Times* surveys show 64% of companies who expect to employ fewer workers in future planning technical innovation, whilst 77% of firms projecting job losses have introduced new technology in the 1980s. Job loss often occurs some time after technological change and some surveys indicate that job loss as a result of technical innovation is increasing (Northcott et al, 1985). Reports state that the information technology industry in the UK is growing at around 12% a year. This compares with a figure of 23% for Japan, 19% for France, 18% for the USA and 15% for West Germany (NEDO, 1984). If an international 'technology gap' becomes significant, an inadequately, geared-up UK economy will be increasingly handicapped and displacement of labour will not be compensated for by growth in demand.

Nonetheless, the major influences on employment levels since 1979 have been broader market and political factors. (In the car industry these factors produced the loss of over 50,000 jobs in British Leyland whilst the introduction of advanced technology actually contributed to the creation of a smaller number of jobs (Willman and Winch, 1985). Moreover, it has been argued that where technological change *has* contributed to job loss it is often the mechanisation of unskilled jobs, not automation that is involved (Penn and Scattergood, 1985). But, of course, the introduction of advanced technology in today's situation can contribute to the *maintenance* and *extension* of large-scale unemployment. And we have yet to see its real impact.)

A recent comprehensive survey highlighted the extent of change. One third of manual workers and two-thirds of office workers in the 2,000 establishments surveyed had experienced the introduction of new technology. Foreign owned companies were more likely to introduce advanced processes than UK firms and the private sector was well ahead of management in the public services and nationalised industries. In the majority of cases there had been no short-term impact on jobs. But where there had been, jobs had been reduced, often substantially. The introduction of advanced technology tended to reduce employment amongst manual workers but the introduction of microprocessors and computers into the office tended, if anything, to increase the size of the work force. The introduction of new technology played a very small part in the overall pattern of manpower reductions, as compared with market demand, cost reductions or reorganisation. Nevertheless, disquiet was expressed at the fact that normally, one would look to workplaces investing in new technology for growth in jobs to compensate for employment loss in declining sectors. This was not happening (Daniel, 1987).

We must steer a path between the alarmist and the sanguine. Certainly in the medium term, new technology is likely to make a contribution to higher levels of unemployment. Already it seems clear that the employment growth in areas like financial services and insurance has been halted, with banks cutting staff levels and closing branches because new technology enables them to provide better services with fewer employees. We can expect similar trends in professional services, such as advertising, data-processing, accountancy and legal services. In contrast, we can expect employment growth in information technology industries, although there is as yet little evidence of a major increase in manpower. Job loss in telecommunications through, for example, the automation of postal sorting may be compensated for by the manufacture, installation and maintenance of new electronic telephone exchanges, videophones and systems of microwave transmission. There will, undoubtedly, be job loss arising from the introduction of CAD/CAM and FMS systems and robots on the shop floor, but changes here are likely in the short term to increase demand for skilled maintenance workers. The picture looks bleaker with regard to office work, where the majority of employees are women, employed in routine clerical activities.

The idea that the service occupations will deliver a host of new jobs does not seem borne out by developments in private services or retailing. Similarly, projection of a growth in the leisure sector sometimes ignores the economic and political situation which also acts as a check on employment growth in the public sector. Gershuny believes that consumers are moving from a 'serviced' to self-serviced mode of provision, using do-it-yourself tools rather than tradesmen, washing machines rather than laundries, videos rather than the cinema. The individualised car's victory over public transport is seen as the potential face of the future. Capital goods would still be produced in conventional fashion, but the economy would see the growth of an informal sector in which production of final commodities and self-servicing would take place in the home. However, what is missing is any attempt to develop the necessary telecommunications infrastructure to take advantage of information technology. This is as essential as roads are to the car, and its creation probably requires a far greater degree of state intervention and support, which at the moment appears unlikely (Gershuny, 1978, 1985).

Existing research directs our attention to broad tendencies which could be limited or reversed. It leaves us unclear as to exactly what the future holds, and past history teaches us the difficulty of predicting the shape of the economic future. The rate of development and diffusion of new technology, and the range of political responses on which so much depends, remain uncertain.

Deskilling and new technology

New technology has been viewed as removing the skill required by many jobs affected, eroding the autonomy of the worker, restricting job satisfaction and contributing further to the degradation of work on the lines proposd by Harry Braverman. In particular, technical innovation has been seen as opening the door to the Taylorisation of the office (Cooley, 1980). Against this, it is argued that microelectronic change provides the basis for job enrichment, enhanced autonomy and for the deployment of a greater range of skills.

Braverman argued that the influence of 'Scientific Management' has been central to management strategies for the effective exploitation of labour. 'Scientific Management' was popularised by F. W. Taylor, an American managerialist of the turn of the century. Taylor claimed that the maximum technical division of labour would produce maximum efficiency. The planning of work should be separated from its execution. Jobs should be broken down into discrete components and performance measured and evaluated. In Braverman's view the dominance of Taylorism has produced deskilling and degradation, a growing 'proletarianisation' of all kinds of work as industrial engineers increasingly remove from white collar as well as manual workers the vital autonomy that make work worthwhile. The trend of technological development and job design is to transfer skill and control from worker to management (Braverman, 1974). Other writers have argued that Braverman exaggerates the importance of *one strategy* for management control and underplays worker resistance. Management may, in reality give greater precedence to other strategies, such as 'responsible autonomy' which seeks to develop employees' loyalty and commitment to management goals by encouraging a degree of discretion in work (Friedman, 1977).

Wilkinson (1983, 48) has castigated 'the folly in the notion that deskilling and increased management control over production processes necessarily leads to increases in efficiency'. He describes how management which regarded its employees as 'lazy, unreliable, stupid and untrustworthy' introduced a new computer-controlled plating line, coating components with aluminium. The control console was installed well away from the electro-plating line and only management had access to it. Despite this, they had to fit the line with a manual override in case of an emergency. This device was quickly utilised by the workers to maintain *their* control over the pace of production.

In another case, management introduced automated rubber-moulding equipment straight from the supplier so that development and adjustments had to be carried out by the workers themselves. As one manager commented: '...development in the production environment meant that the operator would productionise machinery and, rather than management giving production parameters to the operators, the operators would to some extent give them to the management' (Wilkinson, 1983, 50). However, management saw the technical change as providing an opportunity for a fresh start, eradicating past inefficiencies and worker controls. They saw the element of worker participation carrying over to the new equipment. To avoid this in future, they created a separate development area away from the shop floor. In contrast, when the management in an optical company producing glasses purchased computerised precision machinery, they attempted to amelioriate the impact of deskilling. Management encouraged workers to do their own computer programming, maintained a flexible group bonus scheme and introduced a system of job rotation. The conclusions drawn from these studies was that deskilling is unlikely to always meet management purposes, that innovation need not necessarily produce deskilling, that the forms of work organisation contingent on technical change are varied and that there is room for management choice and the injection of workers' goals into the process (Wilkinson, 1983).

Similar conclusions have been reached by surveys of the use of CNC technology in the engineering industry which found differences in implementation by different managements, operating in different markets, with different values and traditions and different degrees of trade union influence (Jones, 1982). Other studies stress that the application of new technology can limit certain types of skills and interests, but provides opportunities for others. In biscuit manufacture, dough mixing was automated and master bakers replaced by unskilled workers. There were fewer variations in the job and less human contact. Operators complained: 'it's much less interesting, more routine, very little scope for human error now. Initially it's more skilled 'till you get to know the set up, then there's a fair amount of boredom' (Buchanan and Boddy, 1983, 187). Microprocessor-controlled weighing of biscuits, in contrast, did not control the process and left a fair degree of autonomy to employees, who felt that the change had increased their job satisfaction.

Human contact, the need for socialisation at work and the employees' view of the job can also be important factors for consideration in the introduction of change. The introduction of word processors can lead to unwanted leisure in the office by reduced typing speeds and lead to reclassification of personal secretaries as either typists in a pool or administrative assistants. This is often resented and, in the case of women tied to repetitive work on word processors, it can represent a loss of interest and autonomy (Bird, 1980; Downing, 1980). Workers complain that 'they were appendages to machines rather than performing functions with other people' and attention has also been drawn to problems of social isolation and a dehumanised environment in processes employing robot assembly (Winterton and Winterton, 1985, 5).

In other cases, microprocessor devices have been specifically designed to limit worker autonomy and measure work. In British Leyland, an electronic machine-monitoring system enabled direct surveillance of individual employees (Scarborough and Moran, 1985). Winterton, 1985, specifically relates the development of technology in coalmining to wider management strategies. A computer system controls coal transport and monitors machinery throughout the pit. At the coal face, sub-systems survey activity and report on the nature and duration of delays. The management have continuously refused to negotiate over computerisation. Here 'deskilling is a conscious design strategy as many control activities as possible are taken by the computer ... it is also designed to reduce workers' autonomy and to increase management control' (Winterton and Winterton, 1985, 12).

Another survey concludes that the overall balance of change as a result of the introduction of advanced technology was towards job enrichment. Restructured jobs provided higher levels of skill and responsibility, a wider range of tasks and more intrinsic job interest. On the other hand, the author states that 'the changes appeared to have a more neutral or even slightly negative effect upon the autonomy of workers as measured by their control over how they did their jobs, the pace of their work and the degree of supervision to which they were subject' (Daniel, 1987, 276). The findings were based upon the views of managers and shop stewards but no information was collected from the workers themselves.

Finally, there is the issue of health and safety. New technology provides the potential for neutralising many of the dangers which arise at work. New equipment can be safer, quieter and cleaner than traditional machinery. On the other hand, robots, for example, will require interlocking barriers to prevent access whilst operating and guards to prevent emission of materials. Deskilling can bring increased stress. The desire to intensively utilise new technology can lead to increased shift working and hazards such as disrupted body rhythms, fatigue, and the social isolation associated with it.

There has been particular concern about the impact of VDUs. These give off small amounts of radiation and continuous working can produce stress, eye and back problems. Workers who spend too long at VDUs have been diagnosed as suffering from 'data processor's disease' or tenosynovitis – pain and numbness affecting fingers, wrists and shoulders. Several reports question the relationship between VDU working and problems in pregnancy. Again, all of these problems can be overcome and trade unions are able to point to a number of agreements regulating, for example, adjustability, clarity, noise, length of operation on VDUs.

The evidence of the impact of new technology on the nature and quality of work demonstrates that management is not simply and uniformly pursuing strategies of deskilling and tighter control. Responsible autonomy is an important card in the pack. But of course 'responsible autonomy' is a strategy of management control, not workers' liberation, and one which can involve an intensification of work. And if some of the more horrific scenarios of new technology as the sinews of a new slavery have not been substantiated, and managerial responses vary according to economic, technological and human constraints, management control of technology remains an important instrument in its domination of the work force.

The impact on the enterprise

Adoption of new technology is seen by observers as facilitating changes in enterprise organisation (see chapter 7). It is argued, for example, that information technology can prompt firms to break themselves down into smaller units carrying on transactions via the market, rather than a complex internal management hierarchy. Many goods and services now internally generated may, in future, be supplied on a subcontract basis, the firm retaining only its 'core' activities. This hiving-off and establishment of 'companies within companies' may go hand in hand with moves to more flexible relationships with labour (Francis, 1986).

Home working or telecommuting could significantly increase as computer terminals become cheaper and more efficent. One agency, F International, already promotes a consultancy and computing service liaising between clients and 1,000 home-based operators. As technology provides the means for carrying out all kinds of business at a distance, the need for the traditional large work unit diminishes. Many companies now have executives working from home and this practice is likely to increase as teleconferencing become less expensive. Rank Xerox, for example, employs specialists working on microcomputers linked to their head office, paid only for specified hours or tasks and tightly controlled by computerised recording of results. Employers utilising home working save on the costs of both plant and labour. Wages in this sector are historically low and there seems to be some evidence that this practice is spreading to the new area of work resourced by information technology. The potential for development in many areas, such as clerical work, and the advantages to management in dividing and isolating the work force, make this an appealing option for future growth. Dispersed workers make for difficulties in unionisation, legal protection for workers is almost non-existent, whilst productivity gains can be higher than in office working and wage rates lower (*Labour Research*, July 1984).

In the flexible enterprise management will shrink, its present pyramid structure will flatten out, and it will gradually change its function as market and technological forms of motivation attain greater precedence. In this scenario, management will move further towards 'responsible autonomy' approaches. Supervision will become less authoritarian and more facilitative, less reactive and more strategic. However, movement towards the flexible firm has been uneven and the speed and degree of change is questionable (see chapter 7).

The trade union response

All of these changes mean big problems for the trade unions. They are confronted with technology in whose design and construction they have played little part, in an economic and political context which has eroded their power. A range of problems, from job loss to smaller size of firm and new contractual arrangements, are posed. On the other hand, increased insecurity, fear of redundancy, unfavourable changes in working conditions and increased work measurement in white collar occupations may provide the preconditions for union recruitment and organisation.

Union awareness of the new challenge burgeoned in the late 1970s. The TUC was definitely for microelectronics. They should be introduced into industry as fast as possible to improve the UK's competitive edge in world markets. Unions should aspire to joint management of the project and share in its ultimate benefits. The TUC attempted to use its privileged position with the Labour government to influence the conditions in which new technology would be introduced. It urged its affiliates to bargain over change at industry and plant level, using negotiations over new technology to push into the area of industrial democracy. With the fall of the Labour government, the TUC sought to establish a national framework with the CBI which would both legitimise its role as a regulator of innovation and ease its affiliates' problems at local level. In the new environment the CBI demurred. It was not prepared to countenance certain aspects of the TUC approach, such as agreement *prior* to the adoption of new technology. It preferred to stand on its own 1980 statement *Jobs: Facing the Future*. This document saw innovation as a matter for management prerogative, not joint regulation. The TUC was left to attempt to implement the approach adopted by the 1979 Congress, and embodied in the policy statement *Employment and Technology*, minus that policy's initial setting of state planning and in a colder climate as far as employers' attitudes were concerned.

The new technologies, the TUC argued in *Employment and Technology*, were, in themselves, 'neither friend or foe'. Whether they worked to the advantage or disadvantage of workers and society would depend on how the techology was introduced and the policies of employers, trade unions and the government. Technological change *could* contribute to higher productivity and increased growth and its impact on employment *could* be controlled and mitigated if unions, management and the state planned technology in partnership – and in the context of wider economic policy.

The end of tripartism meant that from the unions' point of view it was even more urgent that their representatives should push into the realm of management decision-making and become involved with new technology 'at the design stage' or 'before the decision to purchase' (TUC, 1979, 64, 69). Union representatives should seek to control the pattern of change by negotiating specific New Technology Agreements with employers. These should cover:

1. *Change by agreement*: unions should seek to introduce 'status quo' and 'mutuality' clauses limiting management's right to introduce change unilaterally.
2. *Guarantees of job security* for the existing work force. Provisions for retraining of those affected. Satisfactory redundancy provisions as a last resort.
3. *Guarantees on maintenance of earnings and status* for those affected by reorganisation.
4. *Moves towards reduction in working hours* and the 35-hour week. Consideration to be given to control over overtime, longer holidays and earlier retirement.
5. *Full access to information* to be given to shop stewards before decisions on change were reached.
6. *Joint union-management consultation machinery* should be established to consider the adoption and implementation of new technology.
7. *Union control over work.* Unions should be involved in the design of new systems. Computerised work measurement should be eschewed.
8. *Health and safety*: the implications of the new technology for workers' health and welfare should be an important consideration.
9. *Union organisation* should be reviewed. There should be collaboration between unions in negotiations, whilst unions should review their research and knowledge of technical developments and consider the appointment of 'new technology stewards'.

10. *Review procedures* would be needed to enable joint management-union working parties to monitor progress.
How successful have the unions been in meeting these objectives and
influencing the operation of new technologies?

New Technology Agreements

Early surveys of the growth of New Technology Agreements (NTAs)
registered few union successes in terms of reduced working hours and
increased earnings as a result of technical change. Unions were
reasonably successful in avoiding redundancies but job loss occurred
through natural wastage. Many unions were adopting model agreements, adapting the TUC guidelines for their own membership, and
a growing number of agreements were being signed with employers.
But an early verdict was that it would not 'be an over-exaggeration to
conclude that unions have been largely unsuccessful in securing a
share of the benefits of new technology: the rhetoric of model
agreements has not in general been translated in negotiated concessions in clauses of actual new technology agreements' (Manwaring,
1981, 18).

A more extensive survey of over 100 NTAs found that under 10 per
cent of agreements provided for union involvement in the planning
stage of innovation, but around a third assumed union involvement
before implementation. The vast majority of agreements were being
signed by white collar unions (Williams and Moseley, 1981). A CBI
survey of 225 NTAs stated that even in large workplaces, under 20%
of employers negotiated over technical innovation. Overall, 44%
'communicated', 42% 'consulted' and a mere 9% 'negotiated'. Most
NTAs were signed by only one union and nearly 70% provided for
'no compulsory redundancies' (Francis, 1986, 177). However, more
than one third of agreements had no clauses on provision of
information and anything approaching a 'mutuality' clause, by which
management agreed to introduce new technology only if the union
accepted it, was extremely rare. The view that the unions were not
sharing in the benefits of change was confirmed. Moreover, in
practice, unions were exercising little influence, indeed demonstrating little interest, in wider issues such as job design and its impact on
the quality of life at work. The authors of the 1981 study saw the
growth of NTAs as having already passed its zenith (*Labour
Research*, July 1982; Williams and Moseley, 1981).

By 1983, it was reported that only a small proportion of the work force, largely in the white collar field, were covered by NTAs, and it was unions such as ASTMS, APEX, NALGO and TASS which had made the running:

'whereas 1978-80 were years of frantic trade union activity at national level in the production of policy statements, model agreements and booklets for members on the problems of negotiating over new technology, since then there has been a relative silence as the movement has progressed from propaganda to the problems of implementation. Hopes and aspirations of the later 1970s have not been fulfilled ...in many cases, management have felt that they can use their stronger bargaining power to push new technology through unilaterally' (*Labour Research*, November 1983, 296, 297).

A year later, trade unionists felt that 'as a strategy to initiate the involvement of worker representatives in the design of change, technology agreements have not been very successful' (TURU, 1984). The most recent survey of 240 agreements negotiated between 1977 and 1983 noted that both the adoption and content of NTAs had been limited compared with the original TUC objectives. This was related to the recession and its impact on the management-union power balance. NTAs had only been actively pursued by a small minority of white collar unions. Whilst other unions might argue that they handled technological change under their normal bargaining arrangments, it was the inadequacy of these arrangements in dealing with this specific problem which had prompted the TUC initiative in the first place. Only 11% of agreements provided for mutuality and there was doubt as to the extent to which the often vague procedural rights in NTAs were affecting the process of change in practice (Williams and Steward, 1985).

It has been recently noted that 'the relationship between managements' approach towards unions and the existence of new technology agreements is not very strong. It may, however, be that the agreements were signed when management adopted a more supportive approach towards the unions and that this has subsequently changed' (Batstone and Gourlay, 1986, 213). Is the tailing-off of NTAs since their heyday in 1979-82 associated with a hardening of managements' stance as they come to terms with the recession and the new political situation and their impact on the unions? Another recent study found that the most common relationship in the implementation of new technologies was, in fact, consultation rather than negotiation, whilst 50% of the sample of management stated that the unions had not been involved at all (Davies, 1986). This was confirmed by broader research, which found that the incidence of consultation or negotiation was remarkably low: according to the accounts of managers, 'shop stewards were consulted about any stage of the introduction of advanced technical change affecting manual workers in only 39% of cases' (Daniel, 1987, 116). As the manual areas are where unions have been strong, this confirms the view that, on the whole, technological change is being governed by the exercise of management prerogative. Agreements with the unions on advanced technical change never amounted to much, and today 'there can be little doubt that the initiative to sign new technology agreements has run out of steam' (Willman, 1986, 12).

Management and unions

This view is given some support by the fact that even the Institute of Personnel Management, which can be relied upon to adopt a more liberal approach, avoids any endorsement of *negotiated* change and NTAs in favour of 'communication', 'employee involvement' and 'consultation' (IPM, 1983). Moreover, personnel managers have played a very small role in the introduction of recent technical change and, in fact, it is argued that 'one reason for the poor level of consultation over the introduction of technical change may have been the failure of general management to involve professional personnel managers more in the process' (Daniel, 1987, 285). This may also affect the arrangement of work as new technology is introduced.

However, the limited evidence shows that even where unions have been directly involved in innovation, even at its early stages, through participation structures, the impact that they have had on decision-making has been small. The best documented example is the introduction of process change in British Leyland from the late 1970s, involving the launch of the new Metro, intended to recapture the company's declining market share. The changes included CAD, press shop automation, CNC for the engine machining and the introduction of robotic welding in assembling the car body. From 1976 to 1979, a joint participation sub-committee of managers and shop stewards discussed technological and production changes. However, certain decisions on the type of car, productivity targets and production standards had already been taken, and others, such as staffing ratios, were regarded as non-negotiable.

Despite the fact that full-time senior stewards were involved, who regarded it as 'the most successful participation exercise that we took part in', the influence the unions brought to bear on technological change was 'comparatively marginal'. The exercise was an exercise in management conception, and execution, so that individual managers could conclude: 'participation was a success and helped us in selling the changes we wanted' (Scarborough, 1986, 103). Although both 'the management and trade union members of the council sub-committee stressed the free flow of ideas that took place throughout, they felt that the unions had little impact on the overall shape of the ADO 88 (Metro) project. The participation of the unions in the planning process merely led the unions to accept the recommendations of the Red Book almost wholesale and, in particular, the important clause on productivity targets' (Willman and Winch, 1985, 96).

Whilst the impact of British Leyland's economic situation cannot be disregarded, the stewards demonstrated a lack of awareness of the nature and implications of the new technology. Lacking experience of processes such as robotic assembly, they also lacked any back-up technical expertise and were reliant upon management information. They were also constrained by their own union and stewards' committee policies, which saw new technology as progressive and urged its speedy introduction.

Other research has pointed out the inadequacies of the unions in terms of expertise, communications, structure and unity. They are inadequately tooled-up internally to strongly influence the direction of new technology and its application. Union representatives often have difficulty getting hold of relevant information at the right time. When they do, they are often not in a position to assess it. Nor are those who can gain access to, or distil the implications of such information, readily available to union representatives. This produces a reliance on management presentations and an adaptation to their purposes, so that even limited consultation is often an emptier exercise than it might be. Attention has also been drawn to trade unions' failure to avail themselves of many of the advantages of the new technology in terms of improving their information flow and organisational resources (Willman, 1986).

An observation in one recent case-study could apply to a number of unions in a number of industries: 'A complete lack of co-ordination was found between the union representatives in the various operating companies of the same brewing group, which provided management with a major advantage in carrying out technological change in this industry' (Davies, 1986, 184). Unions not only have problems with research resources and internal communications, but the multi-union structure in many workplaces and companies is a particular problem in relation to new technology. The battles in the printing industry and the divisions between the NGA, the NUJ and SOGAT provide the starkest examples. But researchers have found that in the banks where new technology was being introduced union representatives rarely met to discuss the issues and exchange information. In GEC, there were few links between the unions producing new technological systems and shop stewards who would end up using it. And in British Leyland, divisions between craft and general unions and manual and white collar unions and the absence of a joint shop stewards' committee emphasised divisions, inhibited exchange of information and constrained an effective union response to new technologies (TURU, 1981).

Worker resistance?

In several industries attempts by employers to introduce new technology have provoked opposition and industrial action. There are recent examples in the car industry, on the railways and in the Post Office. Advanced technological change has provoked the most extended and bitter resistance in the printing industry because of its radical, far-reaching effects on trade union organisation.

The industry has been affected by the simplification computerisation brings to the printing process, the development of teletext and viewdata and other information systems and the introduction of photo-composition. In the *Messenger* dispute, for example, 4 secretaries trained in 2 weeks were able to set the newspapers. Since the mid-1970s, the capability has existed for tele-ad workers (SOGAT) and journalists (NUJ) to key copy directly into computers so that the paper can be composed on VDUs. The implications for the craft union, the NGA, which organised the compositors whose work would be made redundant by direct input, through a vigorous closed shop, tight control over the work process and high wage rates, need little emphasis. Change has been posed and introduced against a deteriorating background. There was a loss of 63,000 jobs in printing between 1969 and 1976 and the Royal Commission on the

Press, reporting in that year, urged that the introduction of the new technology and the acceptance by the unions of further large-scale job loss was the only way open to cut costs in an inefficient industry.) Both unions and management were also aware of developments in the USA, where employers had used the new technology to decisively weaken union control and break the NGA's sister union, the International Typographical Union.

In 1976, the Fleet Street proprietors and the unions produced a *Programme for Action* in an attempt to introduce change in a coordinated fashion. This was rejected by the members of the print unions and several groups of newspapers decided to go it alone. The Mirror Group moved to bring in a system of photo-composition and facsimile transmission, so that pages composed in London could be printed in Manchester. There would be no direct input – NGA members would set all the type – although there would be redundancies. The system did not work. The *Mirror* had to go back to hot metal and hire extra staff at a cost of £2 million a year.

The *Financial Times* scheme for reform was successfully resisted by the unions. The company decided instead to print a European edition in Germany. The attempt by Times Newspapers to install new equipment led to a year-long lock-out in 1978-1979 which ended in a defeat for the employer. It has been argued that this fiasco and 'about-turn' was motivated by an improvement in the financial position of Fleet Street in the late 1970s, the strength of the unions and the lack of skills and expertise of the management (Martin, 1981). The employers were, however, successful in remoulding the apprenticeship system to reduce costs and allow for retraining.

In the provincial newspaper sector, direct input had been established on the *Nottingham Evening Post* as early as 1973. Elsewhere, the NGA continued to control this function. In 1982, the provincial employers, the Newspaper Society announced *Project Breakthrough* and set a 2-year deadline, on reaching agreement on the introduction of direct input. After the deadline employers would be authorised to change the system over the heads of the unions. The NGA was determined to maintain its closed shop and right not to handle work from non-union sources. In late 1984, in a statement, *The Way Forward*, it modified its policy. If direct input prevailed, the NGA was still determined to follow the work, so that its members would move from the composing room to the editorial and tele-ad area, but it now proposed a 3 union closed shop, together with the NUJ and SOGAT, in the origination area.

The NUJ, whose talks on amalgamation with the NGA had just foundered, was concerned at the Association encroaching on its members' work, and so was SOGAT. Concern turned to active opposition as, in late 1984, the *Portsmouth Evening Post*, now freed by the elapsing of the Newspaper Society's deadline, agreed to transfer NGA compositors displaced by direct input so that they could re-train as sub-editors. NUJ members refused to co-operate and were suspended. As a number of other papers forced direct input through in the face of widespread industrial action by the NGA, the journalists, in retaliation for the NGA's offensive, agreed to work the new system themselves on papers such as the *Shropshire Star*. It was only after a prolonged and bitter dispute that an agreement was put together under TUC aegis. Both unions now accepted that, following the implementation of direct input – and the employers had now won this battle – NGA members transferred to the editorial area would have *dual* NUJ/NGA membership. For a period of 5 years NUJ members would not make up or assemble pages. On the other flank, it appeared by 1987 as if an amalgamation between SOGAT and the NGA was finally on the cards.

In the aftermath of the *Messenger* dispute, the Fleet Street employers returned to the fray. When in 1985-1986 Rupert Murdoch planned his move to Wapping, a sophisticated direct input system produced by the US computer specialists, Atex, was already installed in the new plant and EETPU members had taken the place of NGA members in printing the new *Today* paper, originally owned by Eddie Shah. As Murdoch successfully used the employment legislation to tie up the unions, national newspaper after national newspaper began the detailed planning for moves out of Fleet Street to new greenfield sites, resourced with up-to-date technology. And the print unions reluctantly accepted that further resistance would be wasteful and, indeed, counterproductive.

Or worker co-operation?

In the printing industry the attempt to install new technology, motivated by a desire to cut costs, encountered fierce and sustained resistance. It produced an important remoulding of industrial relations, a change in training arrangements, a stimulus to union amalgamations and the end of national bargaining. However, several recent surveys have found that resistance by workers and unions is a limited phenomenon (Batstone and Gourley, 1986; Edwards, 1985). The powerfully organised newspaper unions saw themselves fighting over control and conditions which went to the root of their members' working lives. In many other areas it seems the installation of new technology is viewed in a different light.

Northcott and Rogers (1984) found that only 7% of their sample had encountered opposition, largely in textiles and printing, and this view is supported by Daniel (1987). Daniel argues that when commentators:

'especially managerially orientated commentators, discuss the reactions of workers and trade unions to technical change, the phrases most frequently used tend to be *worker resistance to change* and *union resistance to change* ... we gained a very different impression ... it was clear that the general reaction was support for change and often enthusiastic support. This was the case on the shop floor as well as in the office. Indeed, the picture we found suggested that commentators should replace their stock phrases with references to *worker support for change* and *trade union support for change* ...' (Daniel, 1987, 263, 264).

Whilst there were pockets of resistance, it was an exception to the general rule, largely isolated cases, which commanded an undue measure of public attention. Failure to innovate had more to do with the failures of management rather than unions and, in fact, the existence of unions could act as a stimulus to the installation of advanced technology. Shop stewards, however, reported that workers were less enthusiastic than they were and the views of the rank and file were not reported in the survey. This enthusiasm is surprising when we note that a large majority of both union and management respondents reported that no increase in earnings was associated with technical change. But the author's analysis of the comparative earnings of different groups in relation to the use of advanced technology showed that employees in workplaces where it had been installed earned more than their comparators elsewhere (Daniel, 1987).

Conclusions

From the late 1970s, a spate of scenarios pondered the potential of the new technologies for the future of work. If their application was used for the good of the majority of the population, then the frozen pattern by which that majority worked, from 16 to 60 or 65, could be transformed. A small, changing minority could provide adequate goods and services for all. Periods of work could be interspersed with periods of leisure and education. All citizens could be guaranteed a basic income. Work could become a free and voluntary activity rather than a matter of necessity and compulsion. Such projection also contained pessimistic variants in which present inequalities and oppressions would continue, but with a far higher level of unemployment than had existed from the 1940s to the 1970s (Handy, 1984; Jenkins and Sherman, 1979).

Today, the optimistic view of the future appears to have little purchase. With sustained unemployment, growing inequality and social polarisation, a patchy record of innovation and the share of the UK's information technology industry in the world market having fallen from 9% in 1970 to 5% today, the optimistic scenario appears a dream as distant as ever. And the social forces which might even begin its realisation are debilitated or inactive. The social regulation, in the form of state planning, essential for real social progress, is conspicuous by its absence. And the trade unions appear in poor shape to design, unaided, the face of the future.

As new technology has been introduced over the last decade, in stuttering fashion, with many conservative employers far from convinced of the need for renovation, the unions have, on the whole, eschewed Luddite approaches to technical change. They have not sought to stop the unstoppable but have, rather, attempted to raise the question 'who benefits?' and to ensure that producers should share in the spoils of progress. Deprived of a supportive, political climate, they have placed the major emphasis on joint regulation of change by collective bargaining. This has not come off. The evidence suggests that trade unions have been accorded only a minimal formal role in the management of change and have, in practice, exercised little influence over the crucial decisions on the nature, shape and implementation of technological innovation.

The unions' failure to attain their targets may have as much to do with the historic limitations of collective bargaining as with a sudden fall from grace in 1979. Nonetheless, the recession and political change have not helped. The 1980s have seen few advances by the Labour movement over the issue of technology and control of work. They *have* seen certain managements turn the hostile, economic and political climate to their advantage and a weakening of those trade unions such as the print unions, who did exercise keen control over the work process. In other areas of industry, whilst management introduced changes in a largely unilateral fashion, there is some evidence that collaboration has had its price, and management's need for co-operation has led to increases in pay and the use of 'responsible autonomy' rather than deskilling strategies.

But as the experiences in the banks or the mines illustrate, the pattern is a diverse one. What stands out is the absence of the unions as important actors in the technological drama. They have lacked the power to strongly influence its impact. They have made few important breakthroughs in the reduction of working hours and have failed in their objective of guaranteeing job security. And they would do well to recall that in the end 'the technology is not socially neutral but embodies and is developed within antagonistic relations of production' (Manwaring, 1981, 22). If trade unions are to go beyond a defensive, reactive and limited civilising of change at the edges, if they are to move to realise the liberating and equalising potential of new technology, then they will have to look beyond collective bargaining. This will necessitate a change of attitudes within the unions so that concern with the quality and design of work is accorded a new attention, new resources and a new legislative framework to stimulate and reinforce trade union action.

In the far more sympathetic climate of the Scandinavian countries, extensive legislation structures the union response to the whole area of change at work. In Sweden, the 1977 *Co-determination Act* and the 1978 *Work Environment Act* make it mandatory for employers to consult and negotiate with trade unions before decisions on change are taken and to provide detailed and accessible information. This is supplemented by national framework agreements covering new technology and local agreements between employers and unions. In Norway, the 1977 *Work Environment Act* and the *Data Agreement* between the Norwegian TUC and the National Employers Federation have produced over 700 local agreements, covering wide sectors of the work force and covering all aspects of technology and the working environment. If, as appears likely, we are in for an immediate future of far more rapid change in all aspects of work, British unions will have to rethink their present philosophy and move in a similar direction.

Further reading

Two recent surveys of this area which are well worth reading are A. Francis, 1986, and C. Gill, 1985. Of the earlier books, C. Jenkins and B. Sherman, 1979, is still stimulating and T. Forester (ed), 1980 and 1985, are useful collections of articles.

There is interesting case-study material in D. Buchanan and D. Boddy, 1983, and B. Wilkinson, 1983. R. Martin, 1981, and P. Willman and G. Winch, 1985, provides interesting analysis of the role of trade unions in technological change in the printing industry and the car industry respectively. J. Winterton and R. Winterton, 1985, provide a good distillation of the problems facing the trade unions. R. Williams and F. Steward, 1985, is the most up-to-date survey of NTAs. The latest general survey of the area is W. Daniel, 1987.

Useful books looking at the wider role of the new technologies are: P. Blackburn et al, 1985; C. Freeman et al, 1982; J. Gershuny, 1978, 1983.

Chapter 5

Trade union democracy

Union democracy has occupied a central position in recent political debate. For the Conservative Party, Norman Tebbit has continually insisted that 'The arrogant misuse of the wealth and power of the trade unions to serve the political ambitions of unrepresentative leaders has been a growing cause of public concern. Trade unions should become more democratic institutions, responsive to the views and wishes of their members.' Union leaders like Eric Hammond have inquired: 'How can unions respond to or reflect their members' interests when their affairs are conducted by leaders and committees accountable only to a thin stratum of activists?' Recently elections have been re-run in the Transport Workers Union and the Civil and Public Services Association because of irregularities in the ballot. Elections in the Seamens' and Building Workers' unions have been the subject of prolonged litigation.

The TUC has denied there is a case worth making. It has hit back at its critics by agreeing that problems are bound to occur in a movement with 9 million members. But the unions are a degree more democratic than the City, the Civil Service, the media or the House of Lords. Nobody elects the judges. Mrs Thatcher rules the country with little over 40% of the popular vote. The much maligned Arthur Scargill was elected President of the Mineworkers' Union in 1981, receiving 70% of the vote on a turnout greater than that in the last 3 general elections.

Are trade union leaders sincere democrats who, in the words of the TUC, ' are accountable to their members every day of the week'? Or do they merit the scathing opinion of Mr Tebbit, who believes that 'by comparision with such trade union leaders, the late Duke of Wellington looks like a trendy liberal'?

Union democracy: an example

In 1976, the National Coal Board decided on a new wage payment scheme. At the 1977 NUM Annual Conference the new scheme was rejected. Despite this, the National Executive announced a ballot of all members. The Kent Area argued that the NEC was breaking the union rules. They took the matter to court. The judges declared that the Executive were not behaving undemocratically: 'what the NEC is proposing to do is to hold a secret ballot of all members. This is the very essence of the democratic process ... a far more satisfactory and democratic method than leaving it to the delegates of a conference'.

In the ballot, a clear majority voted against the new scheme. The NUM Executive refused to accept the result. They ruled that any of the unions' areas which wanted to introduce the scheme could do so. This went against the wishes of the majority expressed in the ballot. Relying on the support the judges had given to the ballot, 3 areas went to court asking for a ruling that the Executive were behaving undemocratically. The court upheld the Executives' action: 'the result of a ballot, nationally conducted, is not binding upon the NEC in using its powers in between conferences', Mr Justice Watkins stated. 'It has no great force or significance.'

The local incentive scheme was introduced. Was this as a result of a democratic decision? Or was it as a result of an Executive which had already made up *its* mind imposing its will upon the membership? Were the judges who thought a national ballot was the essence of democracy right? Or was the judge who believed it was 'of no great significance' on firmer ground? Was it right for the Executive to go against the decision of a more representative gathering of delegates, the Conference and a national referendum of members as exemplified by the ballot?

In early 1984, the Executive of the Scottish and Yorkshire areas voted to support strike action against closures. The National Executive supported the action and sanctioned strikes by any other area under Rule 41 of the NUM constitution. This rule allowed individual areas to call strikes without a national ballot. Rule 43 required such a ballot for *national* action, but was not this just playing with words? Were not the proponents of Rule 41 simply trying to manipulate a national strike into being without allowing the membership a national ballot? Was not the national ballot the guarantee of united action in a naturally fragmented union? Had not the national ballots in 1972 and 1974 laid the foundations for successful action?

Would it not now be fatal to enter upon a prolonged struggle without ensuring that the rules were followed?

Not at all, replied the Executive: if each area decides to call out its own members then, even if that means in aggregation a national strike, the rules have been followed. A national ballot could mean that areas which wanted to take action to oppose closures could be stopped by miners not facing the same problem. Individual areas should have the right to take action and the right to try to convince other areas to support them. Democracy should protect the rights of minorities to take action. And look at what the courts said in 1977 about the lack of importance of the national ballot.

The position of this group was strengthened when a special conference of the NUM voted to support the Executive position. But the problem for the supporters of Rule 41 was that most areas were required by their own rules to ballot before approaching the Executive under Rule 41. And areas like South Wales and Nottingham held ballots which went *against* industrial action. Moreover, when dissident miners took cases to court the attitude of the judges was very different from that of 1977. They now ruled that the national ballot was the foundation stone of democracy. Executive and Conference had no power to call what was really national action in the absence of a vote of all the membership. The controversy over the ballot continued throughout the strike. The procedural arguments were, of course, intimately related to the issues of substance: where one stood on the issue of job loss and what should be done about it. The issue of the ballot had a vital impact on the fortunes of the strike and the legal judgements eventually produced the state takeover of the NUM's assets.

It illustrates clearly that the question of democracy in trade unions is a complex, not a straightforward matter. The NUM, with its different areas and traditions, illustrates the problem in heightened form. But all unions experience similar difficulties in reconciling competing interests and balancing between different forms of decision-making, central control and local autonomy. Moreover, as this example demonstrates, trade union democracy is not some scholastic exercise: it goes to the root of trade union activity.

Why democracy?

Most people believe that unions should be democratic. There are exceptions. It has been claimed, for example, that 'Trade union organization is not based on theoretical concepts prior to it, that is some concept of democracy but on the end it serves .. The end of trade union activity is to protect and improve the general living standards of its members and not to provide workers with an exercise in self government' (Allen, 1954, 15).

This statement is based upon a false dichotomy between union purposes and union democracy. By combining together, individuals increase their power. By acting in disciplined fashion, workers can exercise control over a range of decisions which affect the enterprise. When they join a union, workers give up freedom to act individually. Union democracy provides some guarantee that collective power is used in the interests of the members.

Collective bargaining with employers has been a central means by which unions have acted to defend their members but unions have adopted other methods and goals. NUPE, for example, aims '... to secure for the workers by hand or by brain the full fruits of their labour and the most equitable distribution thereof that may be possible upon the basis of the common ownership of the means of production distribution and exchange..'. One of the NUR's objectives is 'To work for the supercession of the capitalist system by a socialist order of society'.

Different groups inside and *outside* the unions will have different ideas on what the interests of the members are, which goals should take precedence and how they should be pursued. Employers will take an interest in the affairs of an organisation capable of exercising an influence on the future of the enterprise. They will seek to limit union goals and will see the disciplined power of the union as a means of impressing management purposes upon the work force. The state will, in a similar fashion, sometimes see unions as a useful conveyor belt for the implementaion of its policies. Both state and employers will therefore seek to condition union goals and behaviour.

Some writers have emphasised the intimate connection between union goals and union democracy. They have argued that the more limited a union's goals become the more danger there is that democracy will become limited. If unions confine themselves largely to bargaining with the employer and providing services to their members there is less apparent necessity for active participation and more justification for the view that decisions should be left to the professionals (Hyman, 1975). But even where union goals are relatively limited, members can still have an impetus to participate to ensure that settlements on wages and conditions are satisfactory to them. Even within the confines of today's trade union practice, Allen's statement that the end of union activity is to protect their members' living standards begs the question: what policies are to be utilised to achieve this purpose? Is the union to embrace, for example, the aggressive programme of industrial action and political change of Arthur Scargill or the 'no-strike agreements' and 'pendulum arbitration' of Eric Hammond? Only the members directly affected can provide the answers as to which of these conflicting approaches should be adopted.

The rules of democracy adopted by unions are the Marquis of Queensberry rules, formulated to regulate the struggle of competing groups inside and outside the organisation. Union democracy educates members in the art of decision-making. But it is essentially a means to an end – organised action. However, if we accept that unions should be democratic we are still left with the problem of *how* they should be democratic. What kind of system of decision-making should they adopt? As we have seen from the example of the NUM, there are important differences here.

Direct and representative democracy

Democracy is an overworked and imprecise word. But the original craft trade unionists were quite clear as to what it meant. They worked to a literal definition of democracy 'rule by the people'. They attempted to emulate the practice of the city-states of Ancient Greece where all citizens directly participated in taking decisions. In the early unions, all the members had access to the General Meeting, which did its best to deal with as many issues as it could. Only reluctantly were responsibilities delegated. Each of the branches took its turn as the head office and there was regular rotation of official positions. Even when a growth in size and the development of collective bargaining produced more elaborate organisation, the craft unionists were keenly aware of the need to control their officials and tried to develop mechanisms which would involve ordinary members.

The Webbs, writing at the end of the last century, believed that the model of popular participative democracy was irreconcilable with administrative efficiency. There was a tension between the ordinary

members, who would look to their own immediate interests, and the
officials, who were able to bring a wider vision, expertise and
consistency into union activities. It would be disastrous if either were
to completely dominate union decision-making. Once union business
became large-scale and sophisticated, such devices as the mass
meeting, referendum, delegation and rotation of office would
produce incompetence or dictatorship. They prescribed an emulation of parliamentary democracy, government by representative
institutions. The Webbs, therefore, advocated a system of more
limited democracy. For in parliamentary democracy, participation
and control are partial. Citizens elect representatives who are free to
indulge their own views until the next election, unlike delegates, who
must carry out the mandate developed by their constituents.

If the Webbs represented a measured retreat from popular
democracy, Michels represented a headlong flight. He focused on the
processes by which union leaders were able to escape democratic
imperatives. In trade unions, as in other organisations, an 'iron law of
oligarchy' operated. Full-time officials developed a monopoly of
expertise – and used their control over resources and the prestige
their position gave them to impose their own goals on the members
whose ignorance and apathy facilitated this process. Unions were
ruled, not by their members, but by small groups of bureaucrats.

Modern views on democracy

Later students addressed the extent to which members not only *can*
but *do* take decisions. Factors which influence membership participation and control, such as the size and dispersion of membership, skill,
status, education and occupational identity, were analysed. Unions
have been classified as *exclusive democracies* – unions with a
homogeneous and cohesive membership and high participation, like
the traditional craft unions; *aristocracies* in which one group shows
high participation rates and dominates the union apparatus, like the
face workers in the NUM or Co-op workers in USDAW; and
Popular Bossdoms, unions with strong leadership control based on
full-time officials and little rank and file participation, like the big
general unions, typically the TGWU. It has been argued that it is
essential to look at the actual working of the political process in
unions rather than simply measuring constitutions against conceptions of political democracy, and that we should not neglect

examining the extent to which passive members can identify union policy with their own interests (Turner, 1962).

A famous study of an American print union argued that the party system played a healthy role, just as it does in parliamentary democracy. It enabled issues to be organised and presented the voters with a choice between alternative programmes and personnel. It ensured that the government of the organisation was continually open to effective scrutiny, criticism and challenge by experienced judges. This system provided extended opportunities for members to participate in the decision-making process and gain valuable skills and experience. However, this union was seen as untypical and perhaps an anachronism. Its members were of high status, highly skilled and homogeneous and the beneficiaries of a long-established tradition. On paper, its constitution was democratic, and both parties accepted the results of elections, eschewing attempts to entrench themselves in power by changing the rules (Lipset et al, 1956).

More recent studies in Britain have seen the guarantee of democracy in the 'survival of faction', examining factors which make for this, such as the traditions and political culture of the union, the type of technology, its members' work and the strength or weakness of workplace organisation (Martin, 1968; Banks, 1974). The growth of party and faction in British unions has been demonstrated for a range of different unions (Undy and Martin, 1984). It has also been asserted that the common emphasis on union democracy has obscured the need to scrutinise how efficient systems of government are, and that the question of how democratic a union is may be too wide. There may be different means for taking decisions at local and national level. Unions have different channels for decision-making for collective bargaining and non-collective bargaining issues. These different systems, it is claimed, require specific scrutiny (Undy et al, 1981).

Critics have argued that we need a broader, not a narrower, canvas. In their concentration upon internal arrangements and activities, many observers fail to relate these to external pressures from employers and the state. It is impossible, for example, to study union democracy in isolation from the policies of governments. Both external constraints *and* membership action influence the internal political process and the key full-time and lay activists who gave expression and definition to members' collective interests. The unions' decision-making mechanisms play a role in activating or deactivating the membership, making external control by employers and state more difficult or easier (Hyman, 1983).

Some writers have argued that there is a need for unions to rediscover the earlier ideas of direct democracy. The growth of a paper membership, many of whom had little attachment to trade unionism, has acted in combination with the myopic focus of union leaders on bargaining with government to debilitate and demobilise trade unionism. If present trends continue, and branches and district committees become increasingly staffed by a declining minority of activists, then the unions' sinews of mobilisation will wither further. The attempted replication by unions of the institutions of representative democracy has always carried with it the dangers of individualism and the passive member-active leader split of the parliamentary system. Recent legislation is intended to exploit this. There is a need to rebuild popular democracy in the unions (Hyman, 1984; Fairbrother, 1984).

Participation

The structures of many unions illustrate their different histories. The structure of a former craft union like the AEU, still reflects its origin amongst skilled workers and their suspicion of centralised authority, for example. A union like the TGWU still bears the marks of its forerunners, the general unions, which, recruiting a wide range of unskilled, low-paid workers susceptible to high turnover, were built from the top, depending on professional organisers and strong central leadership. But just as the internal structure of the general unions was modified by the amalgamations of the 1920s, so today we are seeing important change.

Participation is a key issue. Evidence shows a low level of sustained membership involvement in formal decision-making. Attendance at branch meetings averages around 7% (Daniel and Millward, 1983). This is similar to figures of 2 decades ago (Goldthorpe and Lockwood et al, 1968). The figure for NUPE has been estimated at 5% and for NALGO, which has less frequent meetings, at over 30% (Fryer et al, 1974). A study of the engineering union over 20 years showed an average attendance of around 7% in a range of 4.5-20%. National elections produce a higher turnout (Undy and Martin, 1984).

The further we move away from the branch, the smaller the numbers of those engaged in active decision-making, although activists may participate at branch, district and also at national level. Nonetheless, national issues provide an impetus for periodic participation. Voting for the General Secretary of the TGWU, for example, has traditionally provided a turnout of around 40% of the membership; in the NUM, the figure has been between 70% and 80%. In the decade until 1982, the annual average turnout for elections for district, divisional and local officers in the engineering union varied between 38% and 24% of those on the electoral roll. In ASTMS, the turnout in Executive election is under 10% and a similar estimate has been made of elections of full-time officers in the GMBATU (Eaton and Gill, 1983).

It could be argued that a significant number of trade unionists take sufficient interest to vote in union elections, but the situation is far from satisfactory. For comparison, around 40% of those eligible vote in local government elections. Against this, it could be argued that when unions campaign to bring issues to their members' attention and when members feel that the issue is important, a high turnout results. Moreover, the variation in participation should lead us to ask why members sometimes participate, and sometimes don't. And we must not forget to relate the low level of branch participation to members' more active involvement in workplace organisation – and their lack of sustained participation in other organisations, such as political parties.

Democracy in practice

Many would claim that unions' decision-making structures look better on paper than in operation. The 1986 Conference of the National Union of Journalists, for example, instructed its NEC to instigate immediate disciplinary action against NUJ members still working at Rupert Murdoch's Wapping plant. The Executive promised to carry out the members' wishes but reported to the 1987 Conference that 'it had discovered procedural difficulties'. The Conference condemned the NEC for ignoring the Conference decision but voted down a proposal that the NEC should resign.

In the light of this kind of common experience many trade unionists would question whether conference is the supreme decision-making body of the union. Real power is concentrated on the Executive. They can interpret conference decisions to their own satisfaction, or argue that changed circumstances have rendered

their realisation redundant and weather the storm at the next
conference, when it is, perhaps, too late to do anything about the
original issue. Or, perhaps, real power resides, not in the Executive,
but in the General Secretary or President. Clegg describes how one
leader 'cast the block vote of his union at meetings of the Labour
Party Conference and the Trade Union Congress as he thought was
right, rather than with close regard for the decisions of his own
conference or the preference of the majority of his union delegates at
the meeting' (1970, 90-1).

All sorts of pressures may be used to ensure that the results of
democratic processes are the right results. A report of the NUJ's 1987
conference states:

The NUJ came under intense pressure at the TUC to remit its motion
criticising the TUC's international department. 'Before it came on the agenda
we had pressure put on by Norman Willis and Mike Walsh (head of the TUC's
international department). Ron Todd, General Secretary of the TGWU,
almost tore my head off. After we remitted the motion other unions did come
up and say they would have supported us', TUC delegate Colin Bourne said.

The Union's TUC delegation was censured but the die was cast.

Conferences can be carefully managed in this fashion. They are
sometimes too large and unwieldy to exercise much influence upon
the detail of policy. Elections, too, can be difficult for those opposing
the existing leadership. In the EETPU, candidates must not send out
any circulars or letters nor allow supporters to do so. They must not
give interviews to the media for electioneering purposes. They must
not visit plants for campaign purposes. Moreover, the Executive can
delete from election addresses any material they are advised is
defamatory or factually inaccurate. It may be felt that in elections in
many unions it is difficult to displace the incumbent. Day-to-day
decision-making may be taken into the hands of full-time officers
whose accountability to the membership is minimised but whose
accountability to the existing leadership is stressed.

In opposition to this, it can be argued that the exceptions prove the
rule; well publicised examples of abuse highlight the fact that for
most of the time unions do operate in democratic fashion. There is an
element of management in union conferences, but this occurs in any
organisation. The Conservative Party Conference is an excellent
example of platform dominance. In most of the elections which
excite controversy, there is speedy investigation and a re-run. Most
of the problems, here, have more to do with the logistic difficulties

sizeable and under-resourced unions face in organising such exercises, rather than chicanery or corruption. The majority of union activists are determined to ensure that union decision-making is above board and seen by the public to be fair. In 1986, when doubts were raised as to the regularity of the election of the General Secretary of the transport workers, it was the victorious candidate, Ron Todd, the man with most to lose, who insisted that the election should be re-run.

Contrasts in union democracy

We cannot look at how different aspects of union democracy operate in isolation. It is not very helpful for trade unionists to be told that the system of company bargaining, through shop stewards, is very democratic and efficient, if the members of their union's TUC or Labour Party delegation – over whom they have minimal democratic control – inform them that they have just voted for a 12 month wage freeze or a general strike. There is a intimate interrelationship between a trade union's industrial and political, organisational and bargaining activities and we need to try to see how the branch, stewards' committees, executive and full-time officers interact in practice. We have also noted that trade union democracy is in a constant state of evolution. It is useful to try to assess its direction.

The large lay member executive of the TGWU may be viewed as extremely democratic in terms of the direct relationship of its members with those they represent. However, when we add a full-time General Secretary, elected by the whole membership for life, to a large conference that meets only every 2 years, we may agree with those who have felt that the structure provides great *opportunities* for the exercise of domination by the General Secretary. With the resources of the head office behind him and the advantages of permanent tenure, he may be able to control the changing non-professional executive. Through direct influence over the appointment of full-time officials, the General Secretary may achieve a high degree of autonomy and attain a mastery over a large and heterogeneous conference.

This was indeed the pattern of control in the TGWU until the late 1970s, with powerful General Secretaries dominating the union through links with the regional and trade group secretaries and ensuring the succession through their choice of deputy. But these structures only provide *opportunities* which may be utilised in different ways according to political and industrial orientation. In the early 1960s, Frank Cousins encouraged a gradual devolution, involving shop stewards on negotiating committees and suporting the extension of workplace bargaining. This process was accelerated by Jack Jones. In one sense this represented an acceptance by the central leadership of a trend which had already strongly developed.

Its consequences were seen in the defeat of the platform over incomes policy at the 1977 Conference and the relative weakness of Jones's successor, Moss Evans, whose illness contributed further to a weakening of central power and the development of factionalism. If the 1974 Labour Government's policies played a role in changing the situation within the TGWU, the differences within the union over attitudes to the Conservative administration and internal dissention in the Labour Party played some role in the growth of factionalism. Personal jockeying for position in an unstable situation was also an important factor. Today, the union is split and the hold of the TGWU General Secretary is more precarious than that of any of his immediate predecessors.

The Engineers

The AEU provides a contrast to the TGWU's disintegrating 'popular bossdom'. Its constitution reflects the model of separation of powers with the policy-making conference, the National Committee, legislating, an Executive elected by the members carrying out its decisions and an elected Final Appeal Court adjudicating on contentious issues. The judgement that this is an extremely democratic organisation is strengthened by the argument that the compact full-time Executive of 7 people is in a strong position to control the Executive officers whose functions are, in any case, divided between a President and a General Secretary. The small National Committee meets annually. It can, thus, claim to play a stronger role than the TGWU conference in limiting the power of the Executive and officials. Power is further dispersed by the strong role given in the constitution to the District Committees and the fact that line officers are elected in the districts and divisions by those whom they will represent – a method which turns the official towards the members, not head office. The rosy picture is completed by the fact that shop stewards have always been strong in the industries the unions covers and active on District Committees.

In the AEU, democracy is facilitated, in practice, by the existence of a 2-party system organised on the basis of clear-cut political differences. This has provided the possibility for a choice of policies to be presented to the electorate in a way hitherto impossible in unions like the TGWU. Its success can be demonstrated by the passing of power from right to left in the mid-1960s and from left to right in the mid-1970s.

However, the position in the AEU has also changed over the past decade. The existing leadership has not hesitated to manipulate and modify this structure to maintain dominance. In response to the Left's success, based upon strong branch organisation, the right wing, which had retained control of the rules' revision committee, pushed through the system of postal balloting. They correctly believed that this would play to their strengths and the Left's weaknesses and mobilise right-wing support more effectively. This system was gradually extended and, in the early 1980s, postal balloting was applied to the election of TUC and Labour Party delegations and the Final Appeal Court. The Right controlled the Executive and National Committee and were determined to limit the influence of the latter body which was one of the bastions of the Left. In two cases, the leadership, in breach of rule, refused to forward correspondence to the Appeal Court which was unable to discharge its functions. The Executive has attempted to erode the powers of District Committees and its hand has been strengthened by the reorganisation and amalgamation of districts and branches the recession has imposed upon the union. Similarly, the economic situation has eroded the ability of workplace organisations to act as a restraint on the central leadership. Further rule changes have been mooted in order to facilitate amalgamation with the Electricians – a union with similar political sympathies to the Engineers, but a very different structure. The devolved structure of the AEU has hidden an increasing concentration of power.

Centralisation in trade unions

Whilst other unions such as the GMBATU and NUPE have in different ways followed a TGWU-style path of devolving power away from the centre, this has been done in a limited and controlled fashion, with independent power at the base of the union restrained by national bargaining structures and the impact of Thatcherism. In other unions, centralisation has been a decisive trend and has attracted both support and criticism.

The electricians' union, the EETPU, is the clearest example of the new model. Its origins were as a craft union and it was organised in similar fashion to the engineers'. However, in the 1960s, after the Communist Party leadership was removed as a result of a ballot-rigging case, a new right-wing grouping took control. They changed the rules, to replace the lay executive elected every 2 years with a full-time Executive elected every 5 years; replaced membership election of full-time officers with Executive appointment; abolished Area Committees; replaced the rank and file Final Appeal Court with an appeal body consisting of Executive members; gave increased power to the Executive to close and amalgamate branches; barred Communist Party members from holding office; and declared that conference decisions were not binding on the Executive.

The leadership of the EETPU justifies its restructuring of the organisation in terms of the dangers of Communist subversion and on the grounds that members are basically interested in success in collective bargaining, not in attending meetings. It claims that the right-wing majority on the Executive and the election, by wide margins, of Eric Hammond as General Secretary in 1982 and again in 1987, demonstrate membership support. Opponents claim the leadership's domination is maintained by their control over appointments, the internal media and discipline. Branches have been suspended because of opposition to the Executive. Elections have been declared invalid and re-runs ordered. Several left-wingers have undergone surprising political conversions in a union described as 'an elective dictatorship'.

Unions on the left

Such essays in remoulding union constitutions to centralise power are not the prerogative of the right wing. An interesting phenomenon is the dominance of left-wing leaders in unions whose members reflect centre or right political tendencies. TASS, the draughtsmen's union, which amalgamated with ASTMS in 1988 to form the giant Manufacturing, Scientific and Finance Union, has traditionally combined a conservative membership with a high degree of union consciousness and organisation. Until the early 1960s the lay member Executive was dominated by the right wing, but by 1963 the 'broad left' led by Communist Party members succeeded in taking control. Their strategy was to gain as many full-time officer posts as possible and full-time officers came to play an increasing role in the 'broad Left'.

By the early 1970s, divisions had opened up within the 'broad Left' based on differences over both Communist Party politics and TASS's industrial policy. The opposition was gradually removed from positions on the Executive and Divisional Councils. Delegates to conference were no longer elected from branches but from divisions. The Executive Committee was no longer based on single divisions, but on more remote regions. The system by which full-time officers were appointed for life – a strong base for leadership power – was maintained. There was hostility to combine committees and, political opponents argued, a reluctance to mobilise the union to defend key militants who were not supporters of the majority line. Left-wing policies on a range of wider political issues were combined with a cautious stance on industrial policy. The opposition saw this as motivated by a desire not to make too many demands upon the membership in terms of action or involvement. It was seen as being based on the view that the members will tolerate certain left-wing policies as long as they are not required to do anything active to implement them. Their trajectory was justified by the leadership by reference to the need not to get too far ahead of the rank and file. Today, it is estimated that more than 90% of conference delegates, the entire national Executive and all the full-time officers are supporters of the 'broad Left'.

There are important differences between TASS and the EETPU in both organisation and policy. Many would argue that both unions leave something to be desired in terms of either representative democracy or popular participatory democracy. Others believe that in today's conditions greater centralisation will become the dominant tendency across the board. It is possible that projected mergers, such as those between TASS and ASTMS, and the EETPU and AEU, will strengthen the trends to concentration and provide an opportunity for changing constitutions.

However, at the level of the TUC, the tendency would appear to be towards decentralisation, with greater autonomy for its affiliates. This greater scope for unions to take their own decisions represents a reversal of the position in the 1970s. Then it was argued that many TUC policies had their origins in the views of a select group of union leaders and their detailed articulation by the Congress House civil service. Their translation into policy by a carefully managed

Congress and the insistence that they then bound all affiliates, meant that policy was emanating from above, not below and that the democracy of individual unions was circumscribed.

The growth of bureaucracy

Both the Left and the Right criticise union leaders, the Left arguing that they fail to represent their members by being too moderate and the Right that they exercise their own militant appetites at the expense of their more conservative members. The first explanation of the bureaucratisation of union leaders was that of Michels. His views often underlie popular discussion today, for he was merely expressing in a sophisticated fashion the view of many that union leaders have more in common with the bosses than with their own members and that the consequences are to be seen in a House of Lords packed with Lords Murray, Scanlon, Basnett, Chappell and many more union leaders, left and right.

This, Michels argued, was *inevitable*. Union bosses became assimilated to the middle class and distanced from the lives and interests of their members. Union policies moved with the social trajectory of the officials in a *conservative* direction. For these leaders' 'their own social revolution has already been effected. At bottom, all the thoughts of these leaders are concentrated upon a single hope. that there shall continue to exist a proletariat to choose them as its delegates and to provide them with a livelihood' (Michels, 1962, 305).

These sentiments were also found in Marxist analysis which developed the idea of 'the trade union bureaucracy', a social stratum with a material interest in the maintenance of capitalism and, hence, the management of their members. The incorporation of union leaders so that they could control their members was also portrayed as a coherent, calculative strategy of state and employers.

Other writers have analysed in more detail Michels's conception of organisational goals replacing original union objectives. In this view, the organisation's need for survival and security as perceived by its leaders stimulates accommodation with employers and the state. The development of sophisticated collective bargaining mechanisms produces a moderate, compromising approach, a need to control, so as to 'deliver' their members, which is the basis of the full-time officials' role. The need for financial stability and unity produces attempts to curb militancy, which can put the organisation or the officials' position in bargaining at risk, yet encourage it when the official requires a bargaining counter in negotiations. These imperatives also breed the need to curb the activities of sectional or oppositional groups. The need for efficiency creates an impetus to greater professionalisation and increased distance between members and apparatus (Fryer and Hyman, 1975). Other studies have stressed the socialisation process which is applied to union leaders, and the pressures for moderate behaviour exercised by the media and public opinion (Allen, 1966; Coates, 1980).

Countervailing pressures
Against this it has been claimed that while bureaucratising processes do operate, their outcome is not inevitable. Unions can only grow away from their members to a certain extent. Rather than iron laws operating, there is a constant struggle in unions between democracy and oligarchy, autonomy and incorporation. Unions which became simply an arm of the state or employers would forfeit the support of their members and would not, therefore, be very useful to management or politicians. In the end, union leaders have to deliver the goods to their members. It they do not, opposition will develop and will mount a challenge, even if checks on the leadership have been attenuated.

In the recent past, the members changed the leaderships of the electricians and engineeers. The General and Municipal Workers' Union was forced to change its policies by rank and file revolts at Fords and Pilkingtons. In the 1970s Walter Anderson, the General Secretary of NALGO, was replaced by an official judged to be more in tune with membership views. In the Civil and Public Service Union there are regular swings between left and right-wing leadership. Even the then all powerful General Secretary of the TGWU was defeated on a central policy issue at the 1977 conference. In recent years, too, we have seen the replacement of the moderate Joe Gormley by Arthur Scargill in the mineworkers' union, and Sid Weighell, resigning under pressure after failing to abide by union policy, in the railway workers' union.

Unions' formal commitment to democracy, the fact that members *expect* their representatives to abide by their wishes, pressures from public opinion, as well as the socialisation of leaders when shop stewards in the norms of shop floor democracy, will constitute an important countervailing pressure to undemocratic manipulation. Finally, it has been stressed that, in the British context, the relative independence and autonomy of the shop steward system has constituted a major barrier to oligarchy and incorporation.

Bureaucracy and rank and file

An alternative argument questions the dichotomy of interests between officials and members. It is asserted that there is a constant overlap and interaction between top level full-time officials, local full-time officials, lay activists and ordinary members. Moreover, each of these categories is characterised by internal differentiation. Even if we can draw a demarcation line between them, is it correct to ascribe different interests and inclinations to militancy to different groups? Isn't it true that in certain cases union officials urge militant action and activists and members do not support them? And, in other cases, union leaders restrain the militancy of activists and members. During the miners' strike, miners in Nottingham were more conservative than their national leaders. Leaders in the TGWU, NUR and ASLEF, who wanted their members to take action to back the NUM, received little support. It is argued:

it is entirely possible that in winter 1979 many ordinary lorry drivers and local authority employees did want to press radical pay claims, while some of their leaders wanted to restrain them out of loyalty to the Labour Government; and that by 1981 these same workers so feared unemployment that they did not want to risk big claims, while some union leaders believed that the government's bluff could be called. And on both occasions there were both workers and union leaders who took the opposite line to the majority of their peers (Crouch, 1982, 173)

In this view, the radicals' attribution of militancy to the activists and membership is just as mistaken as the Conservatives' ascription of militancy to the leaders. Both are partial deductions from a complex whole. In reality, the major differences within trade unionism run through leaders, activists and members and are based upon occupation and industry, political attitudes and conceptions of what trade unionism means and what membership entails. The left-wing union leader has, for example, more in common with left-wing shop stewards than his or her right-wing counterpart.

The counter-argument urges that the danger here lies in liquidating the whole concept of bureaucratisation, which remains a useful means of analysing internal union relations and linking them to external pressures. Because of their functions and position in the union structure, full-time officials do have special interests. We cannot overlook the important distinctions between this group, lay officials and ordinary members. But we cannot predicate an essential antagonism between the interest of professional functionaries and those of ordinary members – though conflicts will arise – nor ascribe all the problems of trade unionism to this antagonism. At times, the officials' commitment to the long-term bargaining relationship with employers or the financial position of the union will lead them to oppose action supported by the members who, unlike the officials, have a direct interest in the outcome. At times, organisational factors may prompt officials to aggression, whereas the members are not prepared to take action. Both groups react to a changing environment. The members are not always straining at the leash, nor are the officials always playing Brutus.

It has been contended, for example, that the acceptance by the unions of the last Labour government's industrial policies cannot be laid at the door of a conservative and undemocratic trade union leadership: 'rather both the vast majority of union leaders *and* members operated within a similar universe of discourse, one in which there was a qualified acceptance, however reluctant, of the force of the government's arguments for wage restraint. This was far less a matter of leadership incorporation than of an entire class's cultural subordination' (Coates, 1980, 211). Nonetheless, as pressure on wages intensified, it is clear that the commitment of union leaders to the social contract and the Labour government was, because of their functions, greater than that of many of their members, whose main impetus was the perceived decline in their living standards.

The bureaucratisation of the rank and file

One important contribution to the argument about union democracy contends that the problem of bureaucracy is not basically rooted in the interests of a specific layer of full-time officers in the unions. Rather, it needs to be seen as a set of relationships pervading all aspects of union practice. The differential distribution of expertise and activism means that there is a dependence on the knowledge and initiative of small groups of leaders by ordinary members at all levels of the union. Over the last 15 years, it is claimed, changes in collective bargaining and union structures have led to an integration of shop stewards, a more passive membership and unfavourable consequences for union democracy. Change has produced formalised agreements and procedures, a new layer of full-time stewards, more extensive facilities, and more hierarchy and centralised control within stewards' organisations. Workplace organisation grew closer to official structures and became more amenable to carrying out official policies. A complex system of links extending from the TUC down to the shop floor facilitated the execution of key policies, such as wage restraint. Whilst this process weakened democracy, it provided an opportunity to overcome sectionalism to deal with centralised challenges from state and employer (Hyman, 1979).

For critics, this analysis underestimates the degree to which full-time stewards previously existed and the extent to which they make for oligarchy. By being more available to members they may make for more democracy. There is little evidence that shop stewards have more influence over their members, or enjoy greater tenure than they did in the past. Management have always provided support for workplace organisation: there is nothing essentially corrupting about facilities. The picture of bureaucratisation is too generalised. In some unions stewards have long been integrated into thc official machine; in others workplace organisation is far from bureaucratised. There is little evidence that changes in workplace structure helped union leaders to push through their policies during the social contract. Pressures generated from the members can just as logically flow up the union structure as down it and lead to greater control *over* rather than *by* the full-time officers. Even steward organisation, sponsored from above, can become independent and autonomous. Hyman's argument, it is claimed, rests upon an inaccurate view of shop steward organisation in the 1950s and 1960s. Prior to the Donovan Report, steward hierarchy, facilities and links with management characterised many workplace organisations and the degree to which they have spread today can be exaggerated. Union leaders were able to carry their members with them in the 1960s without the benefits of bureaucratisation. In so far as 'bureaucratisation' has occurred, it can be, and has been, a force for democratisation in unions like the Transport Workers' (Batstone, 1984; England, 1981).

Special rights

A key question in any democratic system is whether special measures should be taken to secure the involvement and representation of those who have specific disabilities. In the early 1980s, despite the fact that two of Britain's biggest unions, The TGWU and the GMBATU, had almost 700,000 members, there was not a single woman on the GMBATU's 32-person Executive or the TGWU's 89 person executive. The Tailor and Garment Workers' membership was 90% female, yet only 7% of its Executive were women. In the National Union of Teachers, 66% of the membership, but only 9% of the Executive, were women. The picture was the same in other unions and at all levels of the union. In NUPE, for example, 63% of the membership were women but only 8 of 30 places on the Executive and only 7 out of 150 full-time officers' positions were filled by women.

During the 1980s, unions have applied more vigour to adapting their structures to involve women members, although the position remains far from satisfactory. NUPE, which reserved 5 seats on its Executive for women in 1975, was able to report in 1987 that, for the first time, a majority of its Executive were women, at the same time as the GMBATU was planning to reserve a quarter of the seats on its Executive for women. Nearly all unions now have special arrangements to stimulate greater participation by women in the union. The TGWU system of national and regional Womens' Advisory Committees is a typical example. The reserved seats mechanism has become more popular and many unions also organise a special conference limited to women members. Other measures adopted include the appointment of full-time officers with special responsibility for women members, 'women only' education courses and specific publicity and information for women members.

In 1987, the TUC published a 'positive action programme' to follow up its 'Charter for Equality' of 2 years before. The emphasis on structures has led unions to confront the question of how structures work. This has led to an examination of how and when meetings are held. For many women with domestic commitments evening meetings are difficult to attend, there is a need for child-care facilities to be arranged and the procedural rigmaroles, archaic lingua franca and male hostility and sexist assumptions are sometimes forbidding. A recent report produced for USDAW found that 58% of women members believed there was too much jargon at branch meetings, 56% thought they were dominated by cliques and more than 40% thought that they were irrelevant – views supported by many male members. The challenge of women who find their union a problem is doubly valuable in raising questions about democracy which affect all members.

Black trade unionists

At the 1987 biennial conference of the TGWU, for example, there were only 5 black delegates – less than in 1985, and 1983 or 1981. Less appears to have been done by trade unions to adapt themselves to the needs of black workers who also suffer from specific material oppression. Compared with women, black workers are a small minority of trade union members, but despite their commitment, 56% of black workers are union members, compared with 47% of their white counterparts, there are less than 20 full-time officers in the entire union movement. The unions have not been prepared to apply the reserved seats strategy they have used to involve women, to their black members. In the early 1970s, as black trade unionists brought themselves to the attenion of their leaders through a series of strikes, notably at Mansfield Hosiery Ltd, Imperial Typewriters and Grunwick, some changes were made. The TUC established a Race Relations Advisory Committee which was followed by the adoption of a Black Workers' Charter urging unions to negotiate Equal Opportunity Policies with employers.

NUPE established a Race Relations Advisory Committee but argues against a black section on the grounds that it would ghettoise its black members. Also, most unions have followed the example of the TGWU, which opposed the establishment of a black section, although its proponents argued that its necessity was illustrated by the fact that the union's General Secretary, Bill Morris, was the only black official in the union's top leadership. Others have implemented modifications in structure. The National Union of Journalists, concerned at the small number of black journalists and their under-representation in union government, established, in addition to its Equality Council, which deals with equality between the sexes, a Race Relations Working Party. This body consists of 7 members, 5 elected at the union's Annual Delegate Meeting and 2 by the National Executive. Lower union bodies such as chapels and branches have access to the Working Party, which has the right to table motions and amendments for the ADM. The NUJ has also changed its membership forms in an attempt to discover how many black journalists there are in the union. How can you adapt the union to involve black members if you do not know how many you have and who they are?

The meeting of 500 NALGO black members, in 1986, represented the first time a national union had sponsored such a conference. NALGO'S 1985 Conference called for proposals to redress the under-representation of oppressed groups on the NEC. This led to the establishment of a working party which recommended that there should be separate committees to represent women, black, gay and disabled members at both district and national level. Moreover, seats on the National Executive should be reserved for representatives of each of these groups. These proposals encountered opposition on grounds of substance and because they would contravene the 1984 Trade Union Act. At NALGO'S 1987 Conference implementation was deferred.

Positive discrimination

These strategies of positive discrimination have caused controversy. Proponents justify them on the grounds that women and black workers suffer specific discrimination and specific action is required to deal with this. Strategies of positive action are required to ensure that womens' issues or black issues are placed on the agenda. Without special measures the problems these groups face would constitute too great an obstacle to participation for all but a tiny minority. Special conferences are required for confidence-building and strategy creation. They help oppressed workers into the union mainstream where they, in turn, act as an example and incentive to the next generation. Supporters of this approach would agree that it has its limitations. Committees which are, at the moment, 'advisory' should be given more decision-making powers. Too many of the quotas are too small to allow the exercise of adequate influence. Many of the changes introduced to help women should now be applied to black workers. Moreover, positive action is supported by the majority of women and black trade unionists.

Opponents of positive discrimination argue that it is divisive and ineffective, and that women and blacks should look upon themselves as trade unionists, not as *black* trade unionists or *women* trade unionists. All workers have similar problems, whatever their gender or skin colour. Special bodies separate different groups out from the mainstream and constitute in themselves an assertion that women or blacks are second-class and cannot compete on equal terms. This undermines the many who can already adequately operate within the union and inhibits newcomers who could emulate them, if they did not constantly have their alleged inferiority rammed down their throats. Participation in powerless bodies is demoralising. Beneficiaries of reserved seats will be treated as not having got there on their own merits and, thus, as second rate executive members.

Moreover, where will it all end? Gays have now joined blacks, women and disabled people as the recipients of positive discrimination. What about Irish people or Jews? The working-class movement is supposed to be about unity, yet it is becoming increasingly fragmented. Trade unionism is about emphasising what the members have in common, not what divides them.

The real indictment of the positive discrimination strategy is that it has not improved the position of women and black workers. Since 1979, unemployment has increased faster amongst women and black workers than amongst white men. The wage differentials between both these groups and white male counterparts have widened. The major advantages of positive discrimination are reaped, not by oppressed members, but by union leaders who have no intention of seriously assaulting that oppression. They can point to these token measures to show that they are doing something. Women and black careerists are given a vested interest in the status quo and nothing much changes: a 1985 survey of 11 unions showed that only 62 out of 349 Executive seats were occupied by women and of 1,538 full-time officers' jobs, only 87 were occupied by women. Had women been represented in proportion to their numbers, the figures would have been 176 and 592. Also, there is no firm evidence that the majority of women or black members want this ineffective policy.

The politics of union democracy

The industrial unrest of the early 1970s convinced Conservatives that a majority of passive, moderate members were being manipulated by an activist minority of extremists. If the silent majority were able to participate through secret postal ballots, insulated from the 'intimidation' of union meetings, the Conservatives felt that there would be a move to the right and improved industrial relations. Moderates could not be expected to attend meeting after meeting, so a means had to be developed to limit the problem of their absence which played into the hands of the militants. The employment legislation of the 1980s dealt with this issue (see chapter 3).

The Labour Party backed the TUC's opposition to legislation on the grounds that whilst secret ballots had their strengths, the unions should be left to decide for themselves which methods they should adopt. From 1985, however, Labour's policy underwent an important shift. Their leaders emphasised that ballots were popular. For Labour to simply abolish them could be disastrous in electoral terms. Many trade union leaders were willing to go along with this case and the 1986 TUC-Labour Party Liaison Committee document *People at Work: New Rights, New Responsibilities* stated that legislation from a future Labour government would include provision for ballots.

The Liberal Party, in the 1970s, argued for greater participation by union members and supported the idea of postal ballots for elections. They particularly welcomed the scheme for state finance contained in the 1980 Act. The SDP after 1981 was able to give unrestrained expression to the views of Labour's right wing. In late 1982, the SDP MP, John Roper, introduced a private member's bill to regulate the use of a secret postal ballot for elections and for tenure and conditions of Executive members and officers. Like the Conservatives, the SDP showed enthusiasm for referenda to give unions back to their members. The Alliance welcomed the 1984 Trade Union Act's ballot provisions, although they felt that it did not go far enough in placing responsibilities on employers.

Ballots and democracy

The arguments for
1. Union leaders are involved in taking decisions vital to the well-being of economy and society, with minimal accountability. The turnout for voting on important union decisions is low. And *nobody* voted for left-wing leaders like Ken Gill of TASS, who was appointed for life by a left-wing Executive, or Clive Jenkins of ASTMS: he was appointed General Secretary of his union in 1961 and has never had to face the voters since.
2. The closed shop provides a fascinating cameo of the lack of democracy in unions. Until Mrs Thatcher acted, many workers were forced into joining a union without any right to vote in a ballot. The closed shop interferes with the freedom of the individual and the right to work. By constraining management's right to hire and fire and deploy labour in the most effective

fashion, it can inhibit the efficiency of the enterprise. Even from a union point of view, those press ganged into membership are unlikely to become loyal, let alone active members.

3. You cannot significantly improve participation in union decision-making if you insist on members attending meetings. Mass meetings are open to outsiders and to intimidation. They can be stage-managed. 'Meetings at which votes are to be cast can be arranged at times and loccations which are inconvenient for many members. The actual vote may be taken at the end of a long meeting. In these ways members can be discouraged from voting. Furthermore, there are clear risks of manipulation' (Green Paper, *Democracy in Trade Unions*, 1983, 9). Voting by show of hands is not good enough in parliamentary elections and should not be good enough for union elections. Even if members are allowed to vote by ballot box at a meeting, 'an elector may be unduly influenced when being given his ballot paper. He may be afforded insufficient privacy when recording his vote' (*Democracy in Trade Unions*, 9).

4. The secret postal ballot overcomes all these difficulties. It is true that it brings in its wake many practical difficulties, such as the need for increased finance and an accurate up-to-date record of members' private addresses. These problems can be overcome. The government has offered money to limit the cost. It is in the unions' interests to compile a register of members and all unions should emulate those who already utilise the services of an independent scrutineer such as the Electoral Reform Society.

5. The advantages of the postal ballot outweigh the disadvantages. When unions have introduced such systems '… The numbers voting have immediately and significantly increased, for example, the electoral system of the AEU used to involve voting at branch offices. Turn-out was generally in the range 6% – 11%. Since the introduction of postal balloting in 1972 turn-out has increased to between 22% and 50%' (*Democracy in Trade Unions*, 4). The extension of this system will make unions more democratic. Opponents who argue that ballots give members power without responsibility are talking through their hat. The very act of voting is an act of responsibility which demonstrates adequate commitment.

6. Conservatives are reluctant to intervene in the internal affairs of trade unions and have done so only as a last resort. But it is now

essential to extend the ballot-based system of parliamentary democracy to all trade unions. The trade union leaders have been given opportunity after opportunity to introduce postal ballots voluntarily. But they were not even prepared to take public money for this purpose in the period after 1980, although they show no hesitation in snapping up state funds for trade union education. The state has had to act, and the public will eventually benefit, as the system of secret postal ballots gradually produces a new breed of moderate union leaders responsive to the wishes of their members.

The arguments against

1. The evidence for increased turnout in postal ballots is far from impressive. In the AEU, turnout increased compared with branch voting. It then decreased from around 40% of the electoral roll to around 20%. In the 1982 election for General Secretary, 18% of the membership voted by postal ballot as compared with 11% in the 1967 election by branch ballot, and this gives a rough idea of the improvement. Is all the time, money and legislation devoted to postal ballots justified by this limited increase? Evidence from other unions shows the same pattern. If we are simply interested in increasing turnout then *workplace* ballots would appear to represent the best bet, as can be seen from the ballots in the NUM, which regularly passes the 70% turnout mark. Democracy is not, of course, simply about high turn-outs. Postal balloting could weaken democracy in unions by leading to higher turnover in Executive elections, which could make it more difficult for the Executive to control officials who are appointed, not elected.

2. The closed shop is justified by the imbalance of power between the employer and individual employees. Union members give up their specific freedom to opt out, in order to increase their general freedom, by building an organisation which can challenge decisions dictated by the management. This is similar to citizens giving up rights to choose whether or not they should pay taxes in the interests of the public good. The non-union 'free rider' should be regarded in the same way as the tax dodger. If 'free riders' use their individual rights to take advantage of the benefits that their fellow workers' efforts and contributions to the union make possible, why should not those fellow workers use *their* individual rights not to work with that free rider? Admittedly, you can't vote

out the government of the enterprise – your managers – but if you disagree with union policies then you can use your rights in the union to change them.

3. Many of the practical problems associated with postal ballots can be overcome; so can the problems of voting at the branch or workplace. One would also like to see detailed evidence, conspicuous by its absence, of intimidation and manipulation. But the problems of postal balloting should not be underestimated. More than a quarter of the AEU's total members were without a vote in the decade after postal balloting was introduced because they were not on the Electoral Register. The number receiving ballot forms in error, because of changes of address, ensures that it is easier for outsiders to vote than in branch ballots. The detailed intervention of the media leaves the opposition unable to reply in a way they could when voting at meetings. Neither the electorate nor MPs vote by post. And politicians of all parties have declared their opposition to 'government by referendum'. Yet that is exactly what the extension of postal balloting involves for trade union government.

4. Unions ultimately depend on action for their success. They therefore need participation. They need voluntary activists to carry out a whole range of organisational tasks. Their strength depends on their members acting collectively to organise and express the conflicts inherent in the employment relationship. Postal balloting need not deal a death blow to participation but it minimises participation, compared with voting at a meeting. Unions need not only activists but educated activists. Members are in a better position to take decisions when they have listened to the arguments and made their own contribution. If workers vote at the workplace they are in a better position to consider their collective interests than if they vote as isolated individuals at home. Workers are strongest when they regard themselves as a group with collective interests. They are at their weakest when they regard themselves as atomised individuals. Postal ballots could be the thin end of the wedge. If all the important decisions in unions are taken in this way, democracy will wither. If the members become more and more inactive, what guarantee is there that they will take the field when called upon by their union? And a union which has lost the ability to mobilise its membership in action is a broken reed.

5. If the postal ballot is a pallid, dilute force for democracy, its introduction by means of state compulsion weakens the roots of social democracy by restricting the area of legitimate self-government by social groups. The International Labour Organisation's Convention on Freedom of Association states that 'Workers and Employers Organisations shall have the right to draw up their constitutions and rules, to elect their representatives in full freedom, to organise their administration and activities and to formulate their programmes. The public authorities shall refrain from any interference which would restrict the right or impede the lawful exercise thereof'.

6. This legislation has very little to do with democracy at all. It is not about mechanisms, it is about *results*. It is not intended to strengthen participation in unions and strengthen the way decisions are made: its real subject is rather those decisions themselves. Its objective in quite simply to reduce strikes and increase the number of moderates elected to union office. This can clearly be seen from the discussion in the Green Paper *Democracy in Unions* where, for example, increased democracy is seen as a danger — if it produces more strikes. Yet an agnosticism on outcomes has to be the touchstone of the true democrat. Finally, there is no guarantee that the legislation will achieve its designed results. A number of unions have undergone a move to the left using postal ballots. There is no iron law which states that under this system the Right must win. And all the evidence demonstrates that if union members want to take action they will vote to do so, whether in a mass meeting or in a ballot.

Conclusions

During the last decade there has been a move towards more centralised structures in British trade unions. The political relationship with the 1974-79 Labour government pressurised union leaders to centralise authority, often utilising existing mechanisms, ultimately unsuccessfully. The Social Contract has been seen by some as an exercise in limiting union democracy, which played a role in demobilising activists and debilitating their reaction to the post-1979 offensive (Hyman, 1983).

The era of Thatcherism might have been expected to witness a decline in central authority. Certainly this has occurred at TUC level.

It appears, however, as if competing tendencies are at work in the broader movement. Aspects of the employment legislation, such as the provisions on ballots and the union's new liability for unlawful industrial action make for greater control at the top of the organisation. But the termination of links with government might, contrariwise, have been expected to have enhanced local autonomy. Nonetheless, some argue that the greater vulnerability that recession and political assault created in certain sectors of industry produced an appreciation at the grassroots of the need for more centralised control. As the new climate reduced the bargaining power of local units of some unions, there was also a realisation of the extent to which industrial power had been dependent on the bases of the political exchange with Labour (Terry and Ferner, 1986).

However, in other situations, observers have seen an increase in sectionalism, as trade unionists looked less to the wider union as an answer to their problems and more to the enterprise and a close co-operation with its management (see chapter 7). There is, of course, no reason why a greater tendency towards enterprise trade unionism cannot go together with greater centralisation of union structures and augmented hierachical authority. Indeed, it is an important part of the Conservative project to reconcile the two.

An examination of the position today demonstrates that trade unions are far from self-governing utopias. They are action-organisations operating in a hostile society and the consequent tensions mean that democracy is sometimes honoured in the breach. But all the evidence shows that unions provide an important measure of democracy in our society. Compared with other institutions, their democratic credentials are in good order. It is the Conservatives' amplification and distortion of the undeniable weaknesses of union democracy which have facilitated, since 1979, the legislation of a model of state-enforced plebiscatory democracy which is in many ways inappropriate to unions, and which may well restrict still further participation and activism. The Conservative model is best embodied presently in the EETPU, speaking of which Employment Minister Kenneth Clarke opined: 'this to me is what good trade unionism is about'.

Whilst many would question this verdict, and the propriety of a government which opposes democracy in so many other areas of society imposing change on the unions, the Conservative measures and their impact highlight the importance of external influences on union democracy. The ultimate effect of recent changes and the future trajectory of union democracy remain uncertain, but an interim judgement must chalk up another success for Mrs Thatcher, at whose behest protesting unions have been forced to remodel key rules. Yet in the longer term, the rank and file members making their will felt through ballots may prove far less pliant and moderate than Conservative philosophy asserts. And the Conservatives' reluctance to etch even a subaltern role in social control for the trade union bureaucracy may prove to be an expensive political mistake.

Further reading

B. and S. Webb, 1897, raises many questions about trade unions' democracy which remain relevant today. Specific studies include V. Allen, 1954; R. Lipset et al, 1956; R. Michels, 1962; H. Turner, 1962; J. Edelstein and M. Warner, 1975; R. Undy et al, 1981.

R. Hyman, 1971, 1975 and 1983, are excellent discussions of the whole field.

J. Beale, 1982, provides some discussion of positive discrimination while R. Undy and R. Martin, 1984, and P. Fairbrother, 1984, are up-to-date and stimulating studies of current issues.

Chapter 6

Industrial democracy

Industrial democracy was one of the burning issues of industrial relations in the 1970s. The Bullock Report, which recommended that worker-directors should sit on company boards, brought controversy to a climax. Since 1980, many would claim that the subject has been swept under the carpet, as the Conservative governments have opposed any major initiatives. In this, they have had the support of the CBI. The trade unions, for their part, were demoralised by their failure to find a way through the complex problems and the divisions in their ranks that the Bullock debate highlighted. They have had their hands full with other preoccupations.

Yet the issue of participation and democracy at work retains an important significance for at least 3 reasons. The first of these is our membership of the European Economic Community: the EEC's Fifth Directive is still very much on the agenda. First drawn up in 1972, it appears likely that this proposal for legislation will eventually require implementation in all member states. Under its terms, each country will be able to choose from a range of different models of participation. One possibility is that companies would have to ensure that one third or one half of the representatives on their board of directors or a higher supervisory board were elected or co-opted from their work-force. The 1980 Vredling Proposals also cover procedures for disclosure of information. The blueprint for special 'European Companies' requires employee participation. Eight European states already have legislation which meets most of these requirements, including board-level representation for employees.

Secondly, the question of industrial democracy continues to exercise British politicians. The Labour Party-TUC Liason Committee documents *Economic Planning And Industrial Democracy* (1982) and *A New Partnership: A new Britain* (1985) promised legislation to give employees rights to representation at all levels of decision-making in the enterprise. Labour's 1987 manifesto, *Britain Will Win*, stated that a future Labour government would 'encourage the establishment and success of co-operatives of all forms'. Labour and the trade unions now argue that economic planning and industrial democracy are inextricably intertwined. Industrial democracy is not an optional extra to be examined simply on industrial relations grounds, it is a *sine qua non* for the effective management of Britain's economy.

Liberals have had a longstanding commitment to producer co-operatives and to participation schemes in conventional companies. One of the SDP's earliest statements declared support for an Industrial Democracy Act and an Industrial Democracy Agency which would stimulate workers' participation and foster profit-sharing schemes. The 1987 Alliance manifesto asserted that 'opportunity must be provided for participation at top level, for example by employee directors ... we will encourage other forms of industrial participation including co-operatives ... we will extend incentives to employees' share ownership and profit sharing'.

Even the Conservatives, largely suspicious of the whole exercise, have felt it necessary to do something. A series of Finance Acts have made provision for encouraging profit-sharing and wider share ownership. The 1982 Employment Act placed a duty on companies with more than 250 employees to develop arrangements for disclosure of company information to the work force, for consulting employees on important decisions and for the creation of share-ownership schemes.

The third reason is more amorphous but just as important. There is an as yet small, but discernible and growing view that if the strategies of Thatcherism fail there can be no simple return to the 1960s and 1970s. There will be a need for more audacious, far-reaching changes which will give the work force a real stake in the economy and mobilise their intelligence, skills and energies for its regeneration. Industrial democracy would be central to such an approach: indeed it would be the primary catalyst in change.

Participation and democracy

You can see from what we have said up to now that the terms

'participation' and 'industrial democracy' seem to be used inter-
changeably to cover a range of different mechanisms such as
representation on company boards, consultation schemes, information disclosure and co-operatives. Most writers use these terms in this
broad fashion. One influential authority defined industrial
democracy as 'any theory or scheme as long as it is based on a genuine
concern for the rights of workers in industry, particularly their right
to share in the control of industrial decisions' (Clegg, 1960, 3).

Other writers have taken issue with this approach. They have
argued that this kind of imprecision does not help analysis. The
essence of joint consultation, for example, is that management
provides workers with information about decisions they have made
or intend to make and then listens to the workers' views. But
management retains the prerogative to make the decision. In making
it, they may or may not take into account the workers' views. It is not
very meaningful, therefore, to describe such schemes as 'workers'
participation in management decision-making', still less to subsume
them under the heading 'industrial democracy'.

But even schemes for board representation, let alone the ragbag of
other matters, from job enrichment and collective bargaining to
planning agreements and workers' alternative plans, are only
embraced by 'industrial democracy', it is further claimed, by doing
violence to the correct use of this concept. Industrial democracy
should be justified in relation to democratic theory and existing
systems of political democracy. To truly parallel our political system,
it is argued, industry would require a system of self-management in
which decisions within the enterprise would be taken directly or by
means of representative institutions by all employees. *Self- management* would require that the workers should not only have *control* of
the decisions which affect their lives at work but should also *own* the
assets of the enterprise in which they labour. Control without
ownership, it is asserted, is as inadequate as ownership without
control, represented at its most indirect and infirm by traditional
policies of nationalisation. The democratisation of ownership,
economic democracy, is just as essential, in this view, to the
democratisation of the government of the enterprise. But any real
and enduring system of economic and industrial democracy would
require planning and integration between enterprises and major
changes within our society, unattainable within a capitalist
framework.

To those who argue that joint consultation, collective bargaining and workers on the board all represent different means of gradually democratising the enterprise, critics stress the importance of the sponsorship and objective of the particular mechanism or scheme, and the way words can be appropriated by individuals or groups to confuse what is happening and legitimise their own purposes. Real workers' participation in management will lead to a modification of managements' prerogative to take decisions unilaterally. Many consultation or job enrichment schemes have no such objective. They are methods of 'pseudo-participation' used to persuade workers to accept decisions that have already been made by management (Pateman 1970). Having failed to adequately involve the work force in the employers' objectives by welfare programmes, scientific management and the human relations approach, management have resorted to more subtle means of gaining control by consent. By strict criteria, many of the approaches dignified by the term 'workers' participation' or 'industrial democracy' should be filed under the established category 'management techniques'. They leave existing patterns of power in industry intact and seek to elicit the collaboration of employees in their perpetuation.

This argument is an important one. It provides a useful framework against which to evaluate proposals advertised as workers participation and industrial democracy. It seems incontestable that genuine workers' participation will involve a change in the authority structures in the enterprise, and a diminution of managerial power and genuine industrial democracy will require a transformation of industry. All too many of the pretenders, however, aim at reinforcement of managerial authority and the strengthening of the economic and governmental status quo in industry. There is, of course, many a slip between cup and lip, and such strategies can have unintended consequences and provide potential openings for those who seriously desire to create industrial democracy. Nonetheless, distinctions between the purpose and reach of different mechanisms need to be made clear.

Arguments for participation and democracy

Extension of democracy The system of political democracy makes the government of the nation accountable to its citizens. Measured by the canons of political democracy, the government of the enterprise constitutes an oligarchy, even a dictatorship. For those who take the fundamental decisions concerning the enterprise are not answerable, in any formal fashion, to its employees. Collective bargaining between unions and employees does provide workers with a voice in some of the decisions which affect their working lives. The differences between the guaranteed rights of political democracy and the uncertainties of collective bargaining make any direct comparison between the two unsustainable. Collective bargaining is an unsatisfactory mechanism for democratic control as its efficiency depends, to a great degree, on the employees' ability to organise and the employers' willingness to bargain. There is no guarantee of this. The results of collective bargaining are dependent, not on reason or democracy, but rather on the degree of bargaining power employees can bring to bear against their employer at a particular time. This, in its turn, is dependent upon a wide range of economic and political factors over which employees have little control.

Employees spend a large proportion of their lives at work. Their investment in the enterprise is at least as significant as that of the shareholders. They should have a guaranteed voice in decisions which affect their livelihood through a change in the present system of ownership and control. Democracy at work is justified both in its own right and as a means of strengthening democracy in society. The absence of democracy from such a crucial aspect of our lives as work means that democracy as a whole is diminished.

Extension of participation Participation is an essential ingredient in democracy and an essential means of political education. Democracy should involve more than casting a vote in parliamentary elections once every 5 years. If it is to function optimally, democracy needs activists, and that does not just mean MPs or councillors. The power structures governing work give employees limited opportunities to participate in the making of important decisions. Even collective bargaining is often a process carried on *for* rather than *by* most workers. We need to extend democratic accountability to the workplace, otherwise democracy will remain partial and incomplete. Greater participation in industry will, moreover, strengthen the existing system of parliamentary democracy by creating more aware, creative and public-spirited citizens.

Alienation from work Work should be a rich and satisfying experience, allowing immediate satisfaction and the ability to develop our potential. But, for all too many of us, life at work involves toleration rather than gratification. In it we experience tension and boredom. We do not like our jobs. We work largely for the money. Alienation from work is related to the authoritarian nature of decision-making in the enterprise. If we possess a greater degree of autonomy and responsibility in our jobs and we are able to participate in important decisions, we will achieve greater self-realisation. One observer states: 'there is scarcely a study in the entire literature which fails to demonstrate that satisfaction in work is enhanced, or that other generally acknowledged beneficial consequences accrue from a genuine increase in workers' decision-making power'. (Blumberg, 1968, 123).

Greater efficiency and productivity If workers are satisfied at work they are likely to be better motivated and more productive. They possess a vast fund of knowledge which management fails to draw on and a range of abilities management fails to develop. Worker participation improves the flow of information to management and consequently the quality of decision-making in the enterprise. A whole range of studies of experiments in workers' participation demonstrate remarkable increases in productivity. Overall, as the 1982 TUC-Labour Party statement commented, 'accountability in economic decision making is not an inefficient luxury but is essential to improving economic performance'.

Better industrial relations Employees today are better educated, more knowledgeable and critical, less prepared to accept old-style authoritarianism. Attempts by management to go on in the old way have played their part in the generation of low morale and industrial conflict. As the Bullock Committee observed: 'employees have become less prepared to accept unquestioningly unilateral decisions by management and have shown a readiness to challenge a decision if it seems to have ignored their point of view or to affect them adversely'. (Bullock, 1977, 23). A resort to mechanisms of worker participation will facilitate a move from conflict-ridden industrial relations to greater co-operation.

Arguments against participation and democracy

The right of management to manage The enterprise is a team but every team needs a captain. Each individual member of the team does not have to face up to the full consequences of his or her actions. There is an opportunity for shirking at little cost to the individual even though the overall output of the firm suffers. We, therefore, need an individual or group to monitor team performance. This monitor or 'control' will require an incentive not to take it easy, in the form of a right to the profits. In the interests of maximising efficiency, the controller is vested with the property rights in the enterprise from which all management ultimately derive their authority. It is the separation of decision-making from ownership that has led to industrial irresponsibility and economic decline. The 'British disease' would become terminal if decision-making powers were to be further dispersed amongst employees who have no ownership rights, no real stake in the enterprise and no incentive to commit themselves fully to its goals.

Work and politics are different things Our job at work is to produce goods and services for the community and to answer demand in the most efficient and expeditious fashion. What is involved is very different from what is involved in the political process. The management of production requires a range of technical and economic skills, a grasp of a bewildering variety of functions from research and development and accountancy to sales and supervision. It requires complex decisions to be taken speedily and efficiently by experts. At times, it requires an element of secrecy. Everybody can participate fully in the political process but they cannot participate to the same degree in industrial decision-making. If we try to apply political democracy to industry through electing managers, taking decisions through votes of the work force, or bargaining between management and trade unions in the boardroom then we shall fall flat on our faces. Politics may be susceptible to bargaining and compromise. The most important decisions in industry must, in contrast, be dictated by rational economic calculation. Their making must constitute the well demarcated province of professional management. Management-by-compromise has played a role in getting British industry into its present sorry state.

The productivity myth It is doubtful whether increased participation is the answer to the problems of motivation and productivity. Poor productivity is the product not so much of poor motivation on the part of the work force, as of inadequate investment, training, research and development, and outmoded technology. The experiments in participation which showed productivity shooting through the roof are, on the whole, small-scale. Carried out under special circumstances, for short periods, their general implications have been exaggerated. Even if productivity does increase as a result of increased participation, and there is *some* evidence to back this view, this could lead to a variety of results. At one end of the spectrum, the increased efficiency could lead to some workers losing their jobs and the remainder working harder. The assertion that participation mechanisms produce improved industrial relations – a problematic term in itself – also lacks firm evidence to back it.

Workers' participation is a con-trick The initiative for the introduction of participation schemes has generally come from management. Their aim has been to weaken the work force undermine the trade unions, commit the employees to management, goals and ensure that they accept decisions already made by management rather than to democratise the enterprise. Advocates of industrial democracy portray its development in terms of a gradual, organic evolution. In reality, schemes of workers' participation and industrial democracy have come and gone in cycles. It has been popular with the bosses when trade unions have been powerful and popularised as a means of defusing threats to management control. The growth of trade unionism in the 1880s and 1890s, for example, produced a spate of profit-sharing schemes introduced specifically to prevent unionisation. The unrest during the First World War produced the Whitley Councils, designed to canalise and neutralise the challenge from the workers. The Second World War, in its turn, produced the Joint Production Committees. The more recent spate of participation schemes were essentially a manoeuvre to draw the sting of the militancy of the late 1960s and 1970s. If unions fall for participation schemes they will lose their independence and ability to fully and forcefully represent the interests of their members.

Workers on the board

As late as 1967, a TUC working party, chaired by Transport Workers' union leader Jack Jones, saw the major means for future encroachment on managerial prerogative as an extension of collective bargaining. More formal participation mechanisms raised difficult issues of trade union function and independence. Worker-directors were perceived as a subject for small-scale, cautious and voluntary experimentation. But change was rapid. The TUC's reversal of policy took place against the upheavals that characterised industrial relations between 1968 and 1974. The move towards the idea of worker-directors was motivated by the failure of other strategies and a desire to examine more radical possibilities. It was strongly influenced by demands for a greater say in management decisions, emanating from the grassroots, and given voice by left-wing leaders such as Jones and Hugh Scanlon, and greater form by the Institute of Workers' Control, launched in 1968. The unions were also increasingly concerned at the problems the concentration of capital, manifested in the growth of multinationals, the state sponsored mergers of the late 1960s and the spate of closures of the early 1970s posed for classical trade union methods. These developments prompted a rethink in the unions. Britain's entry into the EEC in 1972 and the publication that same year of the Fifth Draft Directive also played a role in changing attitudes.

In 1974, the TUC published a detailed statement, *Industrial Democracy*. The TUC's wide-ranging conception of industrial democracy can be gauged from a document which covered everything from grievance procedures and joint safety committees to worker co-operatives. The document revealed a major transformation in TUC philosophy. There was a need to continue to broaden collective bargaining, which now needed underpinning by legislation. But doubts were expressed as to the ability of collective bargaining to deal with the fundamental processes of decision-making. New forms of control, the TUC felt, were now essential. Company structure should be revised to create a 2-tier board structure with a supervisory board on European lines, overseeing and monitoring the operations of a smaller executive board. In order to give workers 'a degree of joint control over all the major decisions of the company, closures, redundancy, major technological changes, mergers, etc', their representatives appointed through the union machinery should have half the seats on the supervisory board.

The Bullock Report

The TUC change of line was reflected in the incoming 1974 Wilson government. Despite manifesto commitments, they regarded the issue as a 'hot potato'. A Committee of Inquiry, chaired by Lord Bullock, was not established until August 1975 and did not report until January 1977. The Committee's terms of reference demonstrated an unequivocal commitment to the idea of worker-directors. But by the time the report was published, the social contract, whose most radical edge it represented, was well past its zenith.

The committee was split. The majority recommended that single-tier boards should be retained. In private companies with more than 2,000 employees, they should consist of equal numbers of shareholders and employee representatives. The third element in Bullock's '2x + y' formula was a smaller number of directors to be drawn from the ranks of relevant experts, academics, lawyers, accountants and scientists. The employee representatives would be appointed through the 'single channel' trade union machinery. Unions would establish Joint Representative Committees to regulate the new system, but the employee-directors could not be mandated by the shop floor. Finally, company law would be amended so that all directors would be charged with acting in the interests of the shareholders *and* the employees of the company. The 3 employer representatives on the committee produced a minority report. Industrial democracy, they felt, should develop through voluntary means from the bottom up. It should culminate in employee representation on a supervisory board where one third of the directors would be employee representatives.

The report came under strenuous assault from the CBI. The unions themselves were split down the middle. Unions like the NUM, the EETPU, the AEU and the GMBATU all registered strong reservations or outright opposition from a variety of different standpoints. The 1977 TUC Congress produced a woolly compromise resolution. More than a year after the report the government produced a watered-down White Paper. Action on this was, in its turn, delayed by splits in the cabinet and finally the 1979 general election intervened.

The public sector
The Bullock Committee's brief was limited to the private sector. However, worker-directors had been introduced in BSC in 1968. But they sat only on divisional boards, which were purely advisory. They were selected by management from a union list and they were not accountable to the unions. The British Leyland scheme established in 1975 was also limited. In the car division, factory committees elected divisional committees which then elected 11 shop stewards and 4 staff representatives to the Cars Council, where they sat with management representatives. The committees possessed no decision-making powers. It was made clear that the system was quite separate from the collective bargaining structure and that in the event of disagreements

on the participation committees, executive responsibility lay with management.

The experiment in the Post Office, in contrast, was based on a '2x + y' model with equal numbers of management and union representatives and a smaller group of independents. However, employee representatives were appointed by the government from union recommendations, and some were full-time union officials rather than Post Office employees as envisaged in the Bullock blueprint.

And that is about it. Firm employer opposition and Thatcherism has arrested any real development of Bullock-style schemes in British industry. Yet the report and the consequent controversy remain of enduring relevance in their statement of many of the key problems and arguments involved. Bullock is still an essential departure point for any re-examination of the problem of industrial democracy.

Workers on the board – the critique

The employers' opposition The CBI's stance on Bullock represented a well thought-out orchestration of the different positions of finance and industrial capital, the big multinationals and the smaller owners. However, as Labour's commitment to Bullock wilted and as the CBI relating to the developing resonance of Thatcherism moved rightwards, the CBI conference took an even firmer line and jettisoned its commitment to back-up legislation (Strinati, 1982, 171-78).

The unanimity and intensity of employer opposition to Bullock might appear surprising if the report is viewed in terms of radical managerialism. The Donovan Report had been informed by the view that 'to regain control management had to share it', and Bullock could be perceived as simply a further step in this direction. But those sections of capital which would have been affected saw the proposals as potentially too dangerous a constraint, particularly the multinationals, who wished to maintain flexibility in relation to their UK operations. Whilst boardroom representation *might* have advantages to the enterprise, in terms of increased efficiency, it *definitely* constitutes a threat to the status, prestige and prerogative of those who occupy and benefit from existing managerial structures (Coates, 1980; Hodgson, 1984). Certainly, the specific nature of UK trade unionism in the mid-seventies, particularly its strength in the workplace, made acceptance of Bullock a very different proposition for the majority of employers than the introduction of co-determination in Germany, in the face of weak or non-existent trade unionism.

The nub of the CBI's criticism was summed up in the minority report:

'We are completely opposed to the introduction into existing Boards of representatives of special interests of any kind which might provoke confrontation or extend the scope of collective bargaining into top level management. The dilution of management expertise, the confusion of objectives and the risk of a blocking vote seems to us to be a sure recipe for decline in management leadership and initiative; this is basic to our views and it not simply a question of proportions' (Bullock, 1977, 176).

The CBI case was, in essence, the traditional case: management must be left to manage. There was room for consultation and involvement but workers should not be entitled to any determinant voice in strategic decisions.

Having staved off the threat of legislation, the CBI has contented itself with the establishment of an Employee Involvement Audit which periodically surveys the progress of consultative schemes. Research published in the eighties confirms 'that managers of all types were heavily opposed to board level representation' (Cressey et al, 1981, 42; Dowling et al, 1982).

Opposition from the unions Survey evidence which shows that *employees* also place minimal emphasis on participation, compared with more bread-and-butter issues, has not loomed large in discussion. Criticism from the union side has sometimes been based upon left-wing opposition to class collaboration. Alternatively, it stemmed from the right-wing view that trade unions' objectives were restricted and best attained through traditional collective bargaining. Sometimes it appeared to be an amalgam of both.

Many of the criticisms centred on details. It was claimed, for example, that under the '2x + y' formula, union representatives would usually be outvoted. One of the 'independent' experts on the Bullock committee had subsequently resigned to become Director of the CBI. It was also pointed out that Bullock stated that the employee representatives could not be mandated by the unions and that, in certain cases, they would have to maintain confidentiality. In practice, the shareholder representatives would connive to ensure that real decision-making moved away from formal meetings of the Board. The unions should hold out for the TUC proposals – half the seats on the Board.

A second line of attack indicted the intention of the exercise. It was pointed out that Bullock specifically saw participation as increasing profitability, providing a new legitimacy for management and securing enhanced co-operation from the work force in achieving goals set by management. Evidence of the practical realisation of Bullock's theorising could be cited, for worker-director schemes *have* been implemented, albeit with minority employee representation in private industry. A recent survey confirms that such schemes have been initiated by management, incorporated managerial perspectives and achieved little from the point of view of union goals (Chell, 1983). If introduced on a wider scale, such schemes would lead to the incorporation of the unions. Worker-directors would become increasingly isolated from their members and would ultimately urge the acceptance of job loss, more effort for less pay and reduced living standards.

For once management objectives were endorsed, profit maximisation would be the only imperative. The British Leyland participation system was often cited as an example of this process at work. No matter how much supporters of participation talk about what worker-directors can and cannot do, they cannot escape from the central problem: in the end, employers are in business to make a profit and there is a conflict between wages and profits.

In short, attempts to democratise the enterprise without changing the ownership of capital and the wider economic system are doomed to founder in the face of the necessities of capitalist production: 'reform of the authority relations of the factory is impotent in the absence of structural reform of the production relations of society' (Clarke, 1977, 364).

Workers on the board: the justification
One form of counter-argument stresses the short-sightedness and inconsistency of the CBI and the Conservative Party, and the hypocrisy of a position which emphasises the centrality of trade union democracy and ignores the equally important issue of democratising the government of the enterprise. The CBI's defence that 'it is unwise to impose democracy on those who are unwilling or unready to receive it' could be equally applicable to the unions. The Conservatives' opposition to the limited EEC proposals reinforces doubts about their commitment to a gradual and organic growth of democracy at work. If a healthy industrial democracy is only attainable by voluntary means, why should the implementation of democracy in the unions, where it is already more developed than in the enterprise, require the force of law?

Many supporters of board level representation in the unions concede that the Bullock proposals, in themselves, may be far from perfect. Perhaps they can be improved upon. Certainly any system will provide the unions with problems. Vigilance *is* required. But if such proposals were to be implemented the results are not determined in advance. What happens will depend on a number of factors, but at least partly upon the will of the unions to make new arrangements work in a fashion which advances the interests of their members. The purpose of proposing employee representatives on company boards *may* be incorporation. Intentions do not necessarily determine outcomes. It remains an open question as to whether employee representatives will be co-opted by management, or alternatively, will succeed, if they receive adequate backing from the unions, in extending the reach of union interests.

Moreover, such assertions tend to over-emphasise the confidence and unity of the employers and the weakness of labour. Whilst it would be wrong to understate the power of capital, there is no assurance that a changed economic and political situation would not reopen disagreements between the employers as to industrial relations strategies, disagreements perhaps only temporarily elided by the *élan* of Thatcherism. Or, that the unions would not be able to take advantage of such divisions by strategies of which participation at board level could constitute one component.

This is related to a further point: the pursuit of profit does not dictate in any direct fashion *specific* behaviour on the part of the employee-directors. British Steel is different from ICI which is, in its turn, different from EMI or Komatsu. Different firms operate under different product and labour markets. They have different profit levels and different policies and react to problems in different ways. Capital is not a monolith and employers and employee-directors will have a range of discretion in decision-making. It is, moreover, quite possible that in the event of a conflict between shop stewards and employee-directors over strategy, the position taken by the directors might well be just as justifiable, or even more so than that taken up by the stewards. Worker-directors may represent a *step forward* in strategies to transform patterns of ownership and economic regulation (Tomlinson, 1982).

Finally, the evidence that participation experiments have led to incorporation is limited and mixed. The studies carried out for Bullock on board representation in the EEC showed its overall impact was minimal. In British Steel, the findings show that the worker-directors did adopt a managerial approach and did not challenge the financial logic of the corporation. On the other hand, there was little to show that they had played a role in weakening the unions (Brannen et al, 1976; Brannen, 1983). In the case of British Leyland, where there were redundancies and a serious undermining of shop floor organisation, the role played by participation remains undemonstrated. At the time of its introduction the company was already in dire financial straits and the workplace leadership had already committed themselves to support managerial strategies. Studies have found that the scheme acted as a useful propaganda vehicle for management to make their case and that the unions did not find in it an effective instrument for the modification of company policy (Willman and Winch, 1985).

A study of the Post Office scheme found that the employee representatives did challenge management positions but had only marginal impact, although greater than in the case of BSC, reflecting perhaps the stronger representational arrangements. The researchers concluded: 'there was no evidence that the experiment was leading to any greater incorporation of the union into the philosophy and practices of management than might already have occurred through collective bargaining: board representation was not weakening the unions' bargaining strength, or autonomy, or their ability to oppose management in the interests of their members' (Batstone et al, 1983, 11, 120).

The argument for supporting worker-directors, therefore, is based on a rejection of fatalism and the view that their role is not predetermined. The evidence so far which demonstrates that they have little impact could be related to the limited nature and scale of the systems which have been implemented. A national system backed by law and strong trade unions could provide very different results.

The extension of collective bargaining

Critics of worker participation often argue that the development of collective bargaining is a preferable way to develop industrial democracy.

The arguments for
1. Collective bargaining is tried and tested as the central method of

British trade unionism. It is largely responsible for the advances trade unions have made. Not merely are its results impressive, but it enables unions to maintain their independence of management, a matter of incalculable long-term importance. In contrast, worker-directors will be explicitly and intimately involved in management policy and thus constrained in opposing its consequences. Board representation legitimises the view, antagonistic to trade unionism, that industry is a team in which we all have the same interests.

2. Industrial democracy is already substantially embodied in the system of collective bargaining. The basic characteristic of democracy is the existence of an opposition, and the opposition in the workplace to the government of management is the trade union. If the union were to dissolve itself into management through schemes of boardroom representation, there is a danger here we would end up with industrial despotism (Clegg, 1960).

3. Collective bargaining has made inroads into a wide range of issues such as hiring and firing, staffing levels, technology and the speed and content of work. Management prerogative has been challenged over such issues as promotion, pricing, location, mergers and closure. As the TUC–Labour Party Liaison Committee put it recently, 'Collective bargaining has evolved and is evolving to meet new needs and circumstances. New areas continuously arise where collective bargaining can be used to extend joint control into the administration and the execution of corporate policies within the enterprise.'

4. Nonetheless, the immense potentialities of extended collective bargaining remain unrealised. For example, the idea of planning agreements was developed in the 1970s as a means of creating a tripartite agreement between government, employers and unions which would provide the latter with a far closer involvement in enterprise decision-making. Little came of these initiatives under the Labour government, owing to a lack of will, but they have been taken up by radical local authorities. The establishment in the early 1980s of the Greater London Enterprise Board was closely followed by the creation of similar bodies in West Yorkshire, Merseyside and Lancashire. The West Midlands Enterprise Board invested over £10 million in more than 30 companies spanning the industrial spectrum. GLEB adapted the idea of the planning agreement into the 'enterprise plan'.

Whenever it intervened to regenerate local industry it made its assistance conditional upon joint planning by the board, management and unions.

5. The potential inherent in collective bargaining is also illustrated by initiatives stemming from the Lucas Aerospace Shop Stewards Alternative Corporation Plan. The Lucas Combine Committee initiated a research programme which mobilised the knowledge, skills and experience of the work force. The plan sought to draw the sting of the management argument that redundancies were inevitable, by demonstrating that an alternative range of products, which were technically and commercially viable but also socially useful, should be manufactured. It pressed for the replacement of arms production by rail/road vehicles, kidney machines and domestic space heaters. The Lucas plan had 3 main strengths: it raised and popularised the question of the *nature* of production. It moved the unions off the defensive terrain of simply saying 'no' to management decisions by projecting detailed alternatives, which in essence raised the question 'who manages Lucas?'. And it not only pre-empted management decision-making in a series of key areas, but prefigured the socially beneficial purposes for which production could be organised were the creativity of the work force to be given free rein. The popularity of the plan and the degree to which it gripped the imagination of other groups of workers is incontestable and illustrated by the way many other groups of workers took up the idea.

The arguments against

1. Proponents of collective bargaining typically proffer an idealised picture. Collective bargaining has been primarily defensive, failed to raise the share of wages in the gross national product and played a role in bureaucratising trade unions. Nearly all the objections made to workers' participation today can, and have been, levelled at collective bargaining. Collective bargaining legitimises the role of management, secures compliance in their decisions and undermines the independent role of the shop floor. Taken a stage further, these criticisms have been levelled at trade unionism itself. Many of the statements of the supporters of collective bargaining are value-loaded ascriptions rather than justifiable deductions from the evidence.

2. Collective bargaining does not constitute an already existing system of industrial democracy. The existence of an organised opposition is not the essential hallmark of democracy, indeed many democracies have got along fine without this institution. Moreover, the fact that unions are in this model 'an opposition which can never become the government', shows how strained the analogy between collective bargaining and democracy really is. The real determinant feature of democracy is the accountability of the leadership to those they lead (Blumberg, 1968). Collective bargaining provides no formal mechanism for such accountability. In Britain today there is not even minimum legislation requiring employers to recognise unions for the purpose of collective bargaining, and the efficacy of collective bargaining varies tremendously between different industries and work places.

3. Whilst it would be wrong to ignore the achievements of collective bargaining, or downplay its potential, it has typically embraced a limited range of issues and has restricted the use of management prerogative through a negative veto, rather than acting as a channel for the positive assertion of workers' interests. It has operated at the margins. It has done little to influence strategic managerial decision-making on investment, mergers and closures. Its success has declined with the distance travelled from immediate job-related issues. Bargaining over fundamental, primary issues is very different and very much more difficult than bargaining about issues such as wages or hours of work. Unions would be mad to pass up an opportunity to move into the boardroom, closer to the sites of primary decision making. Worker representatives can bargain in the boardroom at least as well as on national and company bargaining committees, which are also remote from their members.

4. The planning agreements of the 1970s achieved nothing. The only full planning agreement developed by the Labour government was with Chrysler. There was no direct trade union involvement in its negotiation. The success of this agreement in involving the company in state planning and extending the ability of the unions to determine strategic decisions was starkly exemplified in the summer of 1978, when Chrysler's US management sold off the UK subsidiary, without even informing the government or the unions until the ink was dry on the sale to Peugeot-Citroen. Whilst

it is, perhaps, too early to pass judgement on the recent spate of local authority initiatives, they are small-scale and suffer from the overall subordination of local to central government and the extensive strengthening of Whitehall dominance since 1980. Witness the fate of the GLC. They do not provide a compelling or persuasive precursor for a national strategy of economic regeneration and increased worker participation in the enterprise.

5. The Lucas Alternative Plan was an inspiring initiative. Nonetheless, mangement refused to negotiate on it and it was never implemented. Instead, management successfully carried through a programme of redundancies. It is difficult to see how the range of alternative products suggested in the Lucas Plan could be produced and marketed successfully by the individual enterprise in the absence of a national system of planning or, at least, extensive state support. The Lucas Plan, rather than reaffirming the possibilities of collective bargaining, embodied in its genesis, a recognition of the limitations of collective bargaining in dealing with concentrated capital and, in its progress, the failure of trade unionists to create an adequate substitute for an outmoded form. A decade after its initiation, it is difficult to see its results as 'a new trade unionism in the making'.

Indeed, workers' plans have fared no better elsewhere. In late 1983, United Biscuits' employees in Liverpool developed what was described as 'the most detailed alternative plan ever prepared by unions in Britain to deal with a closure'. The company stated:

'The alternative plan presented by the unions and the constructive spirit and content of the discussions demonstrates that very difficult decisions can be examined responsibly on the basis of full access to available information. For a small group of shop stewards to achieve in so short a time this level of knowledge and competence in handling that knowledge is most impressive. Sadly their efforts and the efforts of all those who have supported them have not enabled the company to reverse the decision.'

The closure went ahead.

Joint consultation

The 1980 Survey of Workplace Industrial Relations found that joint consultation committees had become more common. This confirmed a study in manufacturing carried out by the Warwick University

Industrial Relations Research Unit, which found that more than 40% of the 1,000 establishments surveyed in manufacturing industry had joint consultative arrangements and that more than 60% of these had been introduced in the seventies (Brown, 1981). More recent research by the Department of Employment shows some consolidation in the 1980s. A third of all enterprises surveyed had such a committee, so they remain a minority interest. A number of such committees in manufacturing had disappeared due to closures, but their decline was being compensated for by an increase in services and the public sector, where the increase was on the margins of significance (Brown, 1981; Millward and Stevens, 1986). Earlier observers saw a decline in joint consultative committees when strong workplace organisation developed in the 1950s and 1960s. Recent research emphasises the sustained use of joint consultation throughout the post-war period (McInnes, 1985).

Recent interest is related to attempts to avoid the enforcement of more real and extensive forms of participation. Some supporters of joint consultation ask why, if participation schemes go in cycles related to union power (Ramsay, 1977), consultation should have continued to develop in the 1980s recession when unions were weakened? Perhaps the answer lies in the perception by the CBI and the Conservatives of the EEC as a replacement threat; as the dangers from Bullock receded, those from Brussels increased. 'Employee involvement' has become the new catchphrase as the government and CBI have given the Bullock usage 'industrial democracy' the widest of berths. This underlines the fact that the growth of consultation in the last decade, as in the past, has been intended to get across management's message, encourage an understanding of 'the facts of life' by employees and turn the flank of aspirations for genuine power-sharing.

Joint consultation has been seen by management as a means of encouraging a joint interest view of the enterprise, as a means of improving communications, encouraging co-operation and picking the brains of the work force. It has been seen by trade unions as a means of undermining their organisations, gaining information as to management intentions and alerting the employer to their views, if constituting no substitute for collective bargaining. The most recent survey claims that it would be wrong to write off consultative committees as management manipulated talking shops: in a third of cases principal consultative committees were used for negotiations.

On the other hand, in 44% of cases, unions nominated no representatives to prinicipal committees and, in 50% of cases, they nominated no representatives to secondary committees (Millward and Stevens, 1986, 139,145).

Given its failure to guarantee employees any influence in management decision-making and its legitimisation of existing prerogatives, it is difficult to see joint consultation as workers' participation or, even more emphatically, as a mechanism of industrial democracy.

Financial participation

In the past the introduction of schemes of profit-sharing and employee share ownership has tended to be related to high levels of employment and industrial unrest. Just a little over a decade ago, the TUC could state that 'company-based schemes of co-ownership and profit-sharing are discredited'. Yet one recent survey found that around one fifth of the companies examined had share ownership schemes (Smith 1986). Another study found that the number of employers surveyed with share ownership schemes had increased from 13% to 23% of their sample between 1980 and 1984 (Millward and Stevens, 1986). It has been claimed that such schemes now cover more than a million employers. Whilst their popularity will continue to increase, their impact upon industrial relations is marginal (Baddon et al, 1987).

Two initial problems encountered have been the limitation of such schemes to senior grades and a generally low participation rate amongst eligible employees. However, the 1986 Workplace Industrial Relations Survey found that only 15% of the schemes they studied were now open to management only, and the the proportion of such schemes covering all employees had increased from 16% in 1980 to 35% today. Nonetheless, participation had not increased and remained at around 15% of those eligible to take up the options. Growth, it seems has been encouraged by recent Finance Acts which provided tax concessions.

In 1986, the government proposed a further stimulus: tax concessions would be granted to companies if at least 5% of an employers' total pay bill related wages to profits. The government cited the relationship in Japan and America between profit-related pay and economic prosperity. They argued that in US industry wages can vary between 85% and 115% of the norm, and quoted several big companies paying out 20% of annual pre-tax profits to the work force. More than 70% of company chiefs polled by the Institute of Directors stated that their company would be seriously interested in the new scheme. The Alliance – David Steel has written a pamphlet on profit-sharing – were said to be annoyed that the Tories had stolen their clothes.

The Labour Party and the TUC have shown more interest in wage-earner funds on the Swedish model as a means of democratising the economy, counterposing these funds as a collectivist alternative to the individualist profit-sharing models. The impetus for the establishment of wage-earner funds came from the Swedish unions. The original proposals provoked widespread opposition from the employers' organisations and the right-wing parties and it was in a watered-down version that the scheme reached the Statute book in 1983. The 5 separate funds are financed by a payroll tax and a levy on profits above a certain level. The funds are linked to the pensions system and enthusiasts claim that over the longer term they will control Swedish investment and decision-making in Swedish industry. At least 5 of the 9 member boards appointed by the government are employee representatives.

The Labour Party and TUC have also seen an important role for occupational pension funds as a means of developing both economic and industrial democracy. A National Investment Bank partly financed by pension funds forms a central part of Labour's economic strategy. The Party claims it would act as a stimulus to industrial regeneration, but also involve employees in decision-making in companies to which it channelled funds. It would be complemented by Local Enterprise Boards, on the model already developed by many local authorities, which could plug in to local government superannuation funds.

The argument for

The schemes give employees a material stake in the enterprise and in the capitalist system. As Mrs Thatcher says: 'an employee should not only be working on the shopfloor or in the office. He should be present at the Annual General Meeting as a shareholder'. They can alter employees' attitudes and help to get away from 'them and us' conceptions by underlining the fact that the future of everybody in our society depends upon profitability, 'the goose that lays the golden eggs'. Whilst these schemes make pay more responsive to market conditions, they can also meet trade union objectives. Profit-related pay can reduce the pressure for redundancies as pay falls in an economic downturn, and give employers an incentive to create jobs in an upturn. It thus meets the Labour Party's desire for a trade-off between pay and jobs.

Profit-sharing and share ownership schemes can stimulate a greater interest in the company's operations and consequently a stronger commitment to its purpose. Increased profit-sharing can play a role in educating employees into an understanding of economics, strengthen the property-owning democracy and stimulate the enterprise culture required for Britain's economic recovery. It is, moreover, possible to build upon profit-sharing and employee share ownership schemes by developing representative institutions to complement profit-sharing. In co-partnership schemes represented by, for example, the John Lewis Partnership. there is an elected central council as well as branch councils which give employees a real say in the organisation.

Even if one rejects conventional profit-sharing and share distribution schemes on the grounds that they increase individualism, strengthen employee dependence on the enterprise and do not increase employee control over decision-making or greater economic democracy, we should still look to more radical proposals on the Swedish model which can meet all of these objectives.

The argument against
These schemes do not change authority relations in the enterprise. Their tiny scale means that even if the new owners did vote in large numbers at AGMs they would be powerless to influence decisions. If progress continues at its present pace, we are light years away from the massive redistribution of shareholding required before any real control is vested in employees. The scale of financial reward yielded by these schemes is small, and they are regarded by employees not as a form of industrial democracy but as producing only an annual bonus.

There are dangers for employees in going further and relating employees' economic rewards in any significant fashion to shares or profit levels. This would increasingly require employees to sink their future in the fortunes of an enterprise over whose operations their control is minimal. What would be the reaction of employees when share values and profits fell? Profits and share values are not simply determined by the efficiency of the work force but by unilateral management decisions. Profits are not, therefore, a particularly good criteria for bonus.

The attitude of most trade unionists towards existing schemes could be summed up by USDAW's statement: 'We are not against them nor are we very enthusiastic about them.' The TUC has taken a harder line and has described employee shareholding schemes as 'not so much an encouragement of individual shareholding as an attack on collective institutions'. As most employee-shareholders soon get rid of their shares, a 'shareholding democracy' remains as far away as ever. And why should employees hold shares in 'their' company as distinct from playing the field? A recent survey of profit-sharing and employees' shareholding schemes found that there was generally no consultation, still less participation in the implementation of the schemes (Baddon et al 1987).

In an economic upturn employers in firms with profit-related pay may have an incentive to take on new labour. But existing employees will want to maximise their pay which depends, in a share economy, on maximising each individuals' share of the profits. Taking on extra workers will cut the individual share of insiders. Existing employees, therefore, will have an incentive to stop an increase in employment. Similar problems will occur over allocation of funds to investment, rather than to profits and, hence, employees' pay. Ironically, the fact that profit-sharing *could* legitimise and extend the participation of employees in management decisions is one major reason why employers are doubtful about new schemes.

As for wage-earner funds, Sweden, like the USA or Japan, is a very different country to Britain. The legislation has been introduced in a different context; for example, workers already have board level representation in Swedish companies. The complexity of the system could mean that the employee representatives either have little say in intricate financial decisions or become absorbed in them and divorced from ordinary employees. It is difficult to see such schemes giving a greater direct say in employment issues to the ordinary shop floor employee. Also, course, all of these schemes for financial participation can suffer from the fact that they discriminate between the private and public sector, dynamic and declining industries, the employed and the unemployed.

Worker co-operatives

The idea of workers sharing in the ownership and the profits of the autonomous enterprise, as well as its government, through a system of 'one person, one vote' has recently attracted new attention and support. For many, worker co-operatives seem to combine the benefits of economic democracy and workers' self-management. In the 1970s, older co-operatives, concentrated in the shoe and textile industries, were joined by new ventures at Meriden, Kirkby Manufacturing and Engineering and the *Scottish Daily News*. These projects originated in struggles against closure by conventional proprietors and were both financially aided by the 1974 Labour government and championed by Tony Benn when Secretary of State for Industry. Labour's Industrial Common Ownership Act, 1976, was intended to stimulate co-operatives in manufacturing industries. The recession of the 1980s provided a further impetus.

Bodies such as the GMBATU and the Welsh TUC established support services for members interested in establishing co-operatives. This was reinforced by support from Labour local authorities. By 1984, the Greater London Enterprise Board had invested over £1 million in 36 co-operatives, providing jobs for 400 people. More than 70 Co-operative Development Agencies sponsored by councils were established in nearly all the big conurbations, and the number of workers' co-operatives was estimated to have increased, by 1987, to more than 1,400, with a work force of around 10,000. They are concentrated in areas such as retail distribution, catering, food-processing, printing and publishing and building and allied services. It has been argued that co-operatives have a similar average performance and a similar life expectancy to the orthodox capitalist enterprise and that their performance record is a good one, given that many are established for job protection rather than to seize opportunities in a growing industry.

The renaissance of interest in co-operatives is illustrated by the intense and continuing publicity accorded to the Mondragon experiment in Spain. Established in 1956, in the Basque country, on the ruins of a small bankrupt firm, the network now covers 150 co-operatives in a range of industries and provides more than 18,000 jobs. It has its own bank, with 84 branches, and its own training and research and development agencies. Mondragon has benefited from intimate links with a homogeneous community. Despite a concentration in hi-tech industries, Mondragon embraces co-operatives in agriculture, education and housing. A General Assembly of workers elects a governing non-executive board which, in turn, appoints management. A social council represents workers through a cell-based system, linked to the governing board. There is no trade union representation, indeed, striking is punishable by expulsion or fines.

Co-operatives have had strong support from both the Labour Party, which in a recent statement asserted that 'worker co-operatives are a pure form of industrial democracy', and the Alliance. The support scheme launched by Mr Kenneth Clarke in 1987 was seen as ending Tory ideological opposition to co-operatives. However, different political philosophies can give very different emphases to co-operatives as the vehicle for defence of jobs, small business-led growth, alternative forms of economic organisation or progenitors and guarantors of alternative life styles. Moreover, co-operatives can take different forms. The Conservatives, for example, are firm supporters of 'employee buy-outs', particularly if the enterprise is in the public sector.

Arguments about worker co-operatives

A question advocates of worker co-operatives often have to address is: why should workers be able to succeed in an economic venture in which capitalist entrepreneurs have failed? A partial answer to this is to point out that, whereas the ownership structure and authority relations in the conventional enterprise alienate employees and limit commitment, the co-operative is, by its nature, liberating because it give all employees a direct responsibility in the enterprise. The co-operators have a real stake in the business and this will stimulate effort and efficiency. Supporters of co-operatives can point to significant increases in productivity and lower unit costs. At KME, for example, there was an increase in output from 7,000 to 13,000 radiators per week and a significant increase in the company's market share.

The injection of public money can also be justified on the grounds of job creation and the alternative costs of unemployment. Unions should support co-operatives because of their rule-book objectives such as the TGWU's 'the extension of co-operative production and distribution', because co-operatives redistribute resources away from monopoly ownership and, because successful co-operatives can raise the self-confidence of workers, question the immutability of established means of industrial organisation and generate demands for more democratic experiments.

It can be argued that this view fails to face unpalatable realities. Co-operatives will encounter serious economic difficulties. Workers will not normally be able to supply adequate capital themselves and will tend to be dependent on external finance. Financial institutions are likely to impose tight constraints and monitoring on loans. Their natural caution, particularly if the co-operative arises from an economic failure, will be boosted by an ideological mistrust of these strange animals. All too often, survival can only be guaranteed through excessive self-exploitation: 'you will have to work like you never worked before' Jack Spriggs, the chairman of the KME co-operative, told its new owners. This can mean that, as at Meriden, co-operators will have to work at below union rates. This not only entails a minimal role for unions in the enterprise. It can then be seen as an invitation to other employers to undermine collective bargaining. It can mean, as at Meriden, that professional management is brought in at professional rates and that orthodox principles of hierachical work organisation, employment differentials and discipline re-emerge. A detailed study of the KME experience found that authority became centralised and that leadership was exercised by a small elite, with little part played by the unions or by the majority of the workers in decision-making (Eccles, 1981). In the end, financial pressures led to the collapse of all 3 'Benn co-operatives' established with such high hopes in the 1970s.

One lesson drawn is that worker co-operatives need well thought-out structures to involve the members in decision-making. But even well-developed democratic mechanisms will not work in the absence of a will to democracy and participative values. Here, the origin of some co-operatives as self-interested strategies for job protection may cause problems, particularly if the strongest motivation comes not from the work force, but from union officials or politicians. In this analysis, the need to counteract the antagonistic non-participative environment draws attention to the enduring value of the established co-operative movement's focus on the importance of education.

The position of some on the Left is more straightforward: 'you cannot build islands of socialism in a sea of capitalism'. Most co-operatives, it is asserted, either fold, or over time, they become conventional enterprises. The first GLC-supported co-operative is often taken as an example of this iron law. When GEC declared its intention of closing Associated Automation, a telephone subsidiary, the GLC purchased the plant and equipment for around £100,000 and turned it over to a co-operative in which the workers invested part of their redundancy payments. Within a year, the new Third Sector Co-operative folded, amongst angry recriminations. The lesson drawn is that co-operatives can distract workers from a fight to force their employer to maintain jobs. The eventual failure of the co-operative confirms that, if Arnold Weinstock cannot make an honest profit, Joe Public certainly cannot. The latter conclusion is also drawn on the Right, where co-operative failures are seen as an affirmation of the benefits of the orthodox capitalist enterprise.

But there are still those who believe that worker co-operatives can play a role in a future strategy for industrial democracy. A pre-requirement is an analysis which does not overestimate or underesti-mate the problems. The failure of co-operatives has been seen as evidence that the road to democratisation is long and hard and that it is simplistic to see the new venture as, of itself, producing a transformation in workers' attitudes and a sudden upsurge in the desire to participate. On the contrary, even with a change of structures, you still need to work at involvement and stimulate participation. On the other hand, it has been argued that there is no iron law stemming from the need for maximisation of profits which inevitably dooms co-operatives from the outset to either collapse or degeneration back to capitalist principles. The framework for profit determination is looser than this view allows, as is demonstrated by the diversity of approaches utilised by conventional firms. Similarly, whilst it is clear that management is necessary as a function, the scope that *does* exist for its development and reform to meet the needs of the co-operative enterprise should not be minimised on the basis of one or two ill-resourced experiments.

Conclusions

Proponents of change are united in their dissatisfaction with the status quo. But deep fissures run between the assumptions and strategies of different groups who often use similar language. Conservatives put forward schemes for the re-establishment of morale, efficiency and productivity, under the existing re-energised government of the enterprise. Reformers are divided. Some see the way forward as lying primarily in an extension of collective bargain-ing. Others favour schemes such as board level representation. Many favour both. Reformers wish to modify the authority structure of the enterprise. But they accept, at least for the present, its existing economic objectives. Radicals wish to change both the government and the economic ends of the enterprise. They divide into those who see workers' participation as a means towards full industrial democracy and those who see it as a trap. The first group are, therefore, willing to examine schemes of participation. The second group argue that workers should preserve their independence, pursuing unilateral workers' control over production in day to day struggles, combined with a wider strategy for socialist transformation.

For the Conservatives, the immediate future holds several problems. There is, as we have seen, evidence to show that employees view involvement schemes as a sophisticated means of controlling the work force. There appear to be powerful barriers to profit-sharing schemes. And there is the continuing background threat from EEC schemes for worker participation.

Advocates of extended collective bargaining have to confront the fact that all the evidence shows continued management domination of strategic decision-making, and the period since 1979 has shown the limitations of this technique in defending, let alone advancing, employee interests. An interest in wage-earner funds on the Swedish model has become fashionable on the Left. However, it must be noted that they represented a novel initiative for a trade union movement with a long history of corporatism, and encountered staunch opposition before implementation in modified form. The funds are, it must be remembered, an integral part of an incomes policy, itself recently under stress. Transplantation to the different environment of the UK would be no easy matter.

From a radical stance it is clear that it is only workers' participation, not industrial democracy, which figures as an immediate political possibility. Supporters of board level representation, whether from a reformist or radical perspective, face many problems, not least the defensive independent caste of British trade unionism. Even if it is accepted that recent years have witnessed a small shift towards a greater strategic concern about the future of the enterprise, British unions are inadequately geared up to operate within the sophisticated apparatuses of multinational capital. And, in this context, organisation skills and knowledge are an essential part of power and participation. Whilst there may be real choices between different policies, different means of implementation and different time scales for boards of Directors and, whilst enterprises may be judged on a range of complex accounting indices and may be long-term profit 'satisfiers', rather than short-term profit maximisers, in the end, there are structural systemic constraints. The enterprise is part of the capitalist system and is required to perform according to the imperatives of that system.

None of this is a decisive argument against worker participation. It underscores the difficulties a weakened trade union movement with a questionable commitment to this path will encounter. The failure to implement Bullock illustrated the limitations of union power in the 1970s. There is little evidence to sustain the view that unions possess sufficient unity and muscle to implement a similar strategy in the 1990s. Employers firmly oppose board level representation across industry. In many sectors they are better equipped to resist it than they were in the 1970s. It is possible that in certain enterprises, in certain sectors, a real degree of participation might be possible. For it to be effective, however, it would require to be made part of a wider industrial strategy. Here we have to note the limitations of past Labour governments in developing industrial policy. As a step towards transforming industry and society the prospects of worker participation in the UK in the immediate future would appear to be severely circumscribed, and the same could be said for co-operative experiments. The increasing recognition that so many of the problems of industrial relations arise from the way work is organised does not make a solution any easier. Nonetheless, if progress *is* to be made on this central question then it remains essential that the issues of workers' participation and industrial democracy continue to figure on the political agenda.

Further reading

Two very good books which discuss generally the ideas of industrial democracy and workers' participation are A. Fox, 1985b and C. Pateman, 1970. Two surveys of recent developments of what is popularly considered workers' participation and industrial democracy are M. Poole, 1986, and T. Schuller, 1985. A good account of the socialist tradition is given in K. Coates and T. Topham, 1970. The revisionist arguments accepted by many in the labour movement on collective bargaining as industrial democracy are put forward in H. Clegg, 1960, and criticised in P. Blumberg,

1968, which contains a valuable analysis of participation experiments.

On worker-directors Bullock, 1977, is still required reading. Studies of the various experiments are covered in E. Batstone and P. Davies, 1976; P. Brannen et al, 1976; P. Brannen, 1983; E. Batstone et al, 1983; and P. Willman and G. Winch, 1985. T. Clarke, 1977, is a good critique of the Bullock Report and participation schemes in general from a traditional socialist standpoint. J. Tomlinson, 1982, outlines a revision of the traditional left-wing case against participation and worker co-operatives.

Recent trends in joint consultation are noted in N. Millward and M. Stevens, 1986, and J. McInnes 1985. The debate about employee financial participation in the enterprise is covered in M. Weitzman, 1984 A useful brief introduction to the wage-earner fund innovations is M. Linton, 1985.

J. Storey, 1980, has some interesting material on the scope of recent collective bargaining. A detailed account of the Lucas alternative plan is given in H. Wainwright and D. Elliott, 1982. Some of the problems involved in collective bargaining as a means of advancing workers' interests and decision-making are discussed in two interesting articles: A. Fox, 1975, and D. C. Wilson et al, 1982.

There is a growing literature on worker co-operatives. Recent publications include T. Eccles, 1981, and K. Bradley and A. Gelb, 1983.

Chapter 7

The state of the unions

The 1980s have seen important changes taking place in industrial relations. Management have been seen as getting tougher, becoming more professional, putting more thought and resources into their industrial relations. Trade unions, it is generally held, have become more divided, weaker, less effective in representing their members' interests. What *has* been happening in industrial relations? Have unions lost the power they had in the 1970s? Have management regained the control over work they lost during the post-war boom? In this chapter we try to find out.

Macho management?

We noted in Chapter 1 some of the different approaches to management. During the 1970s, it was argued that the 'sophisticated modern' approach with its acceptance and encouragement of the union, so that its behaviour could be moulded and turned to the advantage of management, was on the upswing (Purcell, 1979). It could be viewed as the workplace equivalent of political corporatism and many saw it as representing the future. However, as the recession developed, commentators on industrial relations began to note the emergence of a new breed of managers: old-style co-operation with the unions was out, the firm smack of authority was in. Michael Edwardes at British Leyland and Ian McGregor at BSC were seen as the pioneers of the new trend. Edwardes bypassed the unions, communicating directly with the shop floor. He drew up a programme involving 25,000 redundancies and extensive changes in working practice, and circulated a copy to every worker's home: 'politically motivated shop stewards could not be relied upon to present a balanced view to employees' (Edwardes, 1984, 93). Management organised its own ballot on the plan and when shop stewards refused to accept its implementation, imposed it. BL adopted a style in which their first offer was their final offer. They liaised with full-time officers at the expense of shop stewards, took over the platform at union meetings, returned full-time stewards to their jobs and dismissed prominent trade unionists such as Derek Robinson.

At BSC, Ian McGregor organised a successful ballot on his 'survival plan' and bypassed the unions by rejecting national bargaining in favour of local deals. A similar approach was taken by Arnold Weinstock at GEC, where the new style was described as 'autocratic-participative'. Fear of unemployment was seen as breeding a 'new realism' on the shop floor and tipping the bargaining scales significantly in management's favour. A management consultant was widely quoted as commenting to a business seminar that for 2 decades management had had 'a buffeting and bashing from government and unions ... we have an opportunity now that will last for two or three years, then the unions will get themselves together again and the government, like all governments, will run out of steam. So grab it now. We have had a pounding and we are all fed up with it. I think it would be fair to say its' almost vengeance' (Beynon, 1983, 9).

The appointment of Ian McGregor to British Coal, the run-up to the miners' strike and its conduct strengthened the view that something new was happening. Day-to-day relations with the unions in the mines had always been reasonably co-operative. In the wake of the bitter stoppage, far from demonstrating traditional reconciliation, the NCB Chair was widely quoted as stating he wished the strike had gone on longer, declaring: 'people are now discovering the price of insubordination and insurrection. And boy, are we going to make it stick!'. Management refused to reinstate those dismissed, during the stoppage, even when industrial tribunals found that they had been unfairly dismissed and refused to allow pre-strike facilities to union representatives. A spate of small strikes over the disciplining of union representatives and the withdrawal of management concessions came to a head in 1987, when the board imposed a tough new Disciplinary Code with no prior negotiations with the NUM. Opposition from the NUM prompted a national ballot in which

77.5% of miners voted for industrial action, scarcely 2 years after the end of the 12-month long strike.

Supporters of the macho management thesis could also point to developments in the private sector. Critics of British management in its dealings with the unions often cited the national newspapers as an example of the problems caused by appeasement. Yet, in 1986, Rupert Murdoch took on the unions. His final proposals for the move to Wapping represented a clear break with past practice. They provided for a legally binding agreement and a ban on industrial action. They stated that employees would undertake work 'with complete flexibility. There will be no demarcation lines ... The starting and finishing times of an employee may be changed upon ... a day's notice ... manning levels will be determined by the employer ... New technology may be adopted at any time ... There will be no closed shop ...'

Business as usual?

How extensive is macho management? It has been argued that it is mistaken to rely on these well-publicised examples; they are publicised because they are the exception. Examples of the new tough line come disproportionally from the public sector and from companies in financial trouble. One study found that '... if 15% underestimates the number of "macho managers", 23% is likely to exaggerate it. In about a fifth of the plants in the survey, management has made some attempt to reduce the role of the union ...' (Batstone, 1984, 258, 260). Another survey of chief executives found overwhelming evidence that changes in working practices were introduced through negotiations. Seventy-nine per cent of the managers said they had made no changes in the way they dealt with shop stewards: 'The evidence does not then support the view that the emerging trend of industrial relations is based on an aggressive management attack on established trade unions ... a more subtle process seems to have been taking place in which firms have certainly been trying to change working practices but in which co-operation and involvement have been seen as important' (Edwards, 1985, 35).

These findings have been questioned on the grounds that they represent the diplomatic response to be expected from directors and factory managers. A study of personnel managers, who were more centrally involved with industrial relations, found that they believed that management *had* toughened up. There were constant references in their responses to industrial relations improving through fear, and evidence of attempts to bypass the unions through briefing groups, quality circles and communications techniques (Mackay, 1986). When shop stewards have been asked whether they thought management was harder than in the past, they were evenly divided, with clear-cut differences between industries. In British Telecom, 83% of Post Office Engineering Union representatives believed management's approach was tougher, whilst 38% of stewards in electrical engineering, 44% in print, 50% in chemicals and 60% in the civil service thought this was so (Batstone and Gourlay, 1986). In contrast with managers, stewards might be expected to emphasise any change so that these figures could well exaggerate the position.

On the little evidence we have, and as postal surveys and even interviews have strong limitations, we can say only that a tougher stance by management is a discernible but minority trend. In the public sector, political and financial pressure has hardened the industrial relations climate. A similar approach has been taken by a minority of employers in the private sector, impelled by financial pressures or long-term calculation that industrial relations with no unions or weaker unions are more beneficial. However, there is no evidence of a large-scale attempt to confront or uproot trade unions. Most employers want to avail themselves of the new balance of forces to change work organisation but prefer to do this by utilising, or perhaps, outflanking the unions. There remains as yet a disjuncture between the rhetoric and to some degree the policies of the Conservatives and the activities of most sections of management – witness the periodic tensions between government and CBI. Most employers still find unions useful. They are cautious men and see a moderate response today as money in the bank for stability should the balance of forces change in the unions favour tomorrow.

Open shop

Employers who refuse to recognise trade unions do not exercise more than marginal influence upon British industrial relations. Nonetheless, Mrs Thatcher has specifically praised the approach taken by non-union companies such as Marks and Spencer. Moreover, many companies in the private service sector have successfully resisted attempts at unionisation. Whilst 'cases in which companies withdrew negotiating or consultative rights remained very much the exception' (ACAS, 1986), there have been scattered withdrawals of recognition, particularly for white collar groups as at ICI and British Rail, and in printing and publishing. And in the new hi-tech industries, there is a growing list of companies – IBM, Motorola, Maxell and National Semi Conductor – who are determined to keep their industrial relations 'union-free'.

Some have seen, in companies like IBM – it controls 70% of world computer production and only 2.5% of its work force are in unions – the shape of things to come. IBM now employs 19,000 people in Britain. In the late 1970s, a number of unions felt that they had made a breakthrough at its manufacturing plant in Greenock, Scotland. However, in a subsequent ballot organised by ACAS, less than 5% supported union recognition.

This does not seem to be related to a strategy of 'forcible opposition' by the company. They subcontract much of their work and pursue a policy of 'high salary, high job security' for their full-time employees. The company takes great pains with its recruitment policies and, indeed, it has been claimed that it employs the right-wing organisation, The Economic League, to screen job applicants. It claims to follow a 'no-redundancy' policy. Transfer to another job is the worst that can happen. IBM also devote considerable attention to industrial relations. They pursue an 'open-door' policy by which employees always have access to their managers, and if they receive no satisfaction, they can pass speedily to the next level. There is single status throughout the company, an open promotion policy and individual negotiations over pay. Whether IBM, like Marks and Spencer, is a relatively rare example of an employer prepared to devote considerable resources to cultivating a company culture, or a precursor of future trends, remains to be seen.

Strike-free

No-strike deals have attracted attention because of their limitations on the right to withdraw labour. Viewed more widely, they constitute an attempt to create a new model of company trade unionism. As the Director General of the EEF points out, they enable an employer 'to select a moderate and progressive minded union with which he can agree to operate from the outset an industrial relations culture embracing all the different aspects ... that is, employee involvement, harmonisation and flexibility of labour' (Bassett, 1986, 87).

Employers unable or unwilling to resist unions or to devote adequate resources to industrial relations are ensuring that trade unionism will be planted and develop within a framework favourable to company objectives. Moulded with care and precision, it can constitute an effective vehicle for management control. To this end, getting the right union committed to company goals is critical. At Yuasa Batteries, for example, a small company in South Wales, the TGWU had members but was not granted recognition. When, in 1985, the employers felt that their own system of communications was insufficient to effectively monitor the work force, they brought in the EETPU to act as a management conveyor belt, to motivate employees and perform the personnel function.

No-strike deals normally involve one union representing all employees, selected by the employer prior to the establishment of the operation. Closed shops are usually out, and in several cases the selected union has found difficulty in recruiting a majority of employees. In a situation of close union involvement with the management function, there appears to be little point in paying union dues. Whilst the EETPU is identified with this approach, most of the big unions have been involved. Whilst many no-strike deals have been with Japanese employers such as Hitachi, Toshiba and Sanyo, British employers as well as Norwegian and American enterprises, have taken this approach. Such deals normally involve 'single status' between all employees, flexibility between jobs and employee participation. Industrial action is prohibited for the duration of the agreement. In the event of a dispute, both parties agree to *pendulum arbitration*, a system by which the arbitrator cannot 'split the difference' between the two sides but has to choose between the union demand and the employer's final offer as the basis for the arbitration award.

(Supporters of no-strike deals argue that they represent an essential means of coming to terms with the new environment of anti-unionism. They represent the *only way* unions can recruit in expanding sectors of industry. They establish industrial peace. Moreover, there are advantages for the work force; all employees become monthly-paid, salaried staff, using the same car parks, toilets and dining facilities. The new approach combines efficiency and equality. The emphasis on training is particularly positive.) The new company advisory boards give elected workplace representatives confidential information, provide consultation before key decisions are taken and create a co-operative and productive atmosphere.

Critics argue that these agreements involve unions conceding the fundamental human freedom to withdraw their labour and abdicating their responsibilities to become an arm of management. What kind of unionism is possible when the employer picks the union he will negotiate with and workers renounce their fundamental right to strike? Whilst the EETPU argues that there is a ballot of the workforce to ratify the employer's decision, this is a managed exercise: the members play no part in the negotiations. Moreover, whereas other unions have had to reluctantly accept these deals from a backs-to-the-wall position, the EETPU and AEU often press them on management. The consequent publicity encourages more personnel managers to consider their adoption. Undercutting is the name of the game. To keep their members, other unions are forced to sign on the no-strike dotted line, so that the EETPU and AEU are provoking a downward spiral in which basic union principles go to the wall. For employers and employees who support these deals get not a union, but a staff association. In Nissan, only around 20% of the work-force is unionised. ACAS are right when they point out that these deals have tremendous advantages – particularly for employers.

No-strike deals should not be overestimated in terms of their coverage. In 1986, the EETPU estimated that less than 20,000 employees were covered by no-strike provisions and the number of 'model' agreements was less than 30 – and strikes have already occurred in enterprises covered by these arrangements. For their opponents, the fact that they largely involve greenfield sites constitutes the major danger. There is no evidence they make workers better off, nor have they staunched membership loss; the Electricians lost 10,000 members in 1986. Their major importance seems to lie in the explicit challenge they offer to traditional union philosophy.

Flexibility bargaining

Since 1979, management have attempted to increase productivity by reorganising and intensifying the work process. Many of the pioneering efforts occurred in the public sector. In 1980, British Leyland introduced a package aimed at the 'elimination of restrictive demarcations of restrictive practices'. To this end, the memorandum stated: 'any employee may be called upon to work in any part of his plant and to carry out any grade or category of work within his abilities and experience'. This was followed in the same year by a spate of agreements in the private sector such as that at Fairey Engineering, which established separate bargaining units through the plant to create a closer link between pay and performance, a measured day-work payment system, flexible working between different crafts and grades and a 3 shift, 7-day 'Continental' system. In 1982 and 1983 came a series of deals in steel, cars, engineering, oil refining and shipbuilding which led to a relaxation of job demarcations, mobility in and between plants, new wage payment systems, acceptance of new technology and new shift systems.

These initiatives were modelled upon the productivity deals of the 1960s in which management bought greater efficiency through comprehensive establishment agreements. They were often accompanied in a novel development by quality circles – small groups formed to discuss and solve problems of production and suggest new methods of working.

Sometimes their impact seemed dramatic. One Longbridge worker claimed he had worked in 5 different departments in 12 months and done 10 different jobs in one department in 3 months.

'In the past management couldn't shift you without the agreement of the union; now it's done without consultation ... it means that you never get to know any of the blokes, it breaks up any unity. In the old days the target was set by timing the operator; now the target is based on the gross potential of the machine. That means they set the machine as fast as possible and you have to keep up with it. They give you targets you can't reach. The gaffer comes to check your counter every hour; blokes have been suspended for failing to have an adequate explanation of why they haven't reached their target.' (Armstrong et al, 1984, 396-7).

By 1984, productivity in manufacturing industry had grown at an annual rate of around 3% since 1979. Whilst the great shake-out of labour was the most important factor, work reorganisation played a part. This prompted a further growth in flexibility deals. At Nabisco, in 1985, the GMBATU signed a 3 year enabling agreement which allowed for 1,500 redundancies, management discretion to introduce new technology, freedom to move skilled workers between crafts and a commitment that no section would take industrial action without a ballot of the whole plant. Shell Carrington's 1985 agreement removed 14 craft groups and combined 3 grading structures into one – while cutting the work-force from 1,200 to 700. Shell Stanlow's 1986 negotiations replaced an earlier deal with a 3-year agreement increasing shift-working and further reducing craft demarcations. In Wales, Borg Warner agreed to keep its transmission plant open in return for a 6-year pay deal, complete flexibility between crafts and worker responsibility for the machine.

There was no guarantee that such changes would stick or lead to enhanced productivity over the longer term, particularly if union workplace organisation remained strong. The experience of the 1960s was that when one set of 'restrictive practices' was brought out, another soon appeared. However, in the 1980s, flexibility bargaining appeared more intensive and well thought-out. It was, also, often only part of wider changes in work organisation.

Core and periphery

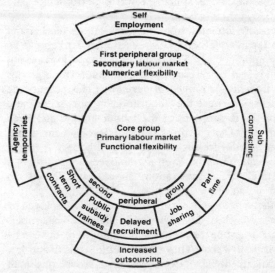

Figure 3 *Source:* Atkinson, 1985.

One of the strategies of the New Right has been the attempt to fragment the working class and weaken trade unionism by encouraging a move to a dual economy and a secondary labour force. It is claimed that in an attempt to adjust to the new competitive market, technological change and the need for a cheap and flexible supply of labour, employers are reducing the number of full-time, permanent employees and replacing them by part-time and temporary employees and subcontractors.

An attempt has been made to systematise these tendencies in the model of the 'flexible firm' (see figure 3). In this model the core workers are motivated by high wages and job security designed to commit them to the organisation. They possess skill and expertise and consist of groups such as managers, designers, sales staff, technicians and craftsmen. Their permanent full-time position is won at the expense of identification with employer goals. Core employees are subject to *functional flexibility*. They must be ready to adapt to changes in technology, and work organisation. This will involve doing different jobs and working in multi-disciplinary teams. It can eventually mean retraining and career change. All core employees have single status and wage systems reward, performance and adaptability.

The core groups are insulated from the wider labour market and are analogous to Japan's 'lifetime employees'. Other workers can be bought in on a temporary basis. The peripheral groups' jobs are not 'firm specific'; they can be resourced from outside. These groups answer the requirement for *numerical flexibility*. This permits the employer to increase or reduce the labour force in more speedy and direct relation to the imperatives of the labour market and keep down costs. *Flexibility of time* involves a greater development of shift patterns, flexitime, '9-day fortnights' and 'annual hours'. A fourth dimension is *financial flexibility*. Even if employees are full-time, a greater proportion of remuneration should be linked to performance.

The *first peripheral group* consists of workers directly employed by the organisation, often less skilled workers filling clerical, supervisory, assembling or testing jobs. They may be full-time, but can be hired and fired at limited cost. They possess little security and few prospects of advancement. The *second peripheral* group consists of part-time workers, those employed on short-term contracts, job sharers and trainees on MSC schemes. The jobs of the *external groups* are not firm-specific. They may involve accountancy skills or cleaning or catering, and the employers' needs can be meet by subcontracting specialist employment agencies or self-employed workers. This approach answers the needs of *numerical flexibility* and *functional flexibility*, as the outside agency will be competitive, specialised and committed.

Those who have developed the idea of *the flexible firm* insist that it is only a model and tool of analysis. Employers are moving in this direction, but 'such changes are as yet pragmatic and opportunist rather than driven by a conscious strategy' (Atkinson, 1985, 14). Growth would represent success for the government strategy of removing rights and power from peripheral groups in society and exposing them to the full rigour of market forces. Some employers have taken steps in this direction. One study observed a small but significant increase in part-time working from 14% in 1980 to 16% in 1984, concentrated in non-manufacturing and the public sector. Temporary, freelance and home-workers were more commonly used in the private sector and there was a relationship between their use and capacity utilisation. They were used by employers to more closely relate output and employment (Millward and Stevens, 1986). A study for the National Economic Development Organisation in 1985 also registered significant progress in the direction of flexibility (IDS Report, 1986, 464).

Reality or aspiration?
There is, then, some evidence of movement in the direction of the core-periphery model but 'rather than systematically moving in this direction, many firms are simply taking advantage of a depressed labour market and implementing some aspects of the model as opportunities arise, without any long-term strategy' (Atkinson, 1985, 22). Some commentators argue that what is happening is a straightforward, small-scale and piecemeal cost-cutting exercise rather than a conscious attempt to buy off a skilled stratum of workers by undermining the conditions of the majority. Talk of the *flexible firm* is seen as creating a false impression of radical change.

Employers faced with a fall in demand which looks permanent may reduce full-time employment. If this is followed by what looks like a temporary upturn they may take on temporary labour, or if the upturn looks more healthy, use secondary labour to increase flexibility and cut costs. But, on the other hand, there will be pressures from workers and unions to answer reductions in demand by shifting work away from the secondary sector into the primary sector. Therefore, 'the question arises as to whether at a particular time in a recession, employers are shedding labour rather than recruiting it' (Batstone and Gourlay, 1986, 8).

The model can be affected by shortages of skilled workers. Definitions of flexibility used by students are diffuse. Moreover, if output rises permanently, an expansion will necessitate more stable, committed labour and lead either to a transfer of workers from the periphery into the core or far greater pressure on core workers. For example, 'manufacturers in the food industry undertaking heavy capital investments may no longer operate with the inefficiencies of the "twilight" or "split shift" system but move to 24-hour operation with seasonal peaks. In so far as they employ "peripheral" workers at all, the change will come within this group. Part-timers will become seasonal workers or disappear' (IDS, *Focus* 39, 1986).

Flexibility is a tactical survival plan related to recession not a strategy which will survive a reduction in unemployment. Subcontracting may be more expensive than using direct labour. Many employers would only be prepared to use sub-contractors in a limited fashion and not to perform essential functions such as maintenance. Subcontracting is likely to remain limited to itstraditional functions such as catering and security. Studies show that employers may be using secondary labour as a supplement to their existing work-force rather than as a substitute for it. The growth of the flexible work-force is exaggerated and, in many cases, where casual and part-time workers are taken on, there is also an increase in the workload of full-time staff. In this view, the 'flexible firm' is likely to remain, at least for the majority of industries, an academic model, and unions will be in a good position to resist attempts at casualisation. The situation in Japan in the post-war period where powerful, well co-ordinated employers were able to undermine the unions is a world away from the UK in the 1980s. On the other hand, given our uncertain economic situation, today's core workers may become tomorrow's unemployed, the casualties in a downturn. There is no way most firms can guarantee jobs for life.

Unions, moreover, may welcome a certain amount of multi-skilling and retraining, producing greater job interest and responsibility. Some may see the exclusion from the primary work-force of weaker groups as a means of strengthening their bargaining power. Union pressure will influence employer strategy. Peripheral workers are concentrated in establishments with a low level of union organisation and there is a relationship between their use and union density (Millward and Stevens, 1986, 210). Whilst these new developments, therefore, represent a challenge to trade unionism in this view, the evidence available shows that they do not, as yet, constitute the catastrophe they are often made out to be.

Trade unions in crisis

According to no less an expert than Norman Willis, General Secretary of the TUC, speaking before the 1987 Congress, Britain's unions face 'a serious crisis ... challenges more profound than at any

Table 8   *Trade union membership, 1968-86*

Year	Membership (all unions 000)	Density	Membership (TUC unions 000)	Density
1968	10,200	44.0	8,875	38.3
1969	10,497	45.3	9,402	40.6
1970	11,187	48.5	10,002	43.4
1971	11,135	48.7	9,894	43.3
1972	11,359	49.5	10,001	43.6
1973	11,456	49.3	10,022	43.1
1974	11,764	50.4	10,363	44.4
1975	12,026	51.0	11,036	46.8
1976	12,386	51.9	11,515	48.3
1977	12,846	53.4	11,865	49.3
1978	13,112	54.2	12,128	50.1
1979	13,447	55.4	12,172	50.1
1980	12,947	53.6	11,601	48.0
1981	12,182	51.0	11,006	46.0
1982	11,593	48.0	10,510	43.5
1983	11,337	47.2	10,082	42.0
1984	10,994	45.7	9,855	41.0
1985	10,716	43.0	9,580	38.4
1986			9,243	38.0

Source: Bain and Price, 1983; Certification Officers' *Reports;* TUC *Reports.*

time in the movement's long history'. There would seem to be strong evidence for this view. The unions have lost 3 million members. Many have financial problems. They continue to face an anti-union political climate. The strike statistics have tumbled. The big battalions like the miners have been soundly beaten. The Conservatives

have successfully saddled the unions with a new framework of law
which severely circumscribes their activities. To what degree does
this popular view of what has happened to trade unions meet the
facts?

Union membership

Table 9   *Union membership, selected years*

Year	Union membership	Union density
1910	2,565	14.6
1913	4,135	22.1
1917	5,499	30.2
1920	8,348	45.2
1921	6,633	35.8
1923	5,429	30.2
1926	5,219	28.3
1933	4,392	22.6
1938	6,053	30.5
1945	7,875	38.6

Source: Bain, 1970.

Tables 8 and 9 make several points. The decline in union membership
is a serious one. It is, however, uneven – compare the TGWU with
NALGO (see table 6). Moreover, it has happened before. Membership loss has been a product of recession in the past, and the situation
has been transformed once recession has given way to economic
upturn. The figures show union density standing at 43%. However,
that figure is based on membership of all unions. If we take the harder
definition, membership of TUC-affiliated unions, the figure comes
down to 38%. These figures undoubtedly *underestimate* membership
loss since 1979, with unions inflating the figures for political reasons.
Membership decline is clearly recession-related. The big drop in
1980-81 was a direct product of the loss of more than a million jobs in
manufacturing industry where the unions were very strong. Nonetheless, the fall in membership has been consistently greater than the fall
in employment. For example, in 1981 and 1982, whilst union
membership fell by 11.6%, employment fell by 5.5%. What worries

trade unionists about the decline is that membership loss related to job loss is not being compensated for by employees in the new jobs that are being created joining unions. In the mid-eighties, the number of employees has been increasing at an annual rate of 150,000 a year. Union membership has been falling at an annual rate of 250,000 a year. As employment has revived, trade unionism has continued its decline. Also of concern to the unions are small signs of membership loss unrelated to unemployment or industrial change: the NUT, for example, lost 23,000 members in 1985-86.)Whilst it is fair to point out that the TUC has more members affiliated than it did in the early 1960s, and trade union density is only now dipping below the average in the 1940s and 1950s, the comparison with the 1970s and 1980s is the important one. And since 1979, the TUC has lost a quarter of its membership.

The decline in union membership is, as yet, not as severe as that encountered in the inter-war recession. Between 1920 and 1928, for example, the unions lost 42% of their membership, and by the low point of the Depression in 1933, union density was at 22.6%, less than half the 45.2% recorded in 1920. This *was* trade unionism on the run. Whereas today, unemployment has had a largely direct effect in taking out jobs in unionised sectors, it had in that period a greater secondary impact in provoking those who kept their jobs to give up their membership.

Yet the effect was temporary. By 1939, density was back at over 30% as unions recruited in the new mass production industries. This underlines the resilience of British unions; in the past they have recovered from their reverses. This observation should provoke caution, but not complacency, for the developing pattern of employment growth in the 1990s is very different from that of the 1930s and 1940s. In fact, many would seriously question the utility of comparisons with the very different economy and society of half a century ago. We are, hopefully, not going to see a move out of today's economic problems accelerated by 6 years of world war. Indeed, some would argue that we are not going to see a recovery involving a return to full employment. Moreover, a change in the political situation cannot be guaranteed. The rate of membership loss has slowed in recent years and by 1987 a number of unions which had suffered seriously – GMBATU, UCATT and USDAW – were registering their first small, but confidence boosting, increases since

1979. If the situation is not as bad as it might be, nor as bad as it has been, it still represents a serious setback for the labour movement.

Union finance

In 1986, the NUM's deficit was at least £2 million. The AEU reported a similar loss, and proposed cutting a third of its full-time staff and sacking 60 full-time officers. UCATT has also encountered financial problems, and, in 1987, the NUJ suspended all conferences and educational activities until cash flow was restored. The NUT proposed to axe a third of its head office staff.

Again, caution is in order. When the NGA and SOGAT declared they were in financial difficulties it was pointed out that if their assets were considered, they were in the millionaire class. Moreover, both unions had encountered specific problems with industrial action and the law, and with payment of unemployment benefits, problems unlikely to recur in the immediate future. The 1985 figures show that TUC affiliates increased their income by 11%, or £3.48 per member, to £332 million. Expenditure went up by 21%, or £6.26 per member, to £331 million. Income consisted of £293 million in membership contributions, £20 million from investments and £18 million from the sale of goods and services. The annual reports of the Certification Officer show an overall decline in unions' financial problems since 1982 and suggest that the problem was not an absolute one, but one of adjustment. Most unions suffered from membership loss, some from the need to pay out large sums in unemployment benefits, some, in addition from big strikes and, therefore, big payouts, and some from brushes with the law. There is now more planning to deal with the first and second problems whilst the unions are exhibiting far greater caution in relation to the third and fourth.

The unions are in the black – but only just. The excess of income over expenditure is slim and precarious. One obvious way out is to further increase membership affiliations. TUC affiliation fees were increased in 1987 and many unions have put up their subscriptions in recent years. But the average annual subscription is still 0.36% of the national average earnings, compared with 1% for unions in Germany and France. This represents a decline from 1.5% of average earnings in 1938 and suggests that an increase to around the 1% mark would be justifiable and realistic. However, in a period of falling membership and intensifying competition, many unions fear resistance. In the absence of such a relatively major increase, unions are likely to continue to keep their heads above water, but not by very much.

Strikes

A high strike rate is often taken as a crude indicator of workers' combativity and trade union strength.

Table 10   *UK industrial disputes, 1974–86*

Year	No. of stoppages	Workers involved (000)	Working days lost (000)
1974	2,946	1,625	14,750
1975	2,332	809	6,012
1976	2,034	668	3,284
1977	2,737	1,166	10,142
1978	2,498	1,041	9,405
1979	2,125	4,608	29,474
1980	1,348	834	11,964
1981	1,344	1,513	4,266
1982	1,538	2,103	5,313
1983	1,364	574	3,754
1984	1,221	1,464	27,135
1985	903	791	6,402
1986	1,704	720	1,920

Source: Department of Employment Gazette, September 1987.

As table 10 illustrates, there has been a downward trend in strike activity since 1979, if we exclude the miners' strike, which accounted for 83% of working days lost in 1984. There is a clear distinction between the aggressive militancy of the 1960s and 1970s and the years of Thatcherism. In 1974, there were nearly 3,000 stoppages. During the 1970s there were never less than 2,000 annually. In 1985 and 1986, there were just under and just above 1,000 and only in 1982 did the figure reach 1,500. The figure of 1.9 million days lost in 1986 was the lowest since 1963. And since 1979 almost all the big battles have resulted in defeat for the unions.

These statistics underestimate the number of small stoppages. There has undoubtedly been a growth of forms of *industrial action short of a strike*. The 1980s figures reflect a declining work-force. But there can be little doubt that they reflect first and foremost the influence of economic recession and the political force of a government willing to face down the unions and determined to see out strikes even if, as in the case of the miners, it takes almost 12 months. The government's preparations for confronting industrial action in the public sector, as reflected in the Carrington Report and the Ridley Report, are well known, whilst the miners' dispute showed a willingness and ability to utilise coercion in a fashion unprecedented since 1945 (Beynon, 1985; Fine and Millar, 1985).

If these figures appear to illustrate a loss in union confidence and an ebbing of power, they should also direct us to the limits of this process. Whilst the unions have suffered important reverses compared with the previous 2 two decades, we are still witnessing national industrial action – absent in the dog-days of the twenties and thirties. And the resilience of the unions is illustrated by the spate of disputes in the miners, the civil service, the schools, the car industry and the Post Office in 1986-87.

Wages

We looked at the government's wages policy in Chapter 2. What has been the response? The image of a battered and depleted trade unionism certainly changes when we look at the pattern of wage increases since 1979. Average earnings lagged behind the rate of price increases in 1979, overtook them in 1980, dropped behind once more, but since 1982 have been running above the rate of inflation, providing a faster rise of real earnings than had occurred through most of the 1970s. In 1986 and 1987, average earnings were increasing at between 7-8% and prices at around 4%.

However, a CBI survey in 1987 of 9,000 pay settlements dating back to 1980 found that just under a third involved unions in accepting changes in working practices and that 60% of employers had clinched at least one flexibility deal during the previous 7 years. The CBI has continually emphasised the dispersion of pay awards, reflecting increasingly the circumstances of individual companies. As we have seen (in chapter 1) differentials have increased. Nonetheless, confronted by a deep recession and mass unemployment, wages have proved intractably resilient.

This may be because the recession has not weakened union bargaining power; indeed some writers argue that the differential between union-determined and nonunion-determined wages has increased in the 1980s (Huhne, 1986). Unions have not been able to successfully resist closures. But those organised plants that have not closed show no decline in density and may be just as powerful, indeed, if there is a concentration of production, more powerful. Reduced demand for products or services may intensify competition between employers and strengthen the union's hand. Employers may wish to build up stocks for an eventually expanded market, when order books begin to fatten. Crucial groups of workers may be viewed as indispensable.

In economic theory, unemployment weakens unions, because it provides a ready supply of alternative labour willing to do the work of existing employees for less money. In the real world, the unemployed may lack the motivation, experience, or skill. Employers may have an inadequate knowledge of external labour markets, appreciate the importance of a stable, integrated work-force and still fear the influence on production of the embittered industrial relations sacking existing employees can produce.

Moreover, as the Industrial Relations Director of Fords noted:

'... if you think about all the de-manning that has been going on, you will realise that the average company has a very rapidly falling wage bill. In addition, labour costs in many companies are not such a significant feature of total production costs as they previously were, because with the use of more technology and the restructuring of work, companies are making savings on their overheads. For example, by raising quality levels, they are cutting scrap costs. In this atmosphere, employers are not keen to risk a strike to cut wage increases' (Rootes, 1986, 7).

This leads us on to the alternative view that the push on wages is coming not primarily from the unions but from management. If they wish to recruit or retain skilled workers they may have to pay more, particularly given regional differences and bottlenecks. Yet even in areas of Liverpool, where unemployment is approaching 30%, there are reports of companies in specialist markets like precision engineering having to scour the north of England for skilled labour. Employers are paying through the nose for their past neglect of training. Furthermore, larger employers wishing to avoid frictions arising from increased differentials may pass on increases to a wider range of employees or be willing to match the going rate. Secondly, in a situation of rising productivity and profitability since 1982, many companies have been willing to pay for co-operation in changing

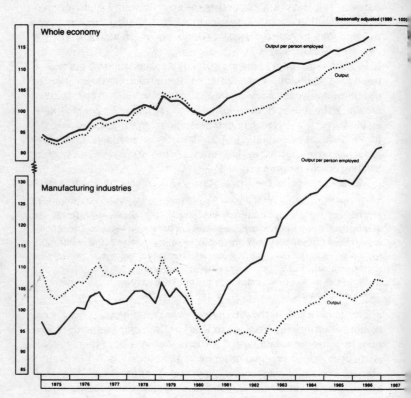

Figure 4   *Source: Department of Employment Gazette: Historical Supplement*

work practices. Flexibility bargaining is reflected in the wage figures. The reason change has been purchased, not imposed, is because employers believe that effective change requires positive rather than hostile attitudes from the work-force, and because they calculate that the costs of ignoring or breaking the union would outweight those involved in continuing to bargain with it.

There is evidence that the traditional view that pay increases are primarily influenced by external economics, rather than internal factors such as profitability, productivity and skill shortages, requires revision. It could be argued, however, that the limited dampening-down of wages in 1979-81 reflected some pressure from rising employment, but its limitations stemmed from the view that the unprecedented levels of employment were strictly temporary and would be reversed in a Thatcher 'U-turn'. The resilience of wages since 1982 could then be explained by the fact that whilst unemployment remained at a post-war high, it did not continue to rise, so that the threat-effect diminished (Nickell, 1987).

Exactly what lies behind the pattern of pay settlements in the 1980s and exactly what it says about trade union power remains unclear. Perhaps it does represent a straight trade-off between wages and unemployment and the unemployed have little reason to acclaim it. Recent findings suggest that companies recognising unions have reduced their work-force in the 1980s, compared with union-free employers (Daniel, 1987). Those who see the level of wage increases as the product of continuing union strength can point to the strenuous attempts of the government and the CBI to dampen down the rate of wage rises. The CBI, for example, campaigned to make 1985-86 'make or break' year and suggested that employers should cut pay settlements by 2% and by a further 2% in 1987 to bring wages below the rate of inflation. The campaign had no discernible effect. It is also suggested that the decline of unions' political power has led to a greater focus on the shop floor and on wages and that the continuing high level of increases shows that unions remain powerful enough to prise a share of increased productivity and profitability from tougher employers.

Those who see buoyant wage increases as employer-led argue that little prising is required. Unions are facing an open door. They point to survey evidence in which employers express satisfaction with the way things are going on the pay front and the fact that in the areas of traditional union power, such as engineering, workers have not done as well as they have elsewhere. Pay increases generate increased productivity and are often self-financing. They must be related to the wider picture of increasing inequality (chapter 1). But if clear conclusions cannot be drawn, it remains difficult to see how trade unions which had been decisively weakened would be able to maintain wages at double the rate of inflation after 8 years of recession and political assault.

Workplace organisation

This argument about wages is intimately related to questions about the existing state of trade union workplace organisation. One view of earlier developments stresses the independence from both management and wider union of shop stewards in the immediate post-war period and emphasises grassroots militancy and the informal nature of workplace industrial relations. From the 1960s, management and unions, in accordance with the recommendations of the Donovan Committee, are seen as stimulating a greater formality in workplace industrial relations, a restoration of management control and more regulated wage systems (Brown, 1981; Daniel and Millward, 1983). However, there are disagreements as to the extent of these developments, the degree to which they represented a sea-change or a continuation of trends already present, and their implications for trade union power.

What changes have the years of recession wrought on the extensive workplace organisation of the 1970s? What evidence there is appears to show that, whilst closures have taken their toll, where there is employment, there is workplace organisation which looks very like it did in the last decade. Overall, 'the gross change in union recognition between 1980 and 1984 is virtually zero in both directions' (Millward and Stevens, 1986, 68) and 'there has been no fall in union density in organised plants' (Batstone and Gourlay, 1986, 72). Even the Hitachis and the Nissans are still prepared to accept trade unionism, albeit on their terms. One survey has suggested that the closed shop *increased* its coverage (Batstone, 1984). However, a more comprehensive study found that the number of workers in closed shops declined from 5.2 million in 1979 to 4.9 million by the middle of 1982, mirroring roughly the drop in employment (Dunn and Gennard, 1984). The most recent examination found a fall in the numbers covered of one million between 1980 and 1984. The significant decline was in private manufacturing industry and amongst manual workers (Millward and Stevens, 1986).

The 1986 *Workplace Industrial Relations Survey* also found an increase in the number of shop stewards, from around 317,000 in

1980 to about 335,000 in 1984, a rise of some 6%. This consisted of a rise of 31% in the public sector and 18% in private services, and a decline of 27% in manufacturing industry. Even the fall in the numbers of full-time stewards in manufacturing appeared to have been compensated for by an increase in both manual and non-manual full-time stewards in the public sector. Moreover, there is evidence that the number of stewards has fallen less than the number of workers, reducing the unit of representation and providing potential gains in efficiency. Stewards' Committees still met regularly, whilst the number of Joint Shop Stewards' Committees and Combine Committees also appeared stable. This backed up the view, presented in other studies, that the structure of workplace organisation had survived intact through the years of change: 'in plants where stewards exist there have been no changes of any significance. If shop steward strength could reasonably have been inferred from such procedural measures in the 1970s, there is no logical basis for hypothesising their present weakness from identical results in the 1980s' (Terry, 1986, 71).

Whether union workplace organisation has maintained the substance, as distinct from the form, of power has proved more difficult to evaluate. The level of wage increases is taken as evidence of strength, the drop in strikes as evidence of weakness – although it could be taken as an index of strength and satisfaction – unions do not need to take industrial action as they are getting what they want without it. Certainly, some writers have detected in managements' supposition that workplace organisation remains a constraint in changing work organisation, evidence of the stability of union power (Batstone, 1984; Edwards, 1984). However, one important change since 1979 seems to be a substantial decline in joint regulation of non-wage issues in the workplace. In 1980, 54% of managers reported negotiations at establishment level over redeployment of labour, whilst 4 years later the figure fell to 29%. There were similar declines in negotiations over physical working conditions, staffing levels and recruitment (Millward and Stevens, 1986, 248).

These developments, which apply to both manual and non-manual groups, added to changes in flexibility, could mean that workplace representatives have ceded a measure of the control over work organisation which was regarded as an important achievement of shop stewards in the last 3 decades. They provide some evidence that, if the institutions of workplace unionism are the same as a decade ago, some of the outcomes are different. Shop stewards' power in the past was not simply based on their ability to increase members' pay – many plants, for example, lacked piecework systems – but on *mutuality*, their ability to negotiate over staffing, redeployment of labour, speed of work and overtime. The picture emerging of union co-operation in changing the organisation of work could represent a process, already well developed, of management regaining control by paying for it. Other evidence, such as the increased contact between steward and union officer, could also be interpreted in terms of workplace organisation losing an element of independence (Millward and Stevens, 1986, 127). The CBI's view is that extensive changes in the organisation of work are occurring, that pay is a crucial lever in securing change and that workplace organisation is 'able to secure only minor modifications in the changes required' (CBI, 1987). The point is reinforced by case studies of management attempts to re-establish control over work which argue that, on a range of issues including wages, the process of bargaining is increasingly ritualistic, with the outcomes decided in advance by management, who, nevertheless, want to see that 'things are done properly' and maintain the influence of workplace organisation (Chadwick, 1983).

This is related to the argument that recent developments disclose a growing potential for 'enterprise trade unionism'. Shop stewards, it is claimed, are becoming detached from the wider union and integrated more with the employer.

'This does not necessarily mean that they necessarily become more docile but that they identify their interests more with the success of the enterprise and less with the job controls, employment anxieties and concern for the poorly organised of the wider union. The structure of trade unionism orginally developed for the strategies of employee solidarity is increasingly being shaped to the needs of employers.' (Brown, 1986, 165).

The resilience of shop steward organisation is striking. Whether workplace organisation has grown less powerful is difficult to estimate within any framework, but our estimations will be influenced by our conceptions of trade union purpose. If we place importance on employee solidarity, the idea of a wider movement, the workplace organisation as an instrument for workers' control, then we will view these tendencies as weakening trade unionism. If we focus only, or primarily, on money, we may view matters differently.

Patterns of growth or decline

The present picture remains susceptible to change from long-term trends which militate against any reversal of the present decline of trade unionism, because they all represent a move from categories where trade unionism is strong to categories where it is weak. Your natural trade unionist in the private sector, it is asserted, is a man in overalls working full-time in a large car factory. The worker of the future is a white collar woman, working part-time in a small office. The problem for the unions is summed up by the fact that Sainsburys now employ a larger UK work-force than Ford.

The first point to make is that these changes do not represent a sudden development since 1980. They have been continuous throughout the post-war period. What we are witnessing is an acceleration of established trends, not a new development, and unions in the 1970s were able to buck these trends achieving the highest membership and the highest density in their history. Moreover, some have argued that the extent of future change is often exaggerated and its implications are often unclear (chapter 4).

It would, however, be wrong to underestimate the degree of change and the problems it can cause for union growth. Compared with manufacturing – over 60% – and the public sector – over 80% – union density in the growth areas is tiny. The Hotel and Catering Industry Board estimates a growth of 120,000 jobs by 1990. The work-force of McDonalds has gone from nowhere to 18,000 in a couple of years. Yet it bears all the stigmata associated with low unionisation: private ownership; small units; part-time workers; high turnover. More than 90% of the new jobs in this area are part-time, whilst turnover is 30% in hotels and around 300% in the fast-food chains.

Recent evidence

We have to take with a pinch of salt many small-scale surveys by development agencies intent on attracting investment. However, a study of companies in a Scottish new town, which might be expected to provide fruitful ground for union recruitment in its new industries, found that union density was 35%. A follow-up survey by the Scottish TUC found that this had declined by 1986 to 20%. This was related not to foreign ownership but to the general decline in plant size, changes in technology, and the nature of the industries (Beaumont and Cairns, 1987). These findings have been challenged by further research, which argues that low unionisation in the electronics industry in Scotland is a myth and that 7 out of 10 electronics workers are employed in offices or factories where unions are recognised. The research covered new companies in Scotland's 'Silicon Glen', as well as established firms. However, it did show that recognition was related to size and that, whilst 89% of companies in Edinburgh and 60% in Glasgow recognised unions, the figure for the new towns was only 16%. Moreover, companies established prior to 1960 were 4 times more likely to recognise unions than those set up since 1984. The level of union recognition was seen as likely to fall away only slightly, as on current trends it would take many years for the smaller new plants to account for a majority of employees (Sproull and McInnes, 1986).

Other research concludes that a relatively high proportion of new companies, particularly in greenfield locations, are non-union. A future decline in membership and density is likely to be influenced to an extent by foreign newcomers, but very largely by small British single establishment companies, who view industrial relations in terms of employee involvement and direct communication with the work-force rather than in terms of collective bargaining and trade unionism (Beaumont, 1987). In the past, the influence pro-union state policy and practice has exercised on employers has helped union growth, and the relationship between being in a union and working in the public sector has been a strong one. The fact that the state now takes a largely negative stance and the nationalised industries are being returned to the private sector add to the unions' gloom.

Out of the gloom?

But the scenarios are not all black. Whilst size of establishment is a vital ingredient in unionisation, 96% of companies in the strongly organised printing industry employ less than 100 people, making up almost half the print work-force. Moreover, two-thirds of Tesco's stores employ more than 100 workers and a third more than 200 workers (Bollard, 1983). The average size of Sainsbury's establishments is even larger. Many supermarkets are, in reality, small factories. Stereotypes can obscure the realities of the work process. Workers in service industries are not all bank clerks or insurance sellers. Refuse collectors, hospital ancillary workers, gas fitters, postal workers, bus and lorry drivers are all groups of employees who will endure into the next century. They are all groups with a strong tradition of trade unionism and they all work in 'services'. Moreover, the negative impact of labour turnover on union growth is mediated through establishment size and employer policy. In the National Health Service, one of the high turnover industries, it has little impact. The same goes for part-time employment:

'of the five industries with the highest proportion of part-time employees only two, distribution and miscellaneous services, are poorly unionised; the other three, health services, local government education and entertainment, are well unionised. Distribution and miscellaneous services are poorly unionised, not so much because of their high proportion of part-time employees as because they have other characteristics, in particular a large number of small establishments' (Bain and Price, 1983, 24).

Where, as in the NHS and in private sector industries, such as food and drink, part-timers work with strongly unionised full-timers, they are in the union, too (Batstone and Gourlay, 1986). Where part-timers are not members, as in distribution, full-timers are not members either. If the size of establishment increases, the problem may diminish.

That unions *do* face a problem in recruiting part-time workers is confirmed by a recent Department of Employment survey which showed that 28% were union members, compared with 51% of full-time employees. The 1986 *Survey of Workplace Industrial Relations* found that private sector firms whose work-force was more than 40% part-time had a union density of 40%, while those with a smaller proportion of part-timers had a higher union density. That the conditions for trade unionism are present can be seen from employee reactions to their work: 'The staff in most stores will tell you that they are greatly overworked, under severe strain and feel physically and mentally drained at the end of the working day' (Smith, 1987, 26). Low pay, speed-up, lack of job security and no legal protection may or may not predispose employees to union membership. They provide suitably inflammable material.

USDAW reports that, as a result of the 1986 Wage Act, allowing for deductions of up to 10% of pay to make up stock or till shortages, it received numerous unsolicited inquiries from Marks and Spencer's stores and that the removal of young people from Wage Council protection provoked a similar response. Ignition will then depend increasingly on union action. The fact that USDAW has recruited a quarter of Harrods' 4,000 employees shows that the problem is not an insuperable one. Union membership in hotels has declined in recent years yet, in the past, recruitment drives have had their successes. In 1976-77, GMBATU increased its membership from 13,00 to 22,000 and the TGWU claimed to have recruited 5,000 members in 6 months. In the 1980s, against a harsher economic and political background, the going is heavier. But, as recent trade union advances in the banking and insurance sector show, there is no iron law governing trade union decline.

The vanishing working class

Some writers have taken the recomposition of the work-force to indicate that the working class is in terminal decline. In this view, trade unions do not merely face tremendous difficulties, but are destined to slowly wither away. Different writers use different definitions of class. The Registrar General's categorisation, for example, is based upon people's occupations and whether they do manual or non-manual work. Many people define manual workers as 'working-class' and white collar workers as 'middle-class'. Others relate class to income and life style, and argue that when manual workers reach a certain stage of affluence they succumb to *embourgeoisement* and become part of the 'middle-class'. Others claim that only productive workers should be classed as working-class, so that all white collar employees and those who carry out manual jobs in local government and public services are middle-class. Here, we assume that the class position of different groups is defined by the relationship to other groups in the organisation of production. In this approach, the working class is constituted by those who have to sell their labour to live, not simply those who work with their hands in factories, or those who are poorly paid.

Blue collar and white collar
Those who argue that the working class is vanishing point to the fact that today, under 40% of employees work in manual occupations, compared with 55% in 1971 and 75% in 1911. Conversely, there are more than 12 million white collar employees and the number is still rising. Who are these white collar employees? They are normally divided into 2 categories, the 'professional-managerial', making up between 20-25% of the employed population, and the 'clerical', making up some 17-18%. The clerical category consists of, amongst

others, typists, filing clerks, secretaries, shop assistants, petrol pump attendants and office machine operators. In the past, the traditional 'clerk' was separated off, certainly, from semi-skilled and unskilled manual workers by better pay and conditions, and particularly, enhanced job security. However, 'by 1978 the average earnings of semi-skilled men have overtaken their clerical counterparts for the first time ... such income advantages that clerical workers enjoyed have been considerably eroded ... in addition to income relativities, many of the traditionally superior employment conditions of clerks have been gained by manual workers' (Crompton and Jones, 1984, 24, 28).

Moreover, it is clear that, in many ways, office work has become 'industrialised'. One study found that over 90% of those on clerical grades were in jobs that were 'entirely rule-bound, although the complexity of the rules varied and required no discretion or autonomy in carrying out their various job tasks' (Crompton and Jones, 1984, 73). Whilst there were opportunities for promotion, these fell largely to the minority of men and are increasingly problematic. The same applies to other employees in this category. Supermarket check-out assistants working laser scanning tills have little control over their work. It is increasingly carried out under large-scale, factory conditions. Like other employees in this category, they are *workers* in the sense that they live by the sale of their labour power.

The clerical category as a whole consists of women – around 70% – who possess few qualifications, come from a working-class background and earn less than the top 30% of manual workers. This, as well as the proletarianisation of the work they do, led to the increase of trade unionism in this group in the 1960s and 1970s and to the dissolution of the 'status superiority' which bonds the small, relatively highly-paid male salariat to their employers. What's in a term? The majority of these workers are, in reality, manual workers, separated from other workers by their now dissolving status rather than by considerations of class. This is not to say that remaining differences, such as the existence of opportunities for promotion, no matter how limited, which may predispose this group to individual rather than collective action, are not of enduring importance.

The professional-managerial category is growing faster than the clerical group. Many are members of the 'new middle class' and exercise a substantial degree of managerial power. But this category also consists of nurses, radiographers, physiotherapists, medical technicians, laboratory technicians and supervisors. A majority of these employees possess little control over resources, over the labour of others, or over their own work: '73% of supervisors exercised no control – or skill – in their own work' (Crompton and Jones, 1984, 76). They have nothing to live on but their salary. They are in trade unions. They go on strike. They are, in a real sense, part of the working class, as are the majority of other groups covered by this category, such as draughtsmen or teachers.

It would be wrong to ignore the changes taking place. They are real, not superficial or temporary, but they are, on the whole, changes *within* the working class. What we are observing is not a withering away, but a *reconstitution* of the working class, a remaking which has been continuous since the advent of capitalism. We have to remember that only a little over a century ago there were more agricultural labourers, domestic servants and workers in trade and transport than there were in factories and mines. As the system of production has been continuously transformed, so it has continuously transformed the working class. But the working class has not been transformed by the fruits of affluence. It has been transformed by changing technology and employment patterns. Affluence may change attitudes, but that is very different from changing structures. The working class is *expanding, not shrinking.* The divisions between full-time and part-time workers, employed and unemployed, men and women, and black and white, represent divisions *within* the working class, divisions which may be limited, or emphasised, by trade union action.

Trade unions and growth

Nonetheless, it must be acknowledged that changes in the class structure placed in their economic setting are more unfavourable to trade unionism than those prevailing earlier this century. However, the extent to which unions recover lost ground, consolidate their position or remain in decline will depend at least to some degree on their own activities. Some writers have seen the role of union leadership as critical in union growth (Undy et al, 1981). Others have argued that government action and employers' policies are crucial and have seen union leadership as a secondary and derivative factor. Unions are at best catalysts – they can only discover discontent and attempt to convince workers that union membership is the answer – but it is a role which is tightly circumscribed by economic factors (Bain and Price, 1983).

Unions and recruitment

The period since 1979 would suggest that this view has been largely accepted by trade union leaders. It has been reported that in the early years of the decade only 10% and 15% of unorganised establishments experienced recruiting activity amongst manual workers and non manual workers respectively: '...generally speaking these results do not indicate extensive attempts by unions to recruit in non-union establishments' (Millward and Stevens, 1986, 70).

As they developed in the post-war period, many unions were geared up to negotiating and servicing members but not to going out to recruit them. Prospective members, who worked in relatively large groups, came to them, not *vice versa*. Shop stewards took care of much of the bread and butter work and the officials appeared when there was an important problem or wage negotiations. Many were already overworked servicing existing, increasingly demanding members, lacked recruitment skills, or lacked a feel for the culture and problems of 'new' groups of workers. There was the hope of a Labour government or a Conservative 'U-turn'. Union leaders, therefore, took their time in appreciating membershp was slipping away and more time in deciding something should be done about it.

Since 1984/85, there has been more action or, perhaps more accurately, more talk about action. The Electricians have pursued no-strike agreements, intended to exploit employers' goodwill, introduced a new range of services and have flown officials to Japan in an attempt to carve out a stake in expanding areas. If this is a strategy aimed at the employer and at 'core' workers, the TGWU has aimed, rather, at the periphery. Officials have been instructed to spend one third of their time on recruitment, and to aim at the fast-growing sectors of the public services and newly privatised industries and services whilst consolidating in existing catchment areas. The *Link-Up* campaign, initiated in 1986, was aimed particularly at temporary and part-time workers and was complemented by an experiment in television advertising. TASS and ASTMS have sought to compete with the EETPU in the new-tech belt along the M4 and have tried mail-shot recruitment around new towns such as Milton Keynes and Bracknell. The GMBATU, in conjunction with a design consultancy, has remodelled its logo, provided plastic membership cards and a video magazine mailed to branches, and launched a campaign to recruit the self-employed. It has organised its *Flare* campaign on the basis of the eroded floor of those legal rights British workers possess and the consequent need for union protection. USDAW, which loses a third of its membership each year through high turnover, has launched a campaign against poverty pay and attempted to involve shop stewards, rather than full-time officers, in recruitment.

In the attempt to increase recruitment the unions have looked to cut rate subscriptions for certain categories of member, an increase in Union speakers in schools, colleges and MSC courses, and the creation of a new category of associate membership by which employees would receive limited services from the union and pay only part of normal dues.

Despite criticism of the 'new realism', 'sweetheart deals' and market-based trade unionism of the ELTPU and AEU, many unions seem intent on following in their wake. The GMBATU offered companies services on a consultancy basis, declaring support for single unionism, single status, flexible working and binding arbitration. UCATT established a finance company to provide members with advice on mortgages, insurance, pensions and investment as well as discounts on car, holiday and health insurance. ASTMS recruitment leaflets stressed: 'If you join ASTMS, there are no political obligations. We are a trade union, not a political party'. The Left-led TASS organised a seminar for employers in the hi-tech Bracknell area. Its publicity noted that

'the growth and prosperity of the region cannot be separated from the needs of local employers to secure a long-term, higher growth rate ... investment by itself will not provide success; it will require the effective management of change. There is an urgent need to establish good in-company communications and industrial relations ... TASS believes it has a lot to offer both sides of industry in this respect'.

There is at least one big problem: are there not other organisations who can provide financial services, management consultancy or industrial training better than the unions? Are these really the kind of services members want from their unions? Perhaps, but certainly not at the expense of what they regard as the unions' central role as a producer of increased wages. Unless the unions can continue to effectively assert and extend their essential role as successful wage bargainers, credit cards, Filofax and videos are unlikely to reverse their present decline. Moreover, if the unions *are* to buck existing trends, they must recruit a sizeable proportion of the quarter of the work-force that now works part-time.

Also, the labour market is still structured in terms of gender, with men in the better jobs and women in the worse jobs. Unions will have to accommodate to a far greater degree the concerns and problems of women workers. The union density of women workers is still only 60% of that of men. Yet, in 1985-86, only 22,000 or 8.6% of the 257,000 new jobs created were filled by part-time male workers. If unions are to recruit more women workers they will have to devote bargaining resources to women's objectives, such as child-care, better employment welfare and Social Security benefits, take a firmer line on minimum wage legislation and adapt their structures to create more involvement by women. The TUC's acceptance, in 1987, of a proposal that an equality department should be established, provided some evidence that the unions were taking the issue of gender more seriously than in the past.

The TUC

The last decade has placed tremendous pressure on the TUC's role in formulating a minimal basis for unions' industrial policy and regulating conflict between them. Three times, over the Conservative legislation, the Wapping dispute and no-strike deals, the TUC has come close to a split. By the late 1980s there was criticism in the unions of the TUC and a feeling that it should be accorded a more residual role. Some trade unionists were concerned at what the TUC's £10 million bureaucracy *delivered*. The big unions felt that Congress House research and education duplicated their own facilities. The escalating increase in affiliation fees led one union, the Metalworkers, to pull out of the TUC. And some observers felt that ACAS was now playing a greater role in inter-union disputes at the expense of the TUC. Having forfeited its political voice, would the TUC also see a reduction in its industrial influence?

Membership loss and recruitment strategies have been a central issue, even if attention has focused on the conflicts over no-strike deals. In the spring of 1984, Hitachi announced that in future they would deal solely with the EETPU at the expense of the other 6 TUC affiliates which had members in the plant. The 6 unions took a formal complaint to the TUC Disputes Committee. They began a successful campaign to tighten up the Bridlington Agreement which governs inter-union competition. Whereas, in the past, unions coming to an agreement with an employer simply had to 'have regard to the interests of other unions', they were now instructed not to agree to such deals unless there was prior consultation and *agreement* with the other unions involved. This produced scarcely a temporary truce. The EETPU was able to justify its members filling printing jobs on the new *Today* newspaper by arguing that this was a new operation and the print unions had no established presence. In 1987, the TUC had to order the EETPU to withdraw from 3 single-union deals at Yuasa, the Japanese battery firm, at Thorn-EMI and at Orion, another Japanese-owned electronics operation, on the grounds that it was infringing the rights of other TUC affiliates. Despite attempts to establish a Code of Practice, single-union no-strike deals remain an issue which could still split the TUC, and even that drastic eventuality is unlikely to restrain intensifying competition, as unions fight for their lives in a shrinking membership market.

Co-ordination of recruitment

In 1987, a paper *Development in Trade Union Organisation* argued that the TUC should become more directly involved in recruitment. The TUC could attempt to make recruitment more efficient by establishing designated organising areas. Individual unions would then be chartered by the TUC and given a clear run for a specified time period at a particular establishment or company. A TUC organising fund would be established to finance campaigns sponsored by the TUC. In chartering unions they would ensure that their recruitment approach met minimum criteria and did not involve 'sweetheart deals'. This initiative met with a mixed response. Some union leaders saw it as strengthening the unions' efforts and ensuring union principles were maintained. Others saw it as intruding on their autonomy, contending that they, not the TUC, possessed the organising know-how, and asserting that once this vital issue was caught up in Congress House bureaucracy, imaginative initiatives would be severely constrained. What was required was patient, day-to-day work at the grass roots level, not grandiose schemes.

At least there is a new awareness and prioritising of the recruitment function. But will it have any practical impact? Objective changes in the industrial and class structure are very important. But they do not *determine* union density: they were working against union growth from 1945 to 1979. Nonetheless, white collar union density increased from 32.6% in 1968 to 44% in 1979, undermining the idea that there was something in white collar occupations that predisposed workers against trade unionism. It has been argued that the reason for the expansion of white collar trade unionism in the 1970s was the squeeze on white collar earnings relative to manual earnings in a situation of rapid price inflation, and against a background of state support for trade unionism which influenced employers (Bain and Price, 1983). Others have claimed that, in addition to an increased need for wage bargaining, other factors, related to the changes in the class situation of non-manual work, need to be taken into account (Crompton and Jones, 1984). Rationalisation, deskilling, changes in job security and conditions of employment relative to manual workers are still continuing in the white collar field. But the economic and political influences which stimulated growth in the 1970s are no longer present. This places a much greater emphasis than was the case throughout the post-war period upon the role of the union as an organiser of discontent. The tide is running against trade unions. But they can still recover lost ground if they seize their opportunities imaginatively and forcefully.

Trade union power

To what degree have the unions suffered a significant loss of power since the seventies? Are trade unions in crisis? Our answers to these questions depend to a large degree on what our conception of trade unionism is. If, like many writers, we take a narrow conception and emphasise workplace organisation and still buoyant wage levels, we might answer both questions in the negative. In this view, little has changed in the last decade (Kelly, 1987; McInnes, 1987). The problem with this position is that in the past the majority of union leaders and activists, if not members, have defined trade unionism in much wider terms, and so have academics. Comparing British unions with those in other countries, they have seen trade unionism as a *movement* attempting to embrace all workers, blue or white collar, skilled or unskilled, full-time or part-time and possessed of a mission to change society. In this view trade unionism has both an industrial and political dimension. For sure, success in both spheres has been limited and there have been continuing controversies about ends and

224 *Trade unions in Britain today*

means. But the fact that the unions, a century ago, broke from the idea that they should only organise a certain skilled and secure section of the labour force, and later broke from a pragmatic involvement in politics and established their own party, were seen as major achievements and guarantees of this tradition.

It seems clear that measured by past philosophies and strengths, British unions, on both the interlinked industrial and political criteria, have suffered a loss of power. Also, even if we base our estimations in far more limited fashion on the stability of workplace organisation and the resilience of wages, we must note the inadequacy of much of the evidence; the relationship of wages to flexibility and labour intensification; the hints of a decline in shop steward control over non-wage issues and of a burgeoning of 'enterprise unionism'; and the growing disparities wage averages conceal. We *are* struck by the continuing underlying strength of *workplace* trade unionism. Nonetheless, our case study of new technology demonstrates its serious limitations in failing to obtain advanced bargaining objectives (chapter 4). But if we simply stop at the workplace and conclude that there has been minimal loss of trade union power and there is no crisis, then we are redefining what trade unionism has meant in the past.

Set against the broader canvas, the picture looks different. A smaller trade unionism may still possess a substantial degree of bargaining power. It is as unlikely to benefit the trade unions' lost 3 million members in the 1980s as the old craft trade unions benefited the majority of workers in the 1880s. In the broader view, a consideration of the wages and conditions of the unemployed takes some gilt off the achievements of employed workers. Increased wages have failed to constrain a significant regressive redistribution of income, wealth and power in the last decade (chapter 1). Moreover, we have already noted the inability of the unions to resist the beginnings of what could be a serious state remoulding of their internal structures (chapter 5). And we have documented the unions' failure to even begin to refashion, in any significant sense, the structure of the enterprise (chapter 6).

We have also observed how broad political developments suggest a diminution of trade union power (chapter 2). A movement which embraces less than 38% of the work-force lacks the credibility to demand an important role in running the country. In 1972 and 1974, the miners were able to defeat a Conservative government. In

1984/85, they were themselves perhaps even more crushingly defeated. Between 1960 and 1973, the unions were able to immobilise legislation from both Labour and Conservative governments. In the 1980s, a far more restrictive legal edifice has been erected and union opposition has been ineffective (chapter 3). In the 1960s and 1970s, Harold Wilson won 4 elections. Since 1979, Labour has lost 3 elections in succession. Once again, the fact that a still shrinking group of members have maintained organisation and conditions with reasonable success, important as it is, looks somewhat less comforting.

Nor can we really content ourselves with the observation that the changes that have occurred are simply cyclical, have been induced by recession and will be reversed in an upturn which, sooner or later, must come. Structural changes unfavourable to trade unionism have accelerated in the recession, and the longer it lasts, the more decisive the remoulding the unions must confront. It is, moreover, impossible to predict that any upturn involving substantial reflation and substantial reductions in unemployment *will come* or that it will come quickly enough to repair the damage to trade unionism that has occurred and that is still occurring. It will certainly not recreate the employment patterns of the post-war boom. We do not know if it will happen, or if it will help unions if it does happen. Will it, for example, lead to a reversal of the trend, very dangerous to trade unionism, towards a smaller size of workplace? A hard-headed stargazer would predict that any economic upturn will be gradual, limited and controlled. But this position is still based upon astrology, a notoriously unreliable art. Right now, the current is still strongly running *against* trade unionism. And the fact that Thatcherism has not yet succeeded in its wider objectives, produced an 'economic miracle', *decisively* cut back the welfare state and slashed public expenditure, should not blind us to its real successes in the trade union field.

Complacency of the 'nothing much has really changed' variety constitutes a danger for trade unions. But an even greater danger is fatalism and defeatism. If a crisis is defined as 'a time of acute danger', both these views are part of the danger. Many other commentators on industrial relations see the prevailing trends towards the free market, new technology, sustained unemployment, growing inequality and a serious decline in trade unionism as inevitable and irreversible. In this view, trade unions have to accept a serious decline in their influence and move more towards the business union model. These trends have happened in countries like the USA or Japan and they will happen here (Leadbetter and Lloyd, 1987; Roberts, 1987). But, as we have seen, many of these trends are contradictory or incomplete. There is no iron law which dictates that unions cannot recruit women, part-time employees. The declining size of workplace in certain sectors can be compensated for by increased size of establishment elsewhere.

There is nothing intrinsic in possessing a mortgage, owning a video or purchasing shares which is antagonistic to holding a union card. A recent MORI poll found, for example, that 80% of union members own their own home, 9% more than the public generally, and only 16% live in council houses. A change of government could reverse many of the trends presently taking place. If we look at the USA or Japan, we must not forget to look at other countries, such as Sweden, which appears to have reconciled powerful trade unions with economic growth and full employment.

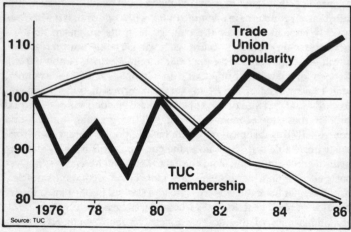

Figure 5 *Source:* TUC.

The position for British unions is a difficult but not an impossible one. A survey by MORI in 1987 found a massive 88% believing that trade unions are essential to protect workers' interests. The Gallup Political Index 1987 found 71% describing trade unions as 'a good thing'. This was the highest rating since 1954 and compares with 51% in 1979. Enhanced popularity mirrors diminished power. It might be cynically observed that the unions only need to lose a few more million members to become as feted as Princess Diana. But the trends also reflect an attachment to trade unionism amongst the British people and a sympathy with their present predicament. If the unions can clarify their philosophy and streamline their organisation they still appear to have room for a comeback.

Alternatives

The organisation, philosophies and traditions of British trade unions leave much to be desired. It could be argued that, in the past, unions concentrated too much on money rather than other social benefits, were insufficiently political, did little for the low-paid and that the insistence on free collective bargaining contributed to making British workers worse off than their foreign counterparts. British unions have no education system to speak of. In other countries the labour movement produces several daily papers. Here the unions cannot even produce a weekly. The fact that, during the miner's strike, several unions found that they did not even have members' addresses, would show trade unionists abroad how deep the problems run. British unions may have much to learn from other countries. Indeed, the crisis of the 1980s perhaps performed one useful function by bringing to the surface competing philosophies of trade unionism. Discussion of these may help unions to reformulate and redefine their role.

In the UK, the idea of *market or business* trade unionism is best exemplified by the EETPU. In this conception, trade unions must explicitly recognise that the welfare of their members is dependent on the success of enterprise goals and enthusiastically co operate with employers to realise these goals. Strikes are unnecessary and harmful. Unions must accept the centrality of profit and relate wages and conditions to the exigencies of the employers' market situation. The job of the workplace union is to support and complement, not challenge management. Management has its job to do and the union role is quite distinct. Business unions identify with management, relate to full-time, skilled employees and support aggressive competition between unions for members. Trade unionism is not so much a movement as a business. It believes in plebiscatory democracy, not activist democracy. Union leaders should provide financial services for their members in a professional fashion. Business unionism rejects class conflict and extensive involvement in politics. Unions should cultivate all political parties and not tie their destiny completely to the Labour Party.

The idea of *semi-syndicalist* or *socialist* trade unionism has been best exemplified in the 1980s by Arthur Scargill and the NUM. Most trade unions have accepted a split in practice between 'the industrial' and 'the political'. Whilst unions are involved in politics, they should concentrate on dealing with employers, whilst the Labour Party concentrates on parliamentary activity. Semi-syndicalist unionism does not accept this distinction, nor Len Murray's view that industrial action should not be used for political ends. The distinction, it is claimed, is artificial. What was the miners' strike about, if it was not about politics? When there is a run on the pound, or an outflow of capital, or the closure of an enterprise, capital is using its power for political purposes, and unions should do the same. Strikes buildup workers' confidence, open their eyes politically and strengthen the movement. Mrs Thatcher is at the root of most of the problems of trade unionists, and they should do their utmost, through industrial and political action, to remove her and replace her with a Labour government. The unions should then use their potentially great power to pressurise that government to introduce socialist measures. In this view, there can be no compromise between employers and workers. And unions are not slot machines, intended to provide benefits for workers, but fighting organisations which require a maximum of active involvement from all members.

Most unions have not met either of these polar cases but they have borne the marks of both of them. *Labourist* trade unions are characterised by contradiction and confusion in philosophy and practice. They have accepted the political-industrial division of labour, but at times have been precipitated into conflict with the state. They have believed that unions should be schools of democracy, but have done little to encourage involvement. They have believed that union involvement with politics should not be pragmatic and limited, but they have rarely mobilised their power to determine Labour Party policy. The political impulse of their leaders has been towards corporatism, but they have been historically confounded by the tension between their demands for free collective bargaining and their demands for a greater degree of economic planning, a tension which contributed more than anything else to the defeats of the Labour governments of the 1960s and 1970s.

Many commentators argue that *semi-syndicalist trade unionism* received its death blow in the miners' strike. It is no longer an option. *Business unionism*, which is related to the TUC's 'new realism', is the model for the future. Certainly *labourist trade unionism* is beginning to fragment, with unions like the AEU following the EETPU's trail and others like the TGWU explicitly rejecting this path. Some of the TUC's labourist majority veer, like the TGWU, towards political trade unionism; others, like the GMBATU, veer politically towards the Right. But both unions are agreed on the need not to desert peripheral workers as the EETPU has. On the other hand, many other TUC unions limit themselves largely to attracting core employees. This is true of TASS and ASTMS, although politically they tend towards the Left. Again, as we have noted, unions like the GMBATU and TGWU have signed deals very close to the no-strike model and unions like TASS and ASTMS employ a recruiting approach very similar to that of business unionism. But the differences of degree and the difference of ideology they have with the 'New Right' unions are important ones.

A further alternative is a revived and stronger *corporatist* trade unionism. In this view, unions should accept that their experience with the last Labour government did not fail because of the inadequacies of corporatism. It failed because it was not corporatist enough. If a new bargain were to be struck by the unions, with Labour to cover the planning not only of wages, but of the economy, and the unions were to offer control over sectional militancy in return for the reduction of unemployment, the electorate would be faced with a compelling alternative. The unions, in this scenario, would have to make an explicit break with the past, but this is justified by the alternative of successive decades of Thatcherism.

The USA

Several recent TUC initiatives are said to have been influenced by American experience and the USA is, of course, the heartland of business unionism, where unions 'give back' part of their wage increases when their employers are in trouble. Can we see the future of Britain's trade unions in America today?

If we can, then it will be a future of declining influence and increased loss of membership. Less than 20% of American workers are trade union members and 60% of overall membership is limited to 5 key areas – government employment, contruction, transport, services and distribution. Less than 25% of the work-force in chemicals and less than 50% in machinery production, gas, electricity and printing are union members. Trade unionism in the USA is geographically confined to the older industrial states in the North East and the Middle West and over 30% of all members work in New York, Pennsylvania and California.

The USA has met the structural changes the UK is now facing far earlier and more intensively. The old industries – steel, railways and textiles – were blitzed there in the 1960s and 1970s. They are facing a continued move from manual to white collar employment, from services to manufacturing and from the old industrial North to the union-free South. They have long been faced with a tough management culture, and the 1970s saw a revival of 'union busting'. Unlike British unions, US labour has never built its own party but acts more as a political pressure group, although it possesses close links with the Democrats. It has never possessed the same conceptions of itself as a movement with a mandate to change society, indeed, at least in the post-war period, it has enthusiastically embraced the social and economic status quo.

Unlike the British unions, the Americans are not facing a sudden recent trauma. US unions really only took off in the 1930s when the Roosevelt 'New Deal' produced the 1933 National Recovery Act and the 1935 Wagner Act, which stimulated growth. Membership, 4 million in 1935, had grown to 14 million a decade later. But, like their Japanese counterparts, American workers suffered a frontal assault from the employers in the post-war period. The *Taft-Hartley* legislation banned closed shops and restricted industrial action. More than 20 states introduced 'Right to Work' laws. The long boom encouraged weakened organisations to identify more closely with the employer and the market approach was strengthened. Density fell from 36% of the work-force in the forties, to 25% by the seventies, 23% by 1980 and less than 20% today. A weakened trade unionism failed to break out of the areas in which it had an historic hold, and in this, it constitutes more of a lesson to be avoided than an example for emulation. It is predicted that, by the year 2000, less than 10% of private sector employees will hold union cards. British unions have had more success in the 1960s and 1970s in bucking the trends to which US unions have succumbed – witness the growth of white collar unionism.

As the US unions begin to accept that they cannot win more members, and instead recruit workers who simply pay an agency fee for services rendered, and the AFL-CIO stresses their friendly society role, many of their British counterparts may have reservations as to the desirability of this model. Nonetheless, if Mrs Thatcher is successful in creating a market economy, British unions could be marked down for a similar future.

Sweden

If supporters of the market option look to the USA and Japan, partisans of corporatism can gain some hope from the Nordic countries. Sweden has long been characterised as the most successful country in the world and has a per capita income second only to Switzerland. In the post-war period it perfected a system of centralised negotiations between employers' organisations and the trade unions. The Swedish TUC, the LO, negotiates a 'frame' agreement with the major employers' association, the SAF. The LO specifically relates its wages policy to full employment, price stability, economic growth and redistribution of income.

During the 1950s and 1960s, the centralised system was successful in reconciling increasing real wages with these objectives and with company profitability. Moreover, through its solidarity policy, the LO was able to achieve a compression of differentials, largely by keeping wages lower than they might have been in the dynamic export sector and keeping them higher than they might have been in the home sector, discouraging new entrants to the market. In Sweden, 90% of the work-force were in unions and 97% of the blue collar work-force were in LO affiliates, whilst white collar employees were organised in a separate federation, the TCO, which generally followed the LO trend. Whilst Sweden has a sizeable public sector – 65% of national income compared with 47% in the UK – the economy continued to be organised essentially on market lines. Moreover, collective negotiations were not tripartite. The SDP, intimately linked with LO, was uninterruptedly in power until 1976. But the government outlined broad economic goals and stayed largely on the sidelines, administering a prod or two when required. Whilst lower-level agreements were then negotiated by employers and unions within the national framework agreement, wage drift was never perceived as a major problem.

From the 1970s, the problems of the world economy increasingly affected Sweden and stability was threatened by a growth in inflation;

a decline in Sweden's share of the world market; stagnation in industrial production; tensions between the private and the now bigger public sector; and between LO and the SDP, which was out of power from 1976-82. Whilst there was an increase in unemployment, it was small by international standards, and Swedish workers remained amongst the best rewarded in the world. However, the unions' turn to relying more on legislation and less on collective bargaining, and the pursuit of industrial and economic democracy personified by the wage-earner funds, gradually led to greater tensions between LO and SAF.

In 1983, the Engineering Employers' and the Metalworkers' Union concluded a separate agreement outside the national frame. This was motivated by employers finding skilled labour difficult to attract, resentment by skilled employees at squeezed differentials and a desire from companies for more flexibility bargaining and, therefore, more local bargaining. In 1985, a second separate engineering deal was negotiated but, in 1986, the engineering unions and employers returned to the national frame. A further change is increased government intervention. In both 1985 and 1986, the Palme and Karlsson governments exercised more pressure on the national negotiations.

There are different views on the degree to which the Swedish system is disintegrating or simply going through stress. Some commentators see the Swedish road as one to be followed in other countries, emphasising the degree to which it has strengthened and unified the working class and curtailed the power of capital. Others go further, and argue it represents more than an effective means of planning wages, employment, profits and growth and see it as a transition to socialism. Others note the limited degree to which control and ownership of the economy has changed, and see in recent problems affirmation of the view that as the working class gets stronger it will press beyond this kind of 'historic compromise' to the replacement of capitalism. Certainly the Nordic countries' ability to reconcile full employment, high wage levels, income redistribution and rising union membership merits attention as against the experience of deregulation, growing unemployment and inequality and dwindling union membership that characterises Japan, Germany, the USA and the UK.

Conclusions

Whilst our evidence is, to some extent, limited and contradictory, it seems that, as yet, there is no dramatic or large-scale transformation of industrial relations of the kind which figures in government rhetoric. Nonetheless, (important changes are taking place with crucial implications for trade unions) A government dedicated to a neo-*laissez-faire* philosophy and the delegitimation of trade unionism, and informed by a remarkable political will; (large-scale unemployment; structural changes in the labour force; the decline of the Labour Party – all of these factors have combined to press British trade unionism towards a turning point) It is doubtful if business unionism and 'new realism' is an answer for more than a minority in the labour movement. It may prove attractive to a skilled, protected minority who may become the 'new model', 'top-hatted' trade unionists in the style of the craft unionists of the last century, presiding over a mass of poorly paid, insecure, disorganised employees. On the other hand, it may be bypassed by individualised union-free employment. Business unionism would certainly appear a recipe for numerical decline and a severe reduction in the political influence and social weight of the trade unions.

In this light, corporatism appears a more attractive proposition. (One recent study of the period 1965-82 found that countries which had strong labour movements and corporatist style wage determination had lower levels of unemployment, less industrial conflict, more limited rates of increase in real wages, but greater increases in the social wage, than free-market collective bargaining comparators. Labour quiescence, however, had little effect on the overall shares of income between labour and capital (Cameron, 1984). When so many are doing so well out of 'free collective bargaining', are British workers prepared for such a trade-off related, perhaps, to proposals for industrial democracy?) Are British trade unions capable of a response which requires the TUC to control union leaders and union leaders to control shop stewards? If, since 1979, there has been a degree of centralisation in some unions in some areas, there has also been a growth of decentralised bargaining, fragmentation of labour markets and company culture, all of which could limit the role of trade union leaders as shop-floor controllers. The decline in union coverage also compromises such a future. Corporatism requires the control of these groups who feel that they do better *outside* such a system. Its attraction to many workers is its promise of decreased

differentials. But the threat this constitutes for other workers lends corporatist arrangement an inherent instability and limited time span. Sweden has a small population, lengthy experience of real corporatism, centralised unions and sympathetic employers. Yet we have seen a tremendous strain placed on their system in recent years.

These are some of the problems advocates of corporatism have to face. They also come under fire from the Left, from advocates of socialist trade unionism who go on to ask why a future Labour government should be any more radical, or successful in delivering the goods to the unions than Wilson and Callaghan were. Moreover, the still fresh memories of their failure make a corporatist approach an unattractive electoral strategy. The measures required to elicit a satisfactory union response – a fundamental redistribution of income and wealth, a commitment to thoroughgoing industrial democracy – are unlikely to be on the agenda of a Labour government led by the party's present leaders. And look at the recent experiences of social democratic governments in Norway, Greece and France. In Spain and New Zealand, Labour governments seem to be operating 'Thatcherism without the Iron Lady'. Alternatively, even a phased reflation of the economy would produce inflation. A reduction in unemployment would put more pressure on prices. There would be a wave of militancy and the strike rate would increase.

Some on the Left see this as hopeful in socialist terms. Such a wave of militancy could push a Labour government leftwards in the direction of more full-blooded planning, nationalisation and workers' self-management. Maybe. But if the Left have failed to elect a Labour government determined to carry out a radical programme, why should the Left then be able to infuse money militancy with socialist consciousness? Why should a right-wing Labour government be pushed leftwards by a strike-wave? Surely the more likely scenario is a re-run of 1978-79 and the election of another Conservative government. The predicament, for socialists, is that they are faced with an overwhelming majority in the unions whose horizons are sturdily bound by the economic and social status quo, and a majority of the conscious political minority whose perspective remains one of mild reform. To change this situation is on the most optimistic estimate, the work not of years, but of decades. Moreover, a Britain moving seriously in the direction of socialism would face massive economic and political difficulties from a hostile world. These constraints may not be insuperable ones. They must be confronted, not ignored or minimised. The immediate problem for left-wing critics of corporatism remains: how do they transform the consciousness of trade unionists, who essentially want more out of capitalism and are far from convinced of the need to move towards an alternative economic and social system?

There are no easy answers to these problems. If they are not to succumb to business unionism, British trade unions will certainly have to become *more* political. They will have to attempt to resolve, once more the tensions between unity and sectionalism, trade unionism as a broad movement and as a wages agency for the employed. What political direction change will take, however, remains conjectural. What *is* clear is that the present predicament of trade unions is not susceptible to glib solutions. Indeed, at the moment, alternatives to the status quo appear to have limited resonance. Thatcherism still holds the stage and the future of trade unionism remains uncertain and insecure.

Further reading

Recent surveys include E. Batstone, 1984; E. Batstone and S. Gourlay, 1986; P. Edwards, 1985, and N. Millward and M. Stevens, 1986; J. Atkinson, 1985 and P. Bassett, 1985, deal with particular aspects of the present industrial relations situation, whilst P. Beaumont, 1987, J. Kelly, 1987 and J. McInnes, 1987, attempt assessments of the present problems facing the unions and possible solutions.

The implications of present changes in the class structure are dealt with in E. Hobsbawm et al (ed), 1981, S. Hall and M. Jacques (eds), 1983, and J. Curran (ed), 1984.

There is a lot of material on Sweden – see W. Korpi, 1978; S. Lash, 1985; R. Petersen, 1987; and J. Stephen, 1979. There is less on recent developments in American trade unionism, but see T. Kochan et al, 1986; R. Miller, 1987; and M. Goldfield, 1987.

Bibliography

B. Abel-Smith & R. Stevens, 1967, *Lawyers and the Courts*, Heinemann

ACAS, 1985, 1986, *Annual Report*

V. Allen, 1954, *Power in Trade Unions*, Longman

V. Allen, 1966, *Militant Trade Unionism*, Merlin

A. Anderson, 1981, 'What provisions do companies make for redundancy?', *Manpower Studies*, Autumn

P. Anderson, 1965, 'Origins of the present crisis', *New Left Review*, 23

P. Anderson, 1987, 'The figures of descent', *New Left Review*, 161

P. Anderson, & R. Blackburn (eds.), 1965, *Towards Socialism*, Fontana

P. Armstrong et al., 1984, *Capitalism Since World War II*, Fontana

E. Arnold & P. Senker, 1982, *Designing the Future*, Engineering Industry Training Board

A. Atkinson, 1972, *Unequal Shares*, Allen Lane

A. Atkinson, 1975, *The Economics of Inequality*, Clarendon Press

J. Atkinson, 1985, 'The changing corporation' in D. Clutterbuck (ed.), 1985

J. Atkinson & N. Meager, 1986a, *New Forms of Work Organisation*, IMS Report 121

J. Atkinson & N. Meager, 1986b, 'Is flexibility just a flash in the pan?', *Personnel Management*, September

R. Bacon & W. Eltis, 1976, *Britain's Economic Problem*, Macmillan

L. Baddon et al., 1987, *Profit Sharing and Employee Share-ownership*, University of Glasgow

G. Bain, 1970, *The Growth of White Collar Unionism*, Clarendon Press

G. Bain (ed.), 1983, *Industrial Relations in Britain*, Blackwell

G. Bain & R. Price, 1983, 'Union growth: dimensions, determinants and destiny' in G. Bain (ed.), 1983

J. Banks, 1974, *Trade Unionism*, Collier–Macmillan

I. Barron & R. Curnow, 1979, *The Future With Microelectronics*, Frances Pinter/PSI

P. Bassett, 1986, *Strike Free: New Industrial Relations in Britain*, Macmillan

E. Batstone, 1984, *Working Order*, Blackwell

E. Batstone & P. Davies, 1976, *Industrial Democracy – European Experience*, HMSO

E. Batstone et al., 1983, *Unions on the Board*, Blackwell

E. Batstone & S. Gourlay, 1986, *Unions, Employment and Innovation*, Blackwell4

J. Beale, 1982, *Getting It Together: Women as Trade Unionists*, Pluto Press

P. Beaumont, 1987, *The Decline of Trade Union Organisation*, Croom Helm

P. Beaumont & L. Cairns, 1987, 'New towns – a centre of non unions', *Employee Relations*, July

I. Benson & J. Lloyd, 1983, *New Technology and Industrial Change*, Kogan Page

J. Bessant, 1983, 'Management and manufacturing innovation' in G. Winch (ed.), 1983

H. Beynon, 1983, 'The politics of the British factory', *Critique*, 16

H. Beynon (ed.), 1985, *Digging Deeper: Issues in the Miners' Stike*, Verso

T. Bilton et al., 1986, *Introductory Sociology*, Macmillan

I. Bird, 1980, *Information Technology in the Office. The Impact on Workers' Jobs*, Equal Opportunities Commission

P. Blackburn et al., 1985, *Technology, Economic Growth and the Labour Process*, Macmillan

R. Blackburn, 1965, 'The new capitalism' in P. Anderson & R. Blackburn (eds.), 1965

R. Blackburn & M. Mann, 1979, *The Working Class in the Labour Market*, Macmillan

P. Blumberg, 1968, *Industrial Democracy: The Sociology of Participation*, Constable

A. Bollard, 1983, 'Technology, economic change and small firms', *Lloyds Bank Review*, January

A. Boltho, 1975, *Japan: An Economic Survey*, Oxford University Press

K. Bradley & A. Gelb, 1983, *Worker Capitalism – The New Industrial Relations*, Heinemann

P. Brannen, 1983, *Authority and Participation in Industry*, Batsford

P. Brannen et al., 1976, *The Worker Directors*, Hutchinson

H. Braverman, 1974, *Labour and Monopoly Capital: The Degradation of Work in the Twentieth Century*, Monthly Review Press

W. Brown (ed.), 1981, *The Changing Contours of British Industrial Relations*, Blackwell

W. Brown, 1986, 'The changing role of trade unions in the management of labour', *British Journal of Industrial Relations*, July

D. Buchanan, 1983, 'Technological imperatives and strategic choice' in G. Winch (ed.), 1983

D. Buchanan & D. Boddy, 1983, *Organisations in the Computer Age*, Gower

Bullock Report, 1977, *Report of a Committee of Enquiry on Industrial Democracy*, Cmnd 6706

A. Burns, 1981, *The Microchip: An Appropriate or Inappropriate Technology*, Ellis Horwood

D. Cameron, 1984, 'Social democracy, corporatism, labour quiescence and the representation of economic interest in advanced capitalist society' in J. Goldthorpe (ed.), 1984

Central Statistical Office, 1986, *Social Trends*, HMSO

Central Statistical Office, 1987, *Economic Trends*, HMSO

M. Chadwick, 1983, 'The recession and industrial relations: a factory approach', *Employee Relations*, November

E. Chell, 1983, 'Political perspectives and worker participation' in C. Crouch & F. Heller (ed.), 1983

J. Child, 1969, *The Business Enterprise in Modern Society*, Collier–Macmillan

J. Child (ed.), 1973, *Man and Organisation*, Allen & Unwin

J. Clark & Lord Wedderburn, 1983, 'Modern labour law: problems, functions and policies' in Lord Wedderburn et al. (eds.), 1983

T. Clarke, 1977, 'Industrial democracy: the institutionalised suppression of industrial conflict' in T. Clarke & L. Clements (eds.), 1977

T. Clarke & L. Clements (eds.), 1977, *Trade Unions Under Capitalism*, Fontana

H. Clegg, 1960, *A New Approach to Industrial Democracy*, Blackwell

H. Clegg, 1970, *The System of Industrial Relations in Great Britain*, Blackwell

R. Clifton & C. Tatton-Brown, 1979, *Impact of Employment Legislation on Small Firms*, Department of Employment Research Paper, 6

D. Clutterbuck (ed.), 1985, *New Patterns of Work*, Gower

D. Coates, 1980, *Labour in Power? A Study of the Labour Government 1974–1979*, Longman

D. Coates et al., 1985, *A Socialist Anatomy of Britain*, Polity Press

D. Coates & J. Hillard (eds.), 1986, *The Economic Decline of Modern Britain: The Debate Between Left and Right*, Wheatsheaf Books

K. Coates & T. Topham, 1970, *Workers' Control: A Book of Readings*, Panther

K. Coates & T. Topham, 1986, *Trade Unions and Politics*, Blackwell

H. Collins, 1982, 'Capitalist discipline and corporatist law part II', *Industrial Law Journal*, September

CBI, 1980, *Jobs: Facing the Future*

CBI, 1987, *Change at Work*

M. Cooley, 1980, *Architect or Bee?*, Langley Technical Services

R. Coombs et al., 1987, *Economics and Technological Change*, Macmillan

P. Cressey et al., 1981, *Industrial Democracy and Participation: A Scottish Survey*, Department of Employment Research Paper 28

R. Crompton & G. Jones, 1984, *White Collar Proletariat*, Macmillan

C. Crouch, 1982, *Trade Unions: The Logic of Collective Action*, Fontana

C. Crouch & F. Heller (eds.), 1983, *Organisational Democracy and Political Processes*, Wiley

J. Curran (ed.), 1984, *The Future of the Left*, Polity Press

W. Daniel, 1987, *Workplace Industrial Relations and Technical Change*, Frances Pinter/PSI

W. Daniel & N. Millward, 1983, *Workplace Industrial Relations in Britain*, Heinemann

W. Daniel & E. Stilgoe, 1978, *The impact of employment protection laws*, Policy Studies Institute

A. Davies, 1986, *Industrial Relations and New Technology*, Croom Helm

Department of Employment, 1983, *Democracy in Trade Unions*, Green Paper, Cmnd 8778, HMSO

L. Dickens et al., 1985, *Dismissed: A Study of Unfair Dismissal and the Industrial Tribunal System*, Blackwell

L. Dickens & G. Bain, 1986, 'A duty to bargain? Union recognition and information disclosure' in R. Lewis (ed.), 1986

M. Dowling et al., 1981, *Employee Participation: Practice and Attitudes in North West Manufacturing Industry*, Department of Employment Research Paper 27

H. Downing, 1980, 'Word processors and the oppression of women' in T. Forester (ed.), 1980

B. Doyle, 1979, 'Trade disputes and the labour injunction yet again', *Modern Law Review*, 42, July

P. Dunleavy & C. Husbands, 1985, *British Democracy at the Crossroads*, Allen & Unwin

S. Dunn & J. Gennard, 1984, *The Closed Shop in British Industry*, Macmillan

J. Eaton & C. Gill, 1983, *The Trade Union Directory*, Pluto Press

T. Eccles, 1981, *Under New Management*, Pan Books

J. Edelstein & M. Warner, 1975, *Comparative Union Democracy*, Allen & Unwin

M. Edwardes, 1984, *Back from the Brink*, Pan Books

P. Edwards, 1985, 'Myth of the macho manager', *Personnel Management*, April

P. Elias & K. Ewing, 1982, 'Economic torts and labour law', *Cambridge Law Journal*, November

J. England, 1981, 'Shop stewards in transport house: a comment on the incorporation of the rank and file', *Industrial Relations Journal*, September–October

Equal Pay and Opportunities Campaign, 1980, *Women and Word Processors*

S. Evans, 1985a, 'Picketing under the employment acts' in P. Fosh & C. Littler (eds.), 1985

S. Evans, 1985b, 'The use of injunctions in industrial disputes', *British Journal of Industrial Relations*, March

S. Evans et al., 1985, 'Unfair dismissal law and changes in the role of trade unions and employers' associations', *Industrial Law Journal*, June

K. Ewing, 1982, Trade Unions, *The Labour Party and The Law: A Study Of The Trade Union Act 1913*, Edinburgh University Press

P. Fairbrother, 1984, *All Those in Favour: The Politics of Union Democracy*, Pluto Press

D. Fatchett, 1987, *Trade Unions and Politics in the 1980s: The 1984 Act and Political Fund Ballots*, Croom Helm

B. Fine & R. Millar (eds.), 1985, *Policing The Miners' Strike*, Lawrence & Wishart

T. Forester (ed.), 1980, *The Microelectronics Revolution*, Blackwell

T. Forester (ed), 1985, *The Information Technology Revolution*, Blackwell

P. Fosh & C. Littler (eds.), 1985, *Industrial Relations and The Law In The 1980s: Issues and Future Trends*, Gower

A. Fox, 1966, *Industrial Sociology and Industrial Relations*, Research Paper No. 3, Royal Commission on Trade Unions and Employers Associations, HMSO

A. Fox, 1973, 'Industrial relations, a social critique of pluralist ideology' in J. Child (ed.), 1973

A. Fox, 1975, 'Collective bargaining: Flanders and the Webbs', *British Journal of Industrial Relations*, July

A. Fox, 1985a, *History and Heritage: The Social Origins of the British Industrial Relations System*, Allen & Unwin

A. Fox, 1985b, *Man Mismanagement*, Hutchinson

A. Francis, 1986, *New Technology at Work*, Clarendon Press

C. Freeman et al, 1982, *Unemployment and Technological Innovation*, Frances Pinter

A. Friedman, 1977, *Industry and Labour*, Macmillan

R. Fryer et al., 1974, *Organisation and Change in the National Union of Public Employees*, NUPE

J. Gershuny, 1978, *After Industrial Society*, Macmillan

J. Gershuny, 1985, 'New technology – what new jobs?', *Industrial Relations Journal*, Autumn

J. Gershuny & I. Miles, 1983, *The New Service Economy*, Frances Pinter

A Giddens & G. McKenzie, 1982, *Social Class and the Division of Labour*, Cambridge University Press

C. Gill, 1985, *Work, Unemployment and the New Technology*, Polity Press

A. Glyn & J. Harrison, 1980, *The British Economic Disaster*, Pluto Press

A. Glyn & B. Sutcliffe, 1972, *British Capitalism, Workers and the Profits Squeeze*, Penguin Books

M. Goldfield, 1987, *The Decline of Organised Labour in the United States*, University of Chicago Press

J. Goldthorpe, 1982, 'On the service class' in A. Giddens & G. McKenzie (eds.), 1982

J. Goldthorpe (ed.), 1984, *Order and Conflict in Contemporary Capitalism*, Clarendon Press

J. Goldthorpe, 1984, 'The end of convergence: corporatist and dualist tendencies in modern western societies' in J. Goldthorpe (ed.), 1984

J. Goldthorpe, D. Lockwood et al., 1968, *The Affluent Worker, Industrial Attitudes and Behaviour*, Cambridge University Press

J. Griffith, 1985, *The Politics of the Judiciary*, Fontana

P. Grout, 1987, 'The Wider Share Ownership Programme', *Fiscal Studies*, August

P. Hain, 1986, *Political Strikes: the State and Trade Unionism in Britain*, Penguin

S. Hall & M. Jaques (ed.), 1983, *The Politics of Thatcherism*, Lawrence & Wishart

C. Handy, 1984, *The Future of Work*, Blackwell

L. Harris, 1985, 'British capital, manufacturing, finance and multinational corporations' in D. Coates et al., 1985

F. A. Hayek, 1980, *Unemployment and the Unions*, Institute of Economic Affairs

A. Heath et al., 1985, *How Britain Votes*, Pergamon Press

B. Hepple, 1983, 'Individual labour law' in G. Bain (ed.), 1983

E. Hobsbawm, 1984, 'Labour: rump or rebirth', *Marxism Today*, March

E. Hobsbawm, et al., 1981, *The Forward March of Labour Halted?*, Verso

G. Hodgson, 1984, *The Democratic Alternative*, Penguin Books

C. Huhne, 1986, 'Why union bashing is not keeping wages down', *Guardian*, 30 January

C. Huhne, 1987, 'Rich take greater share as income gap widens', *Guardian*, 18 December

J. Hutton, 1986, 'Industrial action', *Industrial Law Journal*, December

R. Hyman, 1971, *The Sociology of Trade Unionism*, Pluto Press

R. Hyman, 1975, *Industrial Relations: A Marxist Introduction*, Macmillan

R. Hyman, 1979, 'The politics of workplace trade unionism', *Capital and Class,* Summer

R. Hyman, 1983, 'Trade unions: structure, policies and politics', in G. Bain (ed.), 1983

R. Hyman, 1984, *Strikes,* Fontana

R. Hyman, 1987, 'Trade unions and the law: papering over the cracks?', *Capital and Class,* Spring

R. Hyman & R. H. Fryer, 1975, 'Trade unions: sociology and political economy' in J. McKinlay (ed.), 1975

Incomes Data Services, 1986, *Report* No. 464, January

Incomes Data Services, 1986, *Focus* No. 39, May

IPM, 1983, *How to Introduce New Technology: A Practical Guide for Managers*

N. Swords-Isherwood & P. Senker, 1980, *Microelectronics and the Engineering Industries: The Need for Skills,* Frances Pinter

O. Jacobi et al., 1986, *Technological Change, Rationalisation and Industrial Relations,* Croom Helm

C. Jenkins & B. Sherman, 1979, *The Collapse of Work,* Eyre–Methuen

B. Jones, 1982, 'Destruction or redistribution of engineering skills: the case of numerical control' in S. Wood (ed.), 1982

B. Jones & D. Kavanagh, 1987, *British Politics Today,* Manchester University Press

Sir K. Joseph, 1975, 'Is Beckerman among the sociologists?', *New Statesman,* 18 April

Sir K. Joseph, 1979, 'Solving the union problem is the key to Britain's recovery' in D. Coates & J. Hillard (eds.), 1986

O. Kahn-Freund, 1979, *Labour Relations: Heritage and Adjustment,* Oxford University Press

J. Kelly, 1987, *Labour and the Unions,* Verso

A. Kilpatrick & T. Lawson, 1980, 'On the nature of industrial decline in the UK' in D. Coates & J. Hillard (eds.), 1986

T. Kochan et al., 1986, *The Transformation of American Industrial Relations,* Basic Books

W. Korpi, 1978, *The Working Class in Welfare Capitalism,* Routledge & Kegan Paul

Labour Research, July 1982, November 1983, November 1984, July 1984, August 1985, April 1987, October 1987

S. Lash, 1985, 'The end of neo-corporatism: the breakdown of centralised collective bargaining in Sweden', *British Journal of Industrial Relations*, July

C. Leadbeater & J. Lloyd, 1987, *In Search of Work*, Penguin Books

R. Lewis (ed.), 1986, *Labour Law in Britain*, Blackwell

R. Lewis & B. Simpson, 1981, *Striking a Balance: Employment Law After The 1980 Act*, Martin Robertson

M. Linton, 1985, *The Swedish Example*, Fabian Society

S. M. Lipset, M.A. Trow & J. S. Coleman, 1956, *Union Democracy*, Free Press

R. Loveridge et al., 1986, *Co-Determination, Communication and Control in the Workplace*, Department of Employment Research Paper 54

W. McCarthy (ed.), 1985, *Trade Unions*, Penguin Books

W. McCarthy, 1985, *Freedom at Work: Towards the Reform of Tory Employment Laws*, Fabian Society

J. McKinlay (ed.), 1975, *Processing People*, Iriehart & Winston

J. McIlroy, 1983, *Industrial Tribunals*, Pluto Press

J. McInnes, 1985, 'Conjuring up consultation', *British Journal of Industrial Relations*, March

J. McInnes, 1987, 'Why nothing much has changed: recession, economic restructuring and industrial relations since 1979', *Employee Relations*, Vol. 9, No. 1

L. Mackay, 1986, 'The macho manager: it's no myth', *Personnel Management*, January

I. Maddock, 1980, Introduction to T. Forester (ed.), 1980

A. Manwaring, 1981, 'The trade unions' response to new technology', *Industrial Relations Journal*, July/August

R. Martin, 1968, 'Union democracy: an explanatory framework', *Sociology*, 2, 2

R. Martin, 1981, *New Technology and Industrial Relations in Fleet Street*, Clarendon Press

D. Massey, 1984, *Space and Class: Industrial Location, the Regional Problem and ecline,* Macmillan

D. Massey & R. Meagan, 1982, *The Anatomy of Job Loss*, Methuen

R. Michels, 1962, *Political Parties*, Free Press of Glencoe

R. Miliband, 1969, *The State in Capitalist Society*, Weidenfeld & Nicolson

R. Miliband et al, (eds.), *The Socialist Register 1985/6*, Merlin

R. Miller, 1987, 'The mid-life crisis of the American labour movement', *Industrial Relations Journal*, Autumn

N. Millward & M. Stevens, 1986, *British Workplace Industrial Relations 1980 – 1984*, Gower

M. Moran, 1974, *The Union of Post Office Workers: A Study in Political Sociology*, Macmillan

N. Morris & I. Preston, 1986, 'Taxes, benefits and the distribution of income, 1968–73, *Fiscal Studies*, November

NEDO, 1984, *The Crisis Facing UK Information Technology*

T. Nichols, 1969, *Ownership Control and Ideology*, Allen & Unwin

T. Nichols, 1986, *The British Worker Question*, Routledge & Kegan Paul

S. Nickell, 1987, 'Why is wage inflation in Britain so high?' *Oxford Bulletin of Economics and Statistics*, 49

J. Northcott & P. Rogers, 1984, *Microelectronics in British Industry: Patterns of Change*, PSI

J. Northcott et al., 1985, *Chips and Jobs: Acceptance of New Technology at Work*, PSI

R. Pahl & J. Winkler, 1974, 'The economic elite' in P. Stanworth & A. Giddens, 1974

L. Panitch, 1985, *Working Class Politics in Crisis*, Verso

C. Pateman, 1970, *Participation and Democratic Theory*, Cambridge University Press

R. Penn & H. Scattergood, 1985, 'Deskilling or enskilling? An empirical investigation of recent theories of the labour process', *British Journal of Sociology*, 36, 4

R. Petersen, 1987, 'Swedish collective bargaining', *British Journal of Industrial Relations*, March

M. Poole, 1986, *Towards a New Industrial Democracy: Workers Participation in Industry*, Routledge & Kegan Paul

J. Prior, 1986, *A Balance of Power*, Hamish Hamilton

F. von Prondzynski, 1985, 'The changing function of labour law' in P. Fosh & C. Littler (eds.), 1985

J. Purcell, 1979, 'A strategy for management control in industrial relations' in J. Purcell & R. Smith (eds.), 1979

J. Purcell & K. Sissons, 1983, 'Strategies and practice in the management of industrial relations', in G. Bain (ed.), 1983

J. Purcell & R. Smith (eds.), 1979, *The Control of Work*, Macmillan

H. Ramsay, 1977, 'Cycles of control: workers' participation in sociological and historical perspective, *Sociology*, September

J. Rentoul, 1987, *The Rich Get Richer*, Unwin Books

P. Riddell, 1985, *The Thatcher Government*, Blackwell

B. Roberts, 1987, *Mr. Hammond's Cherry Tree: The Morphology of Union Survival*, Institute of Economic Affairs

P. Rootes, 1986, *Collective Bargaining: Opportunities for a New Approach*, Warwick Papers in Industrial Relations, University of Warwick

H. Scarborough, 1986, 'The politics of technological change at British Leyland', in O. Jacobi et al. (eds.), 1986

H. Scarborough & P. Moran, 1985, 'How new tech won at Longbridge', *New Society*, 7 February

T. Schuller, 1985, *Democracy at Work*, Oxford University Press

J. Scott, 1982, *The Upper Classes*, Macmillan

J. Scott, 1985, *Corporations, Classes and Capitalism*, Hutchinson

P. Senker (ed.), 1984, *Learning To Use Microelectronics*, Science Policy Researcy Unit

C. Smith, 1987, *Recruiting Women To the Trade Union Movement*, TGWU

G. Smith, 1986, 'Profit sharing and employee share ownership in Britain', *Department of Employment Gazette*, September

A. Sproull & J. McInnes, 1986, *Union Recognition in the Electronics Industry in Scotland*, University of Glasgow

P. Stanworth & A. Giddens, 1974, *Elites and Power in British Society*, Cambridge University Press

J. Steffens, 1983, *The Electronic Office: Progress and Problems*, Policy Studies Institute

J. Stephen, 1979, *The Transition From Capitalism To Socialism*, Macmillan

P. Stoneman et al., 1981, *Information Technologies, Productivity and Employment*, OECD

J. Stopford & L. Turner, 1985, *Britain and the Multinationals*, Gower

J. Storey, 1980, *The Challenge to Management Control*, Kogan Page

D. Strinati, 1982, *Capitalism, The State and Industrial Relations*, Croom Helm

A. Taylor, 1987, *The Trade Unions and The Labour Party*, Croom Helm

M. Terry, 1986, 'How do we know if shop stewards are getting weaker?', *British Journal of Industrial Relations*, July

M. Terry & A. Ferner, 1986, *Political Change and Union Democracy*, Warwick Papers in Industrial Relations, Warwick University

J. Tomlinson, 1982, *The Unequal Struggle: British Socialism and The Capitalist Enterprise*, Methuen

TUC, 1979, *Employment and Technology*

TUC, 1982, *Industrial Relations Legislation*

Trade Union Immunities, 1981, Cmnd 8778, HMSO

Trade Union Research Unit, 1981, *New Technology and Trade Union Organisation*, Occasional Paper 71

Trade Union Research Unit, 1984, *The Control of Frontiers: Workers and New Technology*

R. Tur, 1982, 'The legitimacy of industrial action: trade unionism at the crossroads' in Lord Wedderburn & W. Murphy (eds.), 1982

H. Turner, 1962, *Trade Union Growth, Structure and Policy*, Allen & Unwin

R. Undy et al., 1981, *Change in Trade Unions*, Hutchinson

R. Undy & R. Martin, 1984, *Ballots and Trade Union Democracy*, Blackwell

H. Wainwright & D. Elliott, 1982, *The Lucas Plan: A New Trade Unionism In The Making*, Allison & Busby

B. & S. Webb, 1897, *Industrial Democracy*, Longman

F. Webster, 1986, 'The politics of new technology' in R. Miliband et al. (eds.), 1986

K. W. Wedderburn, 1972, 'Labour law and labour relations in Britain', *British Journal of Industrial Relations*, July

Lord Wedderburn, 1985, 'The new politics of labour law' in W. McCarthy (ed.), 1985

Lord Wedderburn, 1986, *The Worker and the Law*, Penguin Books

Lord Wedderburn & W. Murphy (eds.), 1982, *Labour Law and the Community: Prospects for the 1980s*, Institute of Advanced Legal Studies

Lord Wedderburn et al. (eds.), 1983, *Labour Law and Industrial Relations: Building on Kahn-Freund*, Clarendon Press

B. Weekes et al., 1975, *Industrial Relations and the Limits of Law*, Blackwell

M. Weitzman, 1984, *The Share Economy*, Harvard University Press

D. Werneke, 1983, *Microelectronics and Office Jobs*, International Labour Organisation

J. Westergaard & H. Resler, 1976, *Class in a Capitalist Society*, Penguin Books

M. Wiener, 1985, *English Culture and the Decline of the Industrial Spirit 1850–1980*, Penguin Books

R. Williams & R. Moseley, 1981, *Trade Unions and New Technology: An Overview of Technology Agreements*, University of Aston Technology Policy Unit

R. Williams & F. Steward, 1985, 'Technology agreements in Britain: a survey 1977–83' *Industrial Relations Journal*, Autumn

B. Wilkinson, 1983, *The Shop Floor Politics of New Technology*, Heinemann

P. Willman, 1986, *New Technology and Industrial Relations: A Review of the Literature*, Department of Employment Research Paper 56

P. Willman & G. Winch, 1985, *Innovation and Management Control: Labour Relations at BL Cars*, Cambridge University Press

A. Wilson, 1986, 'The future of labour law', *Industrial Tutor*, Spring

D. Wilson et al., 1982, 'The limits of trade union power in organisational decision-making', *British Journal of Industrial Relations*, November

G. Winch (ed.), 1983, *Information Technology in Manufacturing Processes*, Rossendale

J. Winterton, 1985, 'Computerised coal', in H. Beynon (ed.), 1985

J. Winterton & R. Winterton, 1985, *New Technology: The Bargaining Issues*, Universities of Leeds and Nottingham, IPM

S. Wood (ed.), 1982, *The Degradation of Work*, Hutchinson

E. Wright, 1978, *Class, Crisis and The State*, New Left Books

E. Wright, 1985, *Classes*, Verso

Index